Strategic Decision Making

Strategic Decision Making

Niels G. Noorderhaven

Tilburg University

Addison-Wesley Publishing Company

Wokingham, England • Reading, Massachusetts • Menlo Park, California
New York • Don Mills, Ontario • Amsterdam • Bonn • Sydney • Singapore
Tokyo • Madrid • San Juan • Milan • Paris • Mexico City • Seoul • Taipei

© 1995 Addison-Wesley Publishers Ltd.
© 1995 Addison-Wesley Publishing Company, Inc.

Cover designed by Designers & Partners, Oxford
and printed by The Riverside Printing Co. (Reading) Ltd.
Typeset by Colset Private Limited, Singapore.
Printed in Great Britain at Biddles of Guildford.

ISBN: 0–201–59393–9

British Library Cataloguing in Publication Data
A catalogue record for this book is available.

Library of Congress Cataloging in Publication Data applied for.

For Marja Noorderhaven-Rog

Acknowledgements

The publisher would like to thank the following for permission to reproduce material in this book.

Figure 2.1 adapted from J. de Smit (1982), *Planning Rituals; The Development of a Planning Process for the Dutch University System*, Delft University Press, Delft. **Figure 4.2** from A. Tversky and D. Kahneman (1985), The framing of decisions and the psychology of choice, In *Behavioural Decision Making*, Plenum Publishing Corporation, New York. **Figure 4.3** from A. Tversky and D. Kahneman (1992), Advances in prospect theory: cumulative representation of utility, In *Journal of Risk and Uncertainty*, **5**, pp. 297–323. Reprinted by permission of Kluwer Academic Publishers. **Figure 5.6** from R.E. Coffey et al. (1994), *Management and Organizational Behaviour*, Irwin, Illinois. **Figure 6.5** adapted from R. A. Burgelman (1983), A Model of the Interaction of Strategic Behaviour, Corporate Context, and the Concept of Strategy, *Academy of Management Review*, **8**, p. 65. **Figures 7.1 and 7.2** from G. Johnson, (1988), Rethinking incrementalism In *Strategic Management Journal*, published by John Wiley & Sons Ltd, Chichester. **Figure 7.5** adapted from D.J. Hickson et al. (1986), A strategic contingencies theory of intraorganizational power, *Administrative Science Quarterly*, **16**, pp. 216–19, published by Basil Blackwell, Oxford. **Figure 8.4** adapted from Ch.R Schwenk and H. Thomas, (1983), reprinted from *Omega*, **11**, pp. 239–52 with kind permission from Elsevier Science Ltd, Kidlington OX5 1GB, UK. **Figure 8.5** adapted from R.O. Mason and I.I. Mitroff (1981), *Challenging Strategic Planning Assumptions*, Copyright © 1981 John Wiley & Sons, published by John Wiley & Sons, New York.

Box 1.2 adapted from J.A. Byrne (1994), The craze for consultants, In *Business Week*, 25 July pp. 46–50. Quotes from W. Kiechel, *Fortune*, ©1982 Time Inc. All rights reserved. **Box 2.1, Box 6.2, Box 8.1 and 8.3**, adapted from R. Heller (1989), *The Decision Makers*, published by Hodder and Stoughton Ltd, Falmouth. **Box 2.2** adapted from C. J. Loomis, In *Fortune*, ©1993 Time Inc. All rights reserved. **Box 3.1** adapted from S. Sherman, *Fortune*, ©1994 Time Inc. All rights reserved. **Box 3.2** adapted from C. J. Loomis, *Fortune*, ©1993 Time Inc. All rights reserved. **Box 4.2** adapted from F. Rice, *Fortune*, ©1994 Time Inc. All rights reserved. **Box 4.4** adapted from C. Eden and P. Simpson (1989), SODA and cognitive mapping in practice, In *Rational Analysis in a Problematic World*, Copyright © 1989 John Wiley & Sons. Reprinted by permission of John Wiley & Sons Ltd. **Box 4.6** adapted from H. Raffia (1991), Coping with common errors in rational decision making, In *Strategy and Choice*, pp. 341–57 R. J. Zeckhauser, ed., ©1991 MIT Press. **Box 5.1** adapted from D. Kirkpatrick, *Fortune*, ©1993 Time Inc. All rights reserved. **Box 5.2** adapted from T. P. Paré, *Fortune*, ©1994 Time Inc. All rights reserved. **Box 5.3** adapted from *Group Dynamics*, 2nd edition, by D. R. Forsyth. Copyright ©1990 by Brooks/Cole Publishing Company, a division of International Thompson Publishing Inc., Pacific Grove, CA 93950. Reprinted by permission of the publisher. **Box 6.3** adapted from J. Huey, *Fortune*, ©1993 Time Inc. All rights reserved. **Box 7.2** adapted from J.B. Quinn et al. (1988), *The Strategy Process: Concepts, Contexts and Cases*, pp. 262–9, published by Prentice-Hall, Englewood Cliffs NJ, ©1985 James Brian Quinn. **Box 7.5** adapted from D. Cray et al. (1991), Explaining decision processes, In *Journal of Management Studies*, **28**, pp. 13–39, published by Basil Blackwell, Oxford.

Preface

Many books on organizational strategy have been written, and new titles appear on the market regularly. Against this background, the addition of still another title could be seen as superfluous. However, *Strategic Decision Making* is different from the existing textbooks on strategic management. In the first place, the emphasis throughout the book is on the process of strategy formation. This is in marked contrast to the emphasis on the content of strategies which is characteristic of virtually all existing textbooks. Secondly, this book is predominantly descriptive, whereas prescription prevails in most textbooks. Thirdly, this book is more theoretically oriented than most other books, and seeks to bring together – under the unifying theme of strategic decision making – contributions from disparate disciplines, such as approaches from (social) psychology, sociology, management and business strategy.

Given these characteristics, this book is complementary to the typical strategic management textbook. It can be used in specialized courses on strategic decision making (for instance at the PhD level). But it can also be used as an additional textbook in broad strategic management courses (at the BA and MBA level), in order to allow more in-depth coverage of the process aspect of strategic management. In view of the envisaged usage of the book, it is deliberately kept short in spite of the relatively comprehensive coverage of the subject matter. No cases have been included, since these are available in plenty in the existing strategy textbooks (short boxed examples are used to illustrate the concepts and theories discussed). Also not covered are concepts and techniques from traditional schools of thought in strategic management (for example, growth-share matrices, experience curves), as well as from contemporary approaches (for example, resource-based strategy, value chains). Discussions of these concepts and techniques can also be found in existing strategic management textbooks.

The aim of this book is to provide a comprehensive overview of the many factors and conditions that influence the complex processes of strategic decision making within organizations. The first three chapters set the stage, by giving an introduction to the subject (Chapter 1), describing phases and steps in the decision-making process (Chapter 2), and by contrasting rational decision making and undeliberate choice behaviour, or 'programmed choice' (Chapter 3). After that, the book continues to discuss decision-making processes on the level of the individual (Chapter 4), the small group (Chapter 5), and the organization (Chapters 6 and 7), respectively. At a higher level, factors are added to those that play a role at the lower level. Thus, in order to understand decision processes at the level of the small group, we must have knowledge of individual decision making *and* group processes. This means that the subject matter of the chapters gradually becomes more complex. Given their complexity, two chapters are used to describe organizational decision processes. Chapter 6 focuses on the interplay between organizational strategy, structure and culture. An organization's structure and culture influence the decision processes that lead to the formation of a strategy, but that strategy in turn also influences the structure and culture. Chapter 7 discusses conceptual models that have been developed to describe and understand organizational decision processes, as well as empirical research into these processes. This book is written in the belief that an understanding of decision processes is a necessary basis for conscious attempts to improve organizational strategies. Therefore the book concludes with a discussion of techniques and procedures for improving decision making at the level of the individual, the group and the organization (Chapter 8).

Acknowledgements

Many people have contributed to this book. John Bell, who teaches the course on Strategic Decision Making at Tilburg University together with myself, has read first and second versions of most of the chapters. His suggestions have led to many improvements. Sytse Douma, Celeste Wilderom and Rik Pieters, all from Tilburg University, have read one or more chapters in draft versions, and three anonymous reviewers from Addison-Wesley have read the entire manuscript. Their comments have been invaluable. Vincent Driessen, my cheerful and efficient student-assistant, has spent many hours in the library collecting material. Thank you, Vincent. This book is dedicated to my mother, Marja Noorderhaven-Rog, who taught me the morals of decision making on the basis of personal principles rather than strategic considerations. Finally, and once more, I owe Myriam, Philippe and Rebecca an expression of gratitude that goes far beyond the traditional formulae. Will they believe me if I promise that now that this work is finished, I really will spend more time downstairs with them, and less in my study in the attic? Probably not.

Niels Noorderhaven
Berkel-Enschot
October 1994

Contents

1

Introduction

This book is about strategic decision making. It aims to describe and explain the decision-making processes that determine the future state of entities like business firms, government agencies, volunteer groups, and all other kinds of organizations. Clearly, this is a formidable task. According to John F. Kennedy, former president of the United States, it is even an impossible mission, as '[t]he essence of ultimate decision remains inpenetrable to the observer – often, indeed, to the decider himself . . . There will always be the dark and tangled stretches in the decision-making process – mysterious even to those who may be most intimately involved' (De Smit, 1982: 45).

Kennedy was at least partly right: decision-making processes are often of an unfathomable nature. On the other hand, it is possible to pry open the black box: today, a large body of decision-making literature exists, pertaining not only to processes taking place within the brains of individuals, but also to dynamics of group decision making, and organizational decision processes. Although our understanding is still far from complete, it is also true that we now know much more about the processes of decision making than in Kennedy's days.

This book builds on the findings reported in the literature to give a comprehensive overview of decision making, specifically in the context of organizational processes of strategy formulation and implementation. Moreover, on the basis of these insights into the decision process, however fragmentary, suggestions for improving strategic decision making within organizations are made. These can help avoiding common biases and mistakes, and thus contribute to the realization of organizational goals. Nevertheless, at the end of the book it will also be clear that many 'dark and tangled stretches' still remain. No book can make strategic decision making an easy task.

1.1 The concept of strategy

What is 'strategy'?

In order to grasp the subject, an understanding of the meaning of the concepts of 'strategy' and 'decision making' is needed. We will first focus on the concept of 'strategy'.

Strategy and military thought

The word 'strategy' is derived from the Greek 'strategos' – 'the art of the general' (Snow and Hambrick, 1980). Military strategy has to do with 'the practical adaptation of the means placed at a general's disposal to the attainment of the object in view' (Von Moltke, quoted in Liddell Hart, 1967: 320). It entails decisions, the outcome of which is both momentous and uncertain (see Box 1.1).

The example of French military strategy in the First World War can be used to point at a number of important characteristics of strategy and strategic decision making. In the first place, the example shows that the plan for the deployment of means can be altered radically – from defensive to offensive – even if the overall objective remains the same. This is true because this overall objective, for example, the protection of the sovereignty and the independence of the country, can be translated into more concrete goals in many different ways. Thus the choice of a strategy does not follow automatically from the ultimate goals pursued.

Secondly, in the formation of a strategy subjective assessment of imperfect or incomplete information plays an important role. On the basis of defective information concerning the strength of the German troops, or as a result of a wrong interpretation of the available information, the original French strategy was judged to be overly defensive.

Thirdly, the actual implementation of a strategy can lead to quite unexpected results. Dealing with surprises and changing plans when necessary is also part of strategic decision making.

Finally, strategic decision making is not only based on rational calculation but also on moral values (the 'French spirit') and emotions, and possibly also intuition. In the example, values and emotions set the general direction of the strategy; rational calculation was subsequently used in the elaboration of the plan of action.

Military strategy and organizational strategy

The use of military metaphors is common in literature on organizational strategy. This is understandable, for the characteristics of military strategy mentioned above also apply to the strategy of organizations. However, the metaphor has its limitations, as there also is an important difference between military and organizational strategy.

Box 1.1 Military strategy in the Great War

The swift defeat against the German army in 1870 caused the French to adopt a more cautious strategy in the decades preceding the First World War. A great system of fortresses was built along the frontier with Germany, and the plan was to intercept an attack with this line of defence, and to strike back subsequently. However, as time passed a new strategic school of thought rose to ascendancy, which saw this plan as excessively defensive and 'contrary to the French spirit'. A new plan, 'Plan XVII', was adopted, which provided for a headlong offensive against the whole of the German front. Thus, after the outbreak of the war in 1914 the French army developed an all-out offensive. However, the French right wing in Lorraine met with freshly reinforced German troops and was thrown back on the line of defense. The centre was repulsed after a head-on crash with the Germans in the Ardennes. The left wing barely escaped encirclement between the Sambre and the Meuse, and was also thrown back to defensive positions. 'Plan XVII' was finally abandoned after the French army had suffered serious losses, disorganization, and demoralization. Only the failure of their German opponents to fully seize the strategic advantage saved the French from disaster in the first year of the war.

(Source: Liddell Hart, 1967: 151–7)

In military strategy there is always an identifiable enemy – sometimes several. Achieving the ultimate end is nearly always dependent on the enemy not reaching his goals, whether these are defensive or offensive. This is not true of business firms. A business firm has its competitors, but economic competition is not necessarily the same kind of zero-sum game (i.e. what one party gains is a loss to another party) as military warfare is. Moreover, even an organization that has no competitors or 'enemies' can have a strategy. (For a contrary view, see Horwitz, 1979.)

Therefore, organizational strategy can best be specified more broadly as the determination of the function of the organization in its environment. In defining this function, an organization may have to pay attention not only to its competitors but also to any or all of the following groups of actors: clients, suppliers, stockholders, employees, the government, the general public (Mintzberg, 1983a). A business firm will, in its strategy, typically define in which markets it wants to compete, and with which products or services. A government office will demarcate its duties and fields of competence. An organized pressure group will specify the interests it wants to promote and the means it will use to do so. In all cases the relevant environment is defined, as well as the function of the organization within that environment.

Different kinds of strategy concepts

This book focuses on the **process** of strategic decision making. We will, therefore, ask questions pertaining to the processes leading to the choice of goals and means and to processes associated with the effective deployment of these means. We will have to consider conscientiously what demarcation of the concept of strategy is in keeping with this particular focus.

In some uses of the word, strategy is associated with the choice of a course of action in order to reach a given goal in a given situation. In the paradigmatic example of game theory two prisoners, who are accused of committing a crime together, make decisions in order to minimize their sentence (see, e.g., Frank, 1988: 29–30). The choice options and the associated outcomes are given: if both plead not guilty there is only enough evidence to convict them of a less serious offence, for which the penalty is five years in gaol. If both confess they will each go to gaol for 10 years. However, if only one of them confesses (they are held in separate cells), he will serve as witness for the prosecution, and receive a mild sentence of only a year, while the other spends 20 years in prison. Thus the situation, the choice options, the possible outcomes, and the goals (minimize punishment) are all given.

Game theory is a useful tool in the analysis of strategic problems. Some of the principles and applications of this approach will be discussed briefly in Chapter 3. But the concept of strategy used in game theory may be misleading. The goals of a business firm or other organization are not given but have to be decided on. Very general and abstract goals, like 'maximization of shareholder value' or 'provision of optimal services to clients' may be rooted in shared expectations, or laid down in the articles of association. One of the tasks of strategic management is to formulate more concrete goals that will allow the organization to move in the direction of these general and abstract aims (Haselhoff, 1976).

In contrast to the example from game theory given above, in the context of organizational strategy the situation cannot simply be taken as given. True enough, situational factors, like the number and kind of competitors in a market, may be regarded as given at one particular point in time. But as strategy has to do with the choice of the task of the organization, and with the choice of markets in which to compete, strategic decisions made in the present very much shape the situation the organization will be in tomorrow. Thus, regarding the situation as given misses an important aspect of strategy.

Furthermore, strategic decision making in organizations tends to take place in unstructured, open decision situations. This means that the set of options as well as the set of outcomes are at best partially known. As a consequence strategic decision making has to do less with the logic of maximization within constraints than with heuristics for finding feasible solutions (Spender, 1993).

The concept of 'strategy' is sometimes also used in evolutionary biology. In this case, the sets of options and outcomes are open, but there is no question of decision making. For example, females of the great golden digger wasp lay their eggs in a burrow filled with captured and paralysed grasshoppers, which provide food for their offspring when they hatch. The wasps may follow two different strategies: either they dig and fill their burrows themselves, before laying their eggs in it; or they try to use a burrow dug and provisioned by another female digger wasp. These strategies presumably have nothing to do with choice, however, but are genetically determined (Colman, 1982: 251). For any individual animal the strategy is fixed, although at the level of the species a change in the mix of occurring strategies is possible as a result of the forces of variation, retention and selection.

Certain approaches to organizations, for example, organizational ecology, employ a model of strategic choice that comes close to that of evolutionary biology (see, e.g., Carroll, 1988; Hannan and Freeman, 1989). In this book, however, we will persistently assume that strategy is characterized by at least a modicum of intentionality. This means that there is some kind of goal, and that the selection of means is somehow related to this goal. The intentions and goals in question, however, are not necessarily those of the actors normally labelled 'strategists' (top managers, strategic planners, etc.). In some cases strategic initiatives originating from lower levels of the organization may struggle for survival in a process of variation, selection and retention akin to that described in evolutionary biology (Burgelman, 1983). But in these cases, contrary to that of the 'strategy' of genes, intentional choice and behaviour do play an important role.

Intended and realized strategies

The fact that the intentions leading to a strategy may be not only those of top managers, but also those of other organization members, should make us wary of equating strategy with officially promulgated plans. Henry Mintzberg and James Waters have pointed at the fact that many plans never get implemented, and that what an organization actually does often has little to do with its official strategy (Mintzberg and Waters, 1985). In other words, there is a difference between **realized strategies** and **intended strategies**.

On the basis of the distinction between realized strategies and intended strategies, Mintzberg and Waters propose that 'strategy' should be defined as 'a pattern in a stream of actions' (Mintzberg and Waters, 1985: 257; see also Miles and Snow, 1978). In some cases this pattern is fully deliberate, i.e. plans are actually implemented. In other cases, however, the realized pattern of actions has very little to do with the planned strategy. Those strategies are called **emergent** by Mintzberg and Waters.

At the extreme, an emergent strategy could arise without intention. Action in this case is not preceded by decision. More often, however, conscious decisions by one or more individuals will lie at the basis of the strategy. Such a strategy is emergent from the perspective of top management, but deliberate from the perspective of those organization members sponsoring it.

If we want to understand the strategic decision-making process even decisions that fail to get implemented and lead to realized strategies are important. The same can be said of 'non-decisions', instances in which organization members fail to make up their minds. Mental processes associated with strategy formulation are interesting in their own right, as well as the very different kinds of processes that determine whether a strategy gets implemented or not.

Approaches to strategy

The study of organizational strategy has been approached in many different ways. (For overviews, see Chaffee, 1985; Mintzberg, 1990b; Thomas, 1984a.) We will briefly discuss three dimensions in which the various approaches differ, and indicate where on these dimensions our approach can be located.

Content and process

A first distinction that can be made is that between content approaches and process approaches. Content approaches focus on the question which strategy performs best under which circumstances. Work in this vein focuses for example on the influence of accumulated experience on cost structures, or on the relationship between market share and profitability (see, e.g., Allen and Hammond, 1976; Hedley, 1976; 1977; Schoeffler et al., 1974). Process approaches focus on the question of how strategies are made or should be made. Subjects covered include the degree of formalization of the process of strategy formation and the division of roles in the strategy formulation process (see, e.g., Bourgeois and Brodwin, 1984; Langley, 1988; Lyles, 1981). The position of this book on the content–process dimension is unambiguous. The focus is on the process of strategic decision making; very little attention will be paid to the content of the decisions in question.

Prescription and description

The second distinction is that between prescriptive and descriptive approaches. A large proportion of the literature of strategy is of a clearly prescriptive nature, that is, the authors try to formulate instructions for better strategies (content) or improved strategy making (process). The categories of prescription and description are not mutually exclusive. A contribution can first describe actual strategies or strategy-making processes, and subsequently evaluate these findings. This evaluation then forms the basis for prescriptions.

In this book the emphasis is on description. The first seven chapters constitute an attempt to come to grips with various aspects of strategic decision making, on the basis of the descriptive literature. The last chapter, on the other hand, is predominantly prescriptive and summarizes a number of techniques and procedures that can be used to improve strategic decision making in practice.

Formulation and implementation

Thirdly, approaches focusing on strategy formulation only can be distinguished from approaches focusing on strategy formulation *and* implementation. In general, earlier approaches focused predominantly on strategy formulation and tended to disregard implementation. In more recent contributions the implementation of strategy receives more attention, also in approaches that remain predominantly formulation orientated.

Apart from differences in focus, differences in assumptions regarding formulation and implementation exist. In some approaches a sharp distinction between formulation and implementation is assumed; in other approaches both activities are seen as closely interwoven. Virtually all the prescriptive literature falls in the first category. A good example is the textbook by Christensen and colleagues, *Business Policy: Text and Cases* (Christensen et al., 1987). The sharp demarcation between formulation and implementation, and the privileged position of the first, is typical of this approach (Mintzberg, 1990a).

More recently, the implementation process has been given more attention (see, e.g., Johnson, 1988; Mintzberg and McHugh, 1985; Quinn, 1980). In the new view, formulation isolated from implementation is a sterile process. Strategic management demands close interaction between thought and action. We will return to this issue in later chapters (in particular in Chapters 6 and 7); see also Box 1.2.

Although the topic of this text is strategic **decision making** – which could suggest that the emphasis is on strategy formulation – formulation and implementation are seen as equally important. In some cases formulation precedes, and is relatively isolated from, implementation. In other cases the two go hand in hand, and neither can be seen as prior to the other. We will use Henry Mintzberg's concept of **strategy formation** to refer to the broad process of strategy development without implicitly giving priority to either the formulation or the implementation concept (Mintzberg, 1978).

1.2 Strategy and decision making

The preceding section concentrated on the concept of 'strategy'. Now we will examine the concept of 'decision making'.

The concept of 'decision'

What is a 'decision'? The concept has to do with selection and commitment. Before a decision is made two or more alternative purposes or courses of action are competing for preference. If a decision is taken this means that an actor, the decision maker, has selected one purpose or plan and has committed himself to it (Emory and Niland, 1968: 12). Taking a decision is like turning a mental switch: before, various possibilities were considered, but once the decision is taken attention is focused on one option only. Note that a decision may pertain to goals as well as to means.

Box 1.2 Strategy implementation and management consulting

The tendency to put more emphasis on strategy implementation can also be recognized in the management consulting profession. At the beginning of the 1980s, Walter Kiechel criticized management consultants for selling strategic plans and concepts that failed to get implemented. 'The strategy was perfectly good', the consultants would say, 'the client just couldn't implement it'. Slightly more than a decade later, strategy implementation is booming business for the consultancy industry. Working in teams with managers from the client firm, consultants roll up their sleeves 'to perform the nitty-gritty implementation that's needed to deliver results'. That the implementation market is attractive for consulting firms is illustrated by Pittsfield, Massachusetts consulting firm General Systems Co. From 1991 on, General Systems has been working together with Tenneco Inc., Houston, in a 'cost of quality' project. The consultants 'virtually live' in the Tenneco buildings, and General Systems is reported to have pocketed $15 million to $20 million in fees over the years.

(Sources: Byrne, 1994; Kiechel, 1982)

Both selection and commitment are important (Mintzberg, 1981). If there is only one course of action available, no selection can be made, and the concept of 'decision' is hardly applicable. And if a purpose or plan is selected as the best, but the decision maker does not as yet feel committed to it, for all practical purposes no decision has been made. For example, an individual buying a car may, on the basis of a rational evaluation of all alternatives, come to the conclusion that one particular model is objectively preferable, but still lack the inner conviction that this is the best choice. This lack of commitment may be caused by a subconscious criterion (does the car confer sufficient status?) that conflicts with the criteria used consciously. In the case of organizational decision making, the selection of an alternative by an organization member may have to be ratified by another organization member before organizational commitment can be said to exist.

Decision 'making' now simply is the process of selection of and commitment to a purpose or plan of action. The word 'process' implies that decision making is a series of activities with a certain duration. Although a decision itself may be described as an instant – an essentially timeless phenomenon – decision making inevitably has a time dimension (Harrison, 1987). This is true of the selection process, as well as of the commitment process (the process of implementation may be seen as taking into effect the commitment expressed at the moment of choice).

Decision making and management

Decision making is often seen as the central activity of management. Some authors see decision making as virtually synonymous with management (Barnard, 1938; Simon, 1960: 1). But focusing on decisions may lead to an overly rationalistic view of management, and may blind us to other aspects of the managerial task. The concept of 'decision' can easily get in the way if we want to understand what is going on in organizations (Mintzberg and Waters, 1990).

A managerial decision consists of the selection of and commitment to a specific managerial action, but managerial action may also take place without decision. At least, this is true if with 'decision' we refer to a process of deliberate reasoning and weighing of evidence. Many decisions in organizations are 'programmed' by existing procedures, or are made on the basis of routine, without much conscious effort (March and Simon, 1993). Attention to this phenomenon is necessary if we want to understand organizational strategy. In Chapter 3 we will discuss 'programmed choice' and its relationship with rational decision making in the context of strategy.

1.3 Theorizing about organizational strategy

Four basic concepts

Before going into various possible views of organizational reality and con-comitant approaches to organizational strategy, four concepts need to be discussed. These concepts identify the conditions under which theorizing about organizational strategic decision making has meaning.

Complexity

The first concept is that of 'complexity'. If the situation is very simple, for instance because the circumstances clearly dictate one particular course of action, strategic decision making is trivial (Winter, 1987). However, if the number of variables or contingencies on which the strategy depends is suffi-ciently large and if there is not one clearly overriding factor or criterion, a strategy cannot be said to be determined by its environment. An example makes this clear. In a game of chess all possible moves and counter-moves are known, and if the players were able to oversee all possibilities the game would, after the first move, be completely determined. But the number of possibilities that have to be taken into account is enormous. Simon estimated that, assuming that the average length of a game of chess is 40 moves, 10^{120} possibilities must be considered (Simon, 1972: 166; for an assessment of the number of factors that have to be taken into account in strategic decision making, see Bourgeois, 1984). The cognitive limitations of human decision makers cause chess to remain a fascinating game. The same could be said of organizational strategy.

Uncertainty

Another important concept is that of 'uncertainty'. If a situation is complex but certain, decision makers may need a long time, but eventually they will often be able to precisely figure out the optimal strategy. Thus strategic decision making would be reduced to a sum in arithmetic. Frank Knight's distinction between uncertainty and risk is apposite (Knight, 1965). According to Knight, we can speak of 'risk' if the set of possible outcomes as well as the probability distribution is known. In the case of uncertainty, however, not all possible outcomes are known, so probabilistic information is inevitably incomplete. The situation can also be truly indeterminate, for instance because of the presence of other parties with unpredictable behaviour. In game-theory terms this is the case if players change their choice criteria during the course of a multi-period game. Finally, information from different sources may be incommensurable. Human understanding is of a fragmentary nature. A manager may not be able to make sensible combinations of old and new knowledge; indeed his or her existing knowledge base may consist of different fragments that cannot be combined to form a coherent whole (Spender, 1993). We will return to this aspect of uncertainty in Chapter 4.

Rationality

Above we have stressed that strategy is associated with intentionality. Decisions are made and actions are performed with an eye on certain goals. We will also assume that the selection of choices and actions is made in a sensible way, that the ability to reason is exercised. Some relationship between means and ends, as well as between reality and cognition is thus assumed to exist. This means that we associate strategic decision making with the concept of 'rationality'.

However, in order to call a decision rational it is not necessary that it is preceded by extensive analysis or calculation, nor that the influence of emotions is ruled out. 'All that is necessary to make the choice a rational one is that an objective exists and that the decision maker perceive and select some alternative that promises to meet the objective' (Harrison, 1987: 107). Rationality is a complicated concept, the more so, since many different kinds can be distinguished. In Chapter 3 rationality will be discussed in more detail.

Control

Finally, the concept of 'control' is of importance. If managers or other organization members do not have some measure of control over their organizations, no strategy can be said to exist. Without control, any pattern observable in a stream of decisions or actions at the level of an organization is the involuntary outcome of an interplay of causal forces rather than the intentional result of deliberate actions of individuals. The decision-making perspective would not be very useful then.

The control over the organization exercised by the focal actor(s) is a matter of degree. In small private firms the owner-manager usually exerts considerable power. The influence on all parts of the organization of the top manager of a large company inevitably is more limited.

There are almost always people who can exert more influence on the policy of the organization than others. In most cases these people are those invested with formal authority, such as the managers and directors of a business firm, the governor of an institution, the head of an agency. Decision making by these formal leaders is thus a logical starting point for the analysis. In this sense, a managerial perspective is maintained in this book. But the power and influence of managers is limited and we will always have to consider other sources of strategy in order to complete the picture.

Views of organizational reality

In modern organization theory various views of organization and strategy can be distinguished. Proponents of different approaches maintain divergent assumptions about the relation between organization and environment and about the nature of managerial decision making. These assumptions have to do with the view of, and importance attached to, the four concepts discussed above: complexity, uncertainty, rationality and control.

We will discuss three broad categories of theories: external determinism, internal struggle and symbolic action. All three approaches, if pushed to extremes, leave little room for theorizing about strategic decision making. External determinism leads to a view of strategy as the outcome of a computation; the internal struggle approach sees strategy as the unplanned outcome of a tug-of-war; in the symbolic action view strategic decision making is a largely ritual activity.

External determinism

An important part of organizational theorizing is characterized by outside-in explanations: properties of organizations are seen as a reaction to the demands put on the organization by its environment (environment in a broad sense, including, e.g., technology, size, age, and market turbulence). This is true for instance for contingency theories of organization, which posit a deterministic relationship between the environment and structural features of organizations (see, e.g., Burns and Stalker, 1961; Lawrence and Lorsch, 1967; Woodward, 1965).

In the wake of structural contingency theory, deterministic theories of strategy have also been developed. Charles Hofer, for instance, suggested a model based on the product life-cycle concept (Hofer, 1975). In each of the various product life-cycle stages (introduction, growth, etc.) a different kind of strategy can be assumed to be optimal. The task of the strategist would be to correctly interpret the environment, and to select the appropriate strategy. Strategies in this view can be taken from the shelf, ready-made and fit for implementation. Strategic decision making is reduced to a set of calculations.

The deterministic flavour of structural contingency theory has been criticized by John Child (Child, 1972; see also Crozier and Friedberg, 1977; Grandori, 1987). According to Child, contingency theorists fail to acknowledge that organizational decision makers actually *choose* many of the 'contingencies' that supposedly determine the form of their organizations. Furthermore, the complexity of the many possible different combinations of environmental variables precludes a simple calculation of the optimal organizational form.

The same kind of criticism can be levelled at deterministic theories of organizational strategy. Here also, the number of factors that should be taken into account if a decision maker were to calculate the optimal strategy is prohibitively large. Hence the opposite view gains force, according to which strategy making is first and foremost a creative activity (Bourgeois, 1984; Mahoney, 1993).

Internal struggle

Another group of organizational theories focuses on political processes within the organization. These theories form a reaction to approaches that see the structure and policy of an organization as logically determined by objective properties of its task environment. Authors in this school of thought point to the fact that organizations consist of individual actors pursuing private goals (Cyert and March, 1963; Eden, 1992; Mintzberg, 1985; Narayanan and Fahey, 1982; Pettigrew, 1973; 1977). Strategy in this view is not a deliberate plan designed by the organizational leaders, but the outcome of a tug-of-war between all those who have a stake in the organization.

This approach was first developed and applied in the context of public administration (Lindblom, 1959). In this kind of organization performance criteria are more ambiguous than in business firms. Because of a more bureaucratic style, top managers have less discretionary power. In business firms top managers may be expected to be able to exert significant influence on the strategy.

Also, the personal goals of the top managers of business firms (as well as those of many other kinds of organizations) will rarely clash head-on with the overall goals of the firm. It is good for the personal career of a top manager if his or her firm does well. The fact that power always has to be shared may be helpful, too. Other managers and organization members can be trusted to keep watch and prevent the top manager from substituting his or her personal goals for those of the organization as a whole. (In this context the discussion about the incidence of 'corporate plundering' by managers is apposite. See, e.g., Berle and Means, 1932; Stigler and Friedland, 1983.)

Symbolic action

A third school of thought stresses the fact that environmental factors can never directly influence the organization, but only via the perception of decision makers. In a way, this approach embraces the open-system view of received contingency theory (Romme, 1992). Furthermore, the environment is not only interpreted by decision makers, it is also for a large part socially constructed. The organizations and institutions which surround an organization are not objective natural phenomena, but the product of social interaction and sense-making (Berger and Luckmann, 1966; Weick, 1979).

Strategic management in this view is symbolic action: manipulation of symbols and meanings in order to influence the interpretations of organizational members and of actors in the environment. In positive cases this may cause organization members to be more strongly motivated and other 'stakeholders' to have a more favourable view of the organization (Chaffee, 1985; Van Cauwenbergh and Cool, 1982). But in negative cases, if the belief systems of managers are constantly reinforced, strategic decision making becomes a purely ritual activity (Johnson, 1988; Kets de Vries and Miller, 1984; March, 1981).

The strategic triangle

All three approaches – external determinism, internal struggle and symbolic action – shed light on important aspects of management and organization. But a view of organizations in which the concept of strategic decision making assumes an important place has to resist far-reaching claims from each of the three schools of thought discussed above. This is illustrated in Figure 1.1.

Against the claim of external determinism that the strategy of an organization is completely determined by objectively given environmental factors, the strategic decision view puts the argument that in most cases the complexity and uncertainty of the situation preclude an unequivocal interpretation of causal relations. In reaction to the assertion of the internal struggle approach, the strategic decision view states that in most organizations one or more top decision makers have substantially more power than others and that they thus can exert the control over the organization necessary for implementing their preferred strategies (Mazzolini, 1981). The picture of strategic management painted by proponents of the symbolic action approach is qualified by stressing the intended rationality of strategic decision making. It is to the detriment of the organization if the strategic decision-making process becomes a ritual dance. In the long run the position of organizations that lack responsiveness to environmental change becomes untenable (Johnson, 1988).

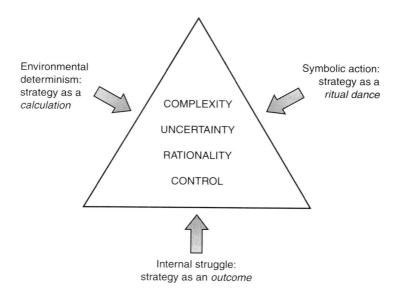

Figure 1.1 The strategic triangle.

1.4 Overview of the book

This chapter and the following two chapters set the stage by explaining basic concepts and by describing the process of decision making and various views on its rationality. Chapter 2 focuses on the decision-making process, and briefly describes the various phases of this process. Chapter 3 elaborates on the concept of rationality, compares various kinds of rationality and discusses the difference between rational decision making and programmed choice, as well as the interaction between both spheres of strategy making.

The next two chapters focus on the rational aspect of strategy and show which factors get in the way of fully rational decision making. The emphasis is on strategy formulation. Chapter 4 describes the psychology of decision making, and deals with issues such as perception, decision heuristics and attitudes towards risk. Chapter 5 discusses the sociology of decision making, and focuses on characteristics of group decision making and the role of power in the decision-making process.

In Chapters 6 and 7, the programmed choice aspect of strategy assumes a central place and organizational strategic decision-making processes are explained. The emphasis is on strategy implementation. Chapter 6 explores the intricate interplay between strategy, structure and culture. Chapter 7 discusses the evolution of models for describing and prescribing organizational (strategic) decision making and presents the findings of empirical research into organizational decision processes.

Chapter 8 describes techniques and procedures that can be used to improve the practice of strategic decision making within organizations. This final chapter deals specifically with the question of how strategic decision making processes can be revitalized.

Chapter summary

■ Strategic decision making concerns the goals of an organization as well as the means to reach these goals.

■ Strategic decision making takes place in open, unstructured decision situations, that is, the sets of options and outcomes are not given.

■ Realized strategies are patterns in a stream of actions that can *post hoc* be distinguished. Intended strategies are the plans of decision makers.

■ A decision is made if an option is selected, and if commitment to the implementation of that option has been expressed.

■ Strategic decision situations are characterized by complexity and uncertainty, strategic decision makers by the intention to make rational decisions and by the ability to exert control over their organizations.

2

The decision-making process

As the focus of this book is on the process of strategic decision making, it is necessary to explore the nature of decision-making processes. This chapter provides a general overview of the various steps that can be distinguished in such processes, and briefly describes the activities that constitute each step.

2.1 Decision making as a process

A structural model of decision making

In many approaches, decision making is not seen as a process, but as a calculation outside the time dimension. In economics in particular, models of the kind illustrated in Figure 2.1 are favoured. We will call this kind of model **logical-structural**, as the emphasis is on the structural aspects of the decision situation (as contrasted with the process aspects), and as the decision maker is assumed to consider alternatives in a strictly logical way.

Elements and relations

In the model in Figure 2.1 three categories of elements, and the relationships between these elements, are distinguished (Ackoff and Emory, 1972). The elements of the decision situation are: the decision maker, outcomes and means leading to outcomes. The decision maker is assumed to be able to rank the outcomes according to his preferences. If the decision maker has no preference, or if he cannot distinguish between different outcomes, no decision situation

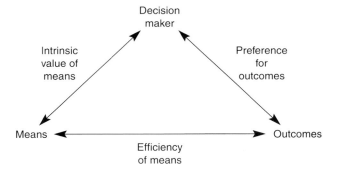

Figure 2.1 A logical-structural model of decision making. (Source: De Smit, 1982.)

can be said to exist. Furthermore, the decision maker is assumed to have information regarding the relationship between means and outcomes. A means leads to a certain outcome with a certain probability and at certain costs.

Problem solving and problem finding

If means are seen as fully instrumental in relation to outcomes, this is all there is to the decision situation. The decision maker can now compare outcomes and efficiencies, and select the most preferable means. This is the kind of decision situation considered in the 'problem solving' literature. The situation is more complex if the decision maker is also allowed to have preferences for means. In this case, these preferences have to be taken into consideration in the selection of means in relation to preferred outcomes. Sometimes, the preference for a given means may outweigh the preference for outcomes. The solution is known, but now the decision maker is looking for an opportunity to apply it. This kind of problem situation may be called 'problem finding'.

In both problem solving and problem finding all the elements and relationships are assumed to be present and fixed. Logical-structural models focus on the short run and view decision making as responding to exogenously given circumstances. The act of decision making is not assumed to lead to new information concerning the efficiency of means or the preference for outcomes. The time dimension may be incorporated into the model to the extent that discounting of future income streams influences the ranking of outcomes. But the decision situation itself is conceptualized as static.

This abstraction is most acceptable in simple decision-making situations. However, if the complexity increases, individual cognitive constraints as well as group dynamics complicate matters, and the abstract model is ill-fitted. In these cases it is better to face up to this complexity and conceptualize decision making as a multi-stage, sequential process.

Process models of decision making

Process models have been developed mainly in psychological approaches to decision making. The basic idea is that decision making is a time-consuming process, in which various kinds of activities, taking place at different moments, can be discerned. The decision process is a sequence of activities (Hauschildt, 1986; for an early formulation of this view, see Dewey, 1933). In most of the process models at least three basic (groups of) activities are distinguished: problem identification, generation of alternative solutions and evaluation of alternatives (Simon, 1965; for a discussion of decision process models in cognitive psychology, see Maule (1985) and for a discussion of strategic decision making process models, see Schwenk, 1984). In the simplest case, the process is assumed to be unidirectional: problem identification leads to the generation of alternatives, which are subsequently evaluated.

Three phases of decision making

Process models differ from structural models in that the decision situation is not assumed to be given, but is constructed by the decision maker, who is no longer assumed to be able to oversee all aspects of the decision situation at the same time. The decision maker first has to recognize the situation as one calling for decision making, that is, he must become aware of the existence of different possible outcomes to which he assigns different preferences.

In the second phase, possible means for reaching a desired outcome are searched for. Here the important difference with structural models is that solutions are not given, but have to be found or generated. This again is a time-consuming process. During this process, the world is not frozen, but all factors are subject to change.

Thirdly, the options generated have to be evaluated against the outcomes they produce. This evaluation may appear to parallel that in the structural model, but whereas all alternatives are typically evaluated simultaneously in the structural models, in the process models several possibilities exist. For instance, each solution may be evaluated immediately after having been generated. Or several solutions may be generated and then evaluated simultaneously.

In simple process models it is implicitly assumed that after the evaluation, the decision itself is a foregone conclusion. Either the first acceptable solution, or – in the case of simultaneous evaluation of several alternatives – the best solution is chosen. We will see below that this is not always a realistic assumption.

Implications

Two important conclusions can be drawn from the discussion of simple process models. In the first place, decision making is seen as a path-dependent process. Interpretations, selections and choices made in earlier phases constrain the decision-making process in later phases. Secondly, although descriptively more sophisticated models may provide for feedbacks from later to earlier phases, real costs and psychic costs are assumed to be associated with returning to previous phases. Therefore, the process is not necessarily iterated as long as would be necessary to reach a solution equivalent to the outcome of a complete structural model, but may very well be aborted at an earlier stage.

However, a process model consisting only of the steps of recognition, generation, and evaluation is incomplete if applied to organizational strategic decision making. The reason is that the model stops where action begins. Action is an inextricable part of strategy, and therefore a satisfactory process model will also have to encompass the *implementation* of the chosen solution.

Furthermore, the act of choice should also be included as an explicit step. In an organizational setting there is often a division of labour prescribing that certain individuals are assigned the tasks of generating and evaluating alternatives, while the actual choice itself is the prerogative of another functionary. This means that the alternative evaluated as best will not necessarily be chosen.

Finally, for a description and explanation of organizational decision-making processes it makes sense to use a more microscopic model, and to distinguish various steps within the main phases of the process. Below we will construct and discuss a process model of decision making that explicitly reflects these insights and considerations.

2.2 Phases and steps in the decision-making process

The process of decision making can be conceptualized in many different ways (see, e.g., Harrison, 1987; Mintzberg et al., 1976; Nutt, 1993; Thomas, 1984a). In order to be satisfactory, at least three more or less distinct phases should be distinguished. First of all, the decision maker should come to realize that there is an opportunity or even a necessity to take a decision, and a first approximate formulation of the problem has to be made. This is the 'awareness' phase. Secondly, the decision maker has to consider what it is that he wants to achieve, and compare and evaluate possible options. This is the 'analysis' phase. Thirdly, true to what was stated above, the act of choice should be considered explicitly, as well as the implementation of the decision and the control of the implementation process. This final phase is that of 'action'.

A conceptual model of decision making

Each of the three phases mentioned above consists of various distinct steps. This brings us to the conceptual model in Figure 2.2. In this model, eight steps in the decision-making process are distinguished. These steps will be briefly described in section 2.3. This discussion will give an impression of the kinds

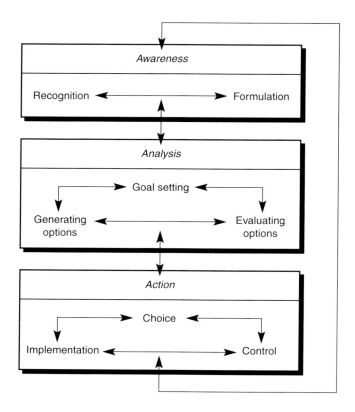

Figure 2.2 A conceptual model of organizational decision making.

of activities that are taking place and of the kinds of mechanisms governing each part of the decision making process. We will first discuss the general outlines of the conceptual model. (This model is derived from the many existing process models, in particular those of Harrison, 1987 and Mintzberg et al., 1976.)

The eight decision-making steps are clustered into three phases. The implication of this clustering is that although all steps are interrelated, the interrelationships between the steps within one decision phase are particularly strong. As far as the direction of influences and the sequence of steps and phases is concerned, the model is deliberately unspecific.

Thus, although the obvious order of phases would be awareness, analysis, action, it is also possible that the decision process starts with action, and that awareness and analysis come only later (March and Simon, 1993: 15). This could be the case if a decision maker initially tries to deal with a problem using a routine response, and only if the expected effects fail to materialize becomes aware of the true nature of the problem and starts to generate and analyse possible solutions.

Especially within the distinct phases, the process of going through the different steps is iterative rather than sequential. For instance, the setting of goals obviously influences the generation and evaluation of solutions. But the evaluation of solutions may also influence the goals, for only in the process of evaluating options it becomes clear which level of aspiration is realistic.

There is more to be said about this conceptual model. In particular, questions regarding the descriptive and normative status of the model are relevant. We will deal with these questions at the end of this chapter. First, we will compare this descriptive model with the kind of model that dominates textbooks on strategic management.

Comparison with the normative-rational model of strategy making

Many strategy textbooks propagate a particular kind of decision process model (see, e.g., Ansoff and McDonnel, 1990; Hill and Jones, 1989; Johnson and Scholes, 1993; Nutt, 1989). Because of its strongly prescriptive nature and the emphasis on systematic rational choice, this model can be dubbed the **normative-rational model** (see, e.g., Bourgeois, 1984; Hitt and Tyler, 1991; and Huff and Reger, 1987). Since the discussion of decision-making models in this chapter is geared to foster an understanding of organizational strategy-making processes, a comparison with the dominant normative model is apposite. Figure 2.3 presents a representative example of the normative-rational model of strategy making.

Many of the steps distinguished in the model in Figure 2.2 are also present in this normative-rational model. However, the awareness phase is not explicitly included. Instead, the SWOT analysis (analysis of strengths, weaknesses, opportunities and threats) is assumed to set the agenda for decision making. A SWOT analysis is a methodical analysis of the issues found to be of interest in the internal and external analysis. Important trends or events in the environment are identified as either opportunities or threats. Characteristics of the organization are divided into strengths and weaknesses. Next, a confrontation of strengths, weaknesses, opportunities and threats takes place, in which questions are raised concerning the potentiality of using strengths for exploiting opportunities and concerning the danger that weaknesses may disable the organization in warding off threats, and so on (see, e.g., David, 1991; Dess and Miller, 1993).

The analysis phase has an important place in the normative-rational model, but goal setting is not normally assumed to be part of this process. Rather, the goals are assumed to be formulated at the very beginning of the decision-making process (see Box 2.1). This is an important difference with the process model adopted here, in which goals are set in close interaction with the generation and evaluation of options.

The act of choice is normally not represented in the normative-logical kind of model. This is not surprising, as the rationality assumption implies that the alternative evaluated as best will automatically be chosen. The generation

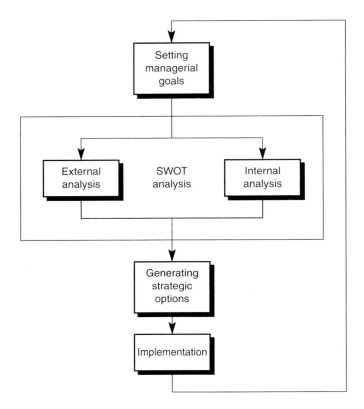

Figure 2.3 The normative-rational model of strategy making.

of options is explicitly included in the model in Figure 2.3, but the normative-rational literature on strategy offers little assistance in this phase of the decision-making process (Mintzberg, 1994: 66–7). In some of the literature, the importance of creativity is stressed (Christensen et al. 1982: 186). In other contributions, standard options in the form of 'generic strategies' are suggested (see, e.g., Porter, 1980). In both cases insufficient light is shed upon the actual process of designing alternative courses of action.

Finally, although a perfunctory feedback loop is a standard feature of normative-rational models, the approach basically assumes a linear sequence of activities. The feedback loop can be understood as indicating that the outcomes of the implementation process, that is, realized strategies, have an impact on the goals governing the next strategy making process. Or, alternatively, the feedback loop can be seen as indicating that in case the implementation leads to unexpected results the process has to be re-iterated. The ideas expressed in the model of Figure 2.2, namely that the various steps in the decision process are closely interrelated and that the process is of an iterative rather than sequential nature, seem to be alien to the bulk of the normative strategy literature.

We will now turn to a more detailed discussion of our process model.

Box 2.1 SWOT analysis and goal setting

Goal setting is normally assumed to precede the SWOT analysis in normative-rational approaches, but that does not mean that the process has no bearing on goals and objectives. Premier Brands arose in 1986 as the result of a highly leveraged management buy-out from Cadbury Schweppes. The company carried a number of brands, like Smash instant mashed potato and Marvel dried low-fat milk, which formerly at Cadbury Schweppes had been regarded as 'dogs', and starved of investment. Premier Brands chairman Paul Judge let all managers write down what they saw as the strengths, weaknesses, opportunities and threats for the business as a whole and for their department in particular. The main aim of this exercise was to set targets much higher than in the past, when the same managers were neglecting these brands. Judge used the SWOT procedure to make everybody aware of the need to change, and to get a focus on the key assets, strengths and priorities of Premier Brands.

(Source: Heller, 1989: 179–82)

2.3 Eight steps in the decision-making process

Recognition

Paying attention

Before decision makers enter into a decision-making process, they will have to recognize a need to do so. In the logical-structural models the decision maker's awareness of the elements of the decision making situation is part of the assumptions. Thus the recognition of the need or opportunity to make a choice is a foregone conclusion. But in practice it is not that obvious (Kiesler and Sproull, 1982). Decision makers have to make sense of weak signals in the form of streams of ambiguous data, like informally voiced opinions, trade gossip, articles in the business press, and so on. Presumably signals that a decision has to be made will have to exceed a threshold value before being noticed (Ansoff and McDonnel, 1990: ch. 5; Mintzberg et al., 1976).

But not only the weakness of signals can cause failure to recognize a decision opportunity or need; information overload can lead to the same problem (Taylor, 1975b). Decision makers have limited cognitive abilities, and therefore cannot attend to everything at the same time. The allocation of managerial time and attention, and the factors influencing this allocation are obviously important factors in the decision-making process (Dutton et al., 1983; March and Sevón, 1988).

Interpretation of signals

The way in which signals are initially interpreted is important for the rest of the decision process. Many firms periodically engage in a SWOT analysis as discussed above. The use of the SWOT analysis as an interpretative scheme has important implications, for it makes a difference whether a trend in the environment is initially interpreted as a threat or as an opportunity (or, more neutrally, as a problem). For example, a technological development that is interpreted as a threat arouses more attention from top management than a technological development perceived as an opportunity. At the same time, when strategic issues are interpreted as threatening, or if the relevant factors are seen as being beyond control, managers tend to be less open to information (Dutton and Jackson, 1987; Starbuck, 1983; Thomas and McDaniel, 1990). More generally, a situation that is labelled as positive will trigger different actions than a situation that is labelled as negative (Smircich and Stubbart, 1985).

While it is clearly important whether a change in the environment is interpreted as a threat or as an opportunity, the distinction between threats and opportunities is all but clear cut. The two are not simply opposites. Rather, both categories are most easily distinguished from events which are not urgent or have little impact. Events which are urgent and important can be interpreted differently, depending on the position and personal characteristics of the decision maker. For instance, if the decision maker has considerable autonomy, he or she is more likely to interpret an event as an opportunity than if his or her actions are constrained by others. Likewise, when the decision maker feels qualified for the job, an event is more likely to be seen as an opportunity. For someone who feels underqualified, almost every change is threatening (Jackson and Dutton, 1988).

Not only processes on the level of individual cognition play a role in the interpretation of signals. Interpretation is also very much a socially influenced process. People watch other people's reactions, and adapt their own interpretation of the situation to the interpretations ascribed to others (Lea et al., 1987: 248). Political interests may also play a role, as participants in the decision process try to influence the interpretation of trends and events to suit their own needs (Narayanan and Fahey, 1982).

A periodic survey of the internal and external environment is important, because without such a procedure it is less likely that important changes are noticed and that the need to come to a decision is realized (see Box 2.2). The default answer in case a relevant issue is not detected is always to continue business as usual. In the case of momentous events this response may be catastrophical. However, the SWOT analysis may be performed in a routine way, without much deliberate managerial attention (Dutton, 1993).

This means that even if new events are observed, they may be interpreted as variations of old, familiar issues, and elicit routine responses. The fact that

Box 2.2 Reading the signs of change at Sears Roebuck

Sears Roebuck, the world's sixth largest corporation in market value in 1972, was the absolute ruler of retailing in the USA for many years. But at Sears the enormous success bred failure. Over the years, a whole library of 'bulletins' was built up, spelling out procedures for dealing with almost any problem. This inevitably brought with it a strong tendency to interpret the environment in terms of these bulletins. To quote a former senior executive of Sears: 'God forbid that there should be a problem that comes up for which there isn't a bulletin. That means the problem is *new!*'. Not surprisingly, this attitude prevented Sears from noticing the rise of a new type of competitor. Well into the 1980s Sears produced competitor analyses which failed to mention Wal-Mart (which in 1990 was to overtake Sears in terms of market share). One commentator called Sears the corporate equivalent of a laboratory 'boiled frog': 'the hapless creature that sits calmly and unsuspiciously in water whose temperature is gradually raised to the killing point'.

(Source: Loomis, 1993)

a strategic issue is detected does not mean that it will be correctly or even adequately understood (Kiesler and Sproull, 1982). This brings us to the next step: problem formulation.

Formulation

Problem formulation is strongly connected to problem recognition. On the basis of the perception developed during the problem recognition phase, the problem will be couched in terms of decision makers, ends and means. This structuring is very important for the further course of the decision process, as it plays a pivotal role in determining what and whom will be included in and excluded from the further course of the decision process (Dutton et al., 1983; Nutt, 1993). The formulation of the problem also has a bearing on the question of whether the decision maker feels that a solution does in fact exist. Apparently unsolvable problems and impracticable solutions are much less likely to initiate further decision-making activities (Mintzberg et al., 1976).

Apart from the structuring of problems in terms of ends and means, it is important how narrowly or how broadly the problem is defined. A problem definition which is too broad fails to direct attention, and may lead to profound but non-committal philosophizing. But a too narrow problem definition leads to an unduly restricted search for solutions (Nutt, 1993). This is a fundamental dilemma: the rewards of 'aggressive' problem definitions, suggesting likely solutions, can only be realized by running the risk of dashing down a false path (Smith, 1989).

Another difficulty at the problem definition phase is that firms tend to categorize problems in terms of their internal organization structure. This means that a problem is conceived as a marketing problem, a production problem, a personnel problem, and so on. Once a problem has been labelled in such a way, the potential decision makers and kinds of solutions are also identified, perhaps prematurely (Hall and Saias, 1980; Nutt, 1993).

Goal setting

Explicit goals?

The issue of goal setting is controversial. The importance of explicitly formulating organizational goals is stressed in the prescriptive strategy literature (see, e.g., David, 1991: 210; Dess and Miller, 1993: 6; Hill and Jones, 1989: 37 – 8; Smith et al. 1991: 65). But are goals really made explicit in real-world organizational decision making? Here we have to distinguish between the official goals and the goals that actually guide the decision process (Perrow, 1961). Official goals can be found in documents such as promulgated mission statements. It is, however, unlikely that business firms would make public all their aims, because in this way they would effectively be giving away their strategy.

From another point of view, the suggestion in the normative strategy literature that organizations need goals in order to direct their activities can be questioned. Individuals sometimes act without conscious goals or preferences: 'We create our wants, in part, by experiencing our choices' (March and Simon, 1993: 15). There is no a priori reason why the same mechanism would not be operative at the level of organizations (Mintzberg and Waters, 1985).

The problem of organizational goals

More fundamental is the question what is to be understood by 'the goals' of an organization. Individuals have drives and aspirations that can conceivably form the basis of operative goals. (These goals in turn act as important motivators of behaviour, cf. Bandura, 1986: 467 – 82.) But the use of the concept of organizational goals seems to be tantamount to a reification of the organization. The organization, as such, does not have goals and does not take decisions; only individuals within the organization do so. How can an organization consisting of individuals pursuing their own personal goals exhibit goal-orientated behaviour?

We do not propose to answer this question here in any detail, but just point out that organizational goals can be conceived of as sets of constraints imposed on choices to be made by organization members, in particular upper level managers. Just like all other individuals, organization members pursue their personal goals, but the situational constraints imposed on their behaviour by the organization promote their decisions to be conducive to the survival and prosperity of the organization (Simon, 1964).

Preference orderings versus aspiration levels

How should we conceive of the kind of goals pursued in practical decision making? In economic theory, as well as in the logical-structural model of decisions, the goals directing decision making are conceptualized as consistent **preference orderings**. This means that if a decision maker is confronted with the choice between two different outcomes, he is always able to express a preference for one of the two, or to state indifference. This is true even if outcomes differ in many dimensions, and if many combinations are possible. Furthermore, preference orderings are assumed to be stable over time: if A is preferred over B today, this will also be true tomorrow.

We will discuss the concept of preference orderings and the assumptions underlying this concept in the next chapter. Here we will only indicate that it is unlikely that goals in the form of preference orderings guide practical decision processes. With preference orderings, one can only say that the goals have been reached if an optimal solution – given the situational constraints – has been found. Optimality gives no direction to the decision-making process, for one can decide about optimality only if all the alternatives are known and have been evaluated and compared – but then the decision process is also completed. As in practical situations the number of possible solutions is often unknown or unlimited, and as the consequences of many alternatives are highly uncertain, it is no surprise that goals explicitly stated as optimum solutions appear to be rare (Hauschildt, 1986).

Decision makers need a goal concept that enables them to take shortcuts and to economize on information requirements. Such a goal concept is that of an **acceptable level** or **level of aspiration**. Instead of searching for an elusive optimal solution, decision makers focus on a target stating acceptable levels of achievement in specified dimensions. As soon as a solution meeting the requirements is found, the search process can be discontinued. This style of decision making is called 'satisficing', to distinguish it from the 'maximizing' of logical-structural decision models (Cyert and March, 1963; March and Simon, 1993).

Goal finding

It should be obvious from the above, but it bears repeating: in strategic decision making, goals cannot be assumed to be given. Experimental data suggest that at the level of the individual, preferences are inconsistent and imprecise, and change over time (Fischhof et al., 1980; March and Olsen, 1976). This has to do with the fact that it is very difficult to know what one prefers if one does not know what is feasible. It makes sense to assume, therefore, that goal setting takes place in close interaction with the generation and evaluation of alternatives: 'decision-makers develop their goals in a continuous dialectical process with their search for alternatives and their view of the situation' (Hauschildt, 1986: 12). This will apply *a fortiori* at the level of organizations, where goals have to be constructed by a plurality of participants.

Operationalization of goals

A great deal of words could be used to work out the difference between various levels and kinds of goals. A common distinction is that between the 'mission', and the 'goals and objectives' of an organization. The mission is a broad statement of purpose, expressing the *raison d'être* of the organization (Johnson and Scholes, 1993: 186–7). Goals and objectives are more concrete and specific translations of these general statements.

Mission statements are most of the time formulated as open objectives, that is, they are formulated in such a way that actual achievements cannot unambiguously be measured against them. Goals and objectives are often, but not always, formulated as closed objectives, that is, performance towards them can be measured (Johnson and Scholes, 1993: 190). This is for instance the case if they are formulated as acceptable levels or aspiration levels.

In the case of closed objectives, three dimensions are important. In the first place, goals refer to a future state of reality. The organization wants to achieve something, for example, to raise its market share by a certain percentage. This is the dimension of achievement in the sphere of reality. Secondly, certain financial goals or constraints apply. This is achievement in the financial sphere. Thirdly, both types of achievements are placed within a time-frame.

All three dimensions of goals are highly relevant. If the organization succeeds in reaching its goal in the sphere of reality, for example, a product innovation is realized, but it fails in the dimension of finance (the innovation is too expensive) or in the time dimension (the innovation is too late), the success of the strategy is questionable. Note that a statement of financial goals without goals in the sphere of reality will not do. A simple statement like 'our company aims to double its profits every five years' can only lead to choice and action if supplemented – explicitly or implicitly – with goals pointing at specific real achievements.

Generating options

In contrast to the logical-structural model, the assumption in the process model is that options (or alternatives, or means) are not always given, but often must be found or developed. This brings into focus the economics of information and the nature of the processes leading to solutions.

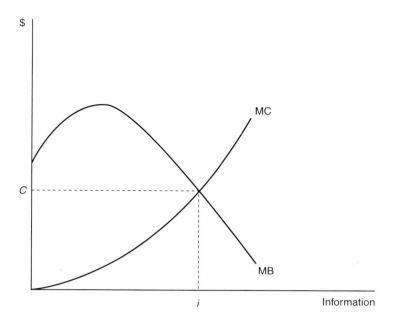

Figure 2.4 Marginal costs and benefits of information.

Economics of information

At the outset, decision makers mostly have only limited information about feasible options and their consequences. They can decide to gather more information, but there are costs associated with this process. Normally, one will begin gathering the information that is most easily accessible. This will often be information available within the organization itself. The next step is to acquire information that is readily available in the market, for example, information in the form of standard marketing surveys. Gradually, however, a decision maker will have to invest more and more time and money for acquiring additional information. For instance, a custom-made market survey is more expensive than general surveys produced on a routine basis. The upshot is that the cost of information tends to rise exponentially (see Figure 2.4).

On the other hand, the benefits of the information gathered may be assumed not to rise continuously. The marginal benefit of information, that is, the extra value to the decision maker of an additional bit of information, will rise initially, but after a while it is likely to decline. The reason for this is that the first bits of information help the decision maker to build a frame of reference. This frame of reference then helps to categorize and interpret the information that is subsequently acquired (Johnson and Russo, 1984; Van Raaij, 1988). For instance, when buying a washing machine, a consumer may use the initially acquired information to categorize the obtainable appliances in price ranges, in front-loaders and top-loaders, and according to programme options. These categories help him or her to interpret and make the most of additional information, and therefore the marginal utility of information will rise for some time.

However, after a while the marginal utility of information is likely to decline, as new information tends to duplicate the information already available. This means that theoretically an optimum exists, namely at the point at which the marginal utility of information equals its marginal cost. Up to that point, the benefit of additional information outweighs the cost of acquiring it. Past that point, the value added by additional information is insufficient to justify the costs.

The *practical* usefulness of Figure 2.4 is limited, however. It is very difficult to estimate the costs and benefits of chunks of information. It is therefore also very difficult for decision makers to assess their position on the curves, and to decide whether the optimum has already been reached or not. But the idea that information gathering will not continue indefinitely or until the information is deemed to be complete has a strong intuitive appeal.

Apart from cost considerations, search processes are often restricted because of time limitations. If a firm spends too much time gathering information competitors may take the lead and realize first-mover advantages. A too-prolonged search for information may also be self-defeating because as time passes the information initially acquired becomes outdated, so that part of the search process would have to be repeated (Ölander, 1975). For instance, when looking for a second-hand car, a prospective buyer would have to check regularly whether the cars viewed at the beginning of the search process are still available.

The nature of search processes

Our knowledge about the nature of the processes leading to the generation of alternatives is limited. Given information costs and time pressure, it is likely that in many cases decision makers will try to find short-cuts to the nearest possible solution. This is what Cyert and March call 'simple-minded search' (1963: 121). Solutions will be looked for in the neighbourhood of problem symptoms and in the neighbourhood of the current alternative (if available). Both tendencies lead to incrementalist decision making rather than to the radical redesign that is propagated in the normative strategy literature, and that is consonant with the spirit of the logical-structural decision-making model.

A more differentiated approach to organizational decision making assumes that the nature of the search process depends on the nature of the problem. In some cases a limited, simple-minded search process will be satisfactory. In other cases, however, more resources will be spent and new and better solutions will be actively sought for. If a ready-made solution cannot be found, decision makers will – if the problem is seen as important enough – engage in design activities, in order to construct a custom-made solution (Mintzberg et al., 1976). In all cases, the output of this step in the decision-making process will be at least one possible solution. This solution will then have to be evaluated before a decision can be made.

Evaluating options

The evaluation of options forms the heart of the logical-structural model. In a way, this *is* the logical-structural model. All the previous steps are abstracted from, as the decision situation is taken as given. All the subsequent steps are seen as irrelevant, as the decision is assumed to follow inescapably from the evaluation and action from the decision.

Parallel and sequential search and evaluation

The discussion of the generation of alternatives, however, has shown that this process may be restricted because of information costs and/or time limitations. The result may be that at first only a single option is developed and considered for evaluation. Only if this option is rejected in the evaluation process are other solutions searched for. One may also question the ability of decision makers to generate options without simultaneously evaluating them. Perhaps every potential option is initially evaluated before time is invested in developing it further. In an organizational context, this process of preliminary evaluation does not preclude a subsequent more formal evaluation of one or several alternatives. This is the case, for instance, if a staff department submits proposals to a line manager for decision.

Both observations lead to the conclusion that in many cases options will be developed and evaluated **sequentially** rather than **simultaneously**. This concurs with the view on goals as aspiration levels and with satisficing decision making as discussed above.

Modes of evaluation

The actual evaluation of alternatives can be performed in many ways (see Harrison, 1987: 56–8; Tversky, 1972; Van Raaij, 1988: 93–7). In the unlikely case that alternatives are evaluated against a single criterion, two possibilities exist. Either all alternatives are compared, and the alternative with the highest score is selected. Or the alternatives are evaluated one by one, until a solution is found that satisfies the objective stated in the form of an acceptable level.

The decision situation is more complicated if alternatives are evaluated against more than one criterion. Two main categories of multi-attribute evaluation models can be distinguished: compensatory models and non-compensatory models. In the **compensatory** models, the scores on the various attributes are in some way combined into an overall score. This means that a low score on one criterion can be compensated by a high score on another criterion (and vice versa, of course). The scores on the various criteria may simply be added, or submitted to a transformation (e.g. multiplication with a weight factor) before addition.

In the **non-compensatory** models, no attempt is made to combine the scores on the different dimensions. Many non-compensatory models have been suggested in the literature. In the **lexicographic model**, the various criteria are first arranged in order of importance. Next all options are evaluated against the most important criterion, and the option with the highest score is selected. Only if there is a draw, is the next criterion in order of importance taken into consideration, and so forth.

In the **conjunctive model** the decision maker first sets a minimum score for each criterion. Subsequently, the options are evaluated one by one on all criteria. As soon as an option which satisfies all criteria is found it is selected, and the evaluation process is discontinued.

The **elimination-by-aspects** procedure also starts with setting minimum scores on all criteria. But next, these criteria, as in the lexicographic model, are arranged in order of importance. Subsequently, all options are evaluated against the most important criterion. If several options meet the minimum score on this criterion, the decision maker moves on to the next criterion, until one solution is selected.

Two variants of the **disjunctive model** can be distinguished: **maximax** and **maximin**. In the maximax procedure, the option with the highest score on any criterion is selected. In the maximin procedure, the option with the highest minimal score on any criterion is selected.

More evaluation models can be distinguished, but most of them are variations of those discussed above. All the non-compensatory models enable decision makers to economize on information and cognitive capabilities. This is especially true of the very simple models, such as the disjunctive mode. This kind of evaluation may seem to be absurd, but under some circumstances, for example, high information costs and severe time pressure, using them may make sense. The non-compensatory models also put lower requirements on the data. For many compensatory models to be applicable ratio-scale data, allowing multiplication, have to be available. But the non-compensatory models can be used with ordinal data (Van Raaij, 1988). A decision maker can also combine various models, and start, for example, with elimination-by-aspects in order to limit the set of acceptable solutions. From that set the best solution can be chosen by using the lexicographic mode (Van Raaij, 1988).

Evaluation mode and decision outcome

A simple numerical example shows the relevance of the evaluation mode. Depending on the model used, different options may be chosen. Figure 2.5 shows the scores of three hypothetical options (I, II, II) on three hypothetical criteria (A, B, C).

If a compensatory model is used, with simple summation of the scores on all criteria, option I will be chosen. But if the conjunctive mode is used, with a minimal score of three on all criteria, option III is selected. In the case of elimination-by-aspects, with B-A-C as the order of importance of the criteria, and with minimal scores of four (C), three (B), and two (A), option I is selected again. But if the lexicographic model is used with the same order of criteria (B-A-C), option III is selected. The maximax version of the disjunctive model leads to the choice of option II, but the maximin version to option III.

This is only a simple hypothetical example, of course, but it is suggestive for the importance of the mode of evaluation for the outcome of the decision

		Criterion:			Chosen with:
		A	**B**	**C**	
	I	2	3	6	Linear mode; elimination-by-aspects
Option:	II	7	2	1	Maximax
	III	3	3	3	Conjunctive mode; lexicographic mode; maximin

Figure 2.5 Evaluation example.

process. A particular mode of evaluation may be used automatically, without the decision maker being conscious of its limitations. But the evaluation mode may also be chosen in order to manipulate the outcome of the decision process, to rule out certain alternatives, or to push forward a favoured solution.

The act of choice

In an organizational setting the option evaluated as best is not automatically chosen. A staff department of strategic planning may select two or three options, point out advantages and disadvantages of all three, and leave it to top management to decide. The act of choice after the evaluation process has been finished may amount to rubber stamping a decision that for all practical purposes already has been taken. But it may also involve a thorough screening of the criteria and weights used in the evaluation, and possibly a referral to an earlier phase of the decision process.

Even if evaluation and choice are in one hand, the option evaluated as best is not necessarily chosen. The outcome of the cerebral process of evaluation may not correspond to the intuition of the decision maker. The option coming out of the evaluation phase as the best, may not 'feel good', and be rejected in favour of another option (Janis, 1989: 72).

In any case, choice indicates a commitment to action. The selection of and commitment to a particular solution constitutes a fact that forms a barrier against returning to the earlier phases in the decision-making process. At the level of the individual this barrier consists in an unwillingness to return to a state of indecision, and an eagerness to come to action. At the level of the organization social mechanisms discourage re-opening an issue. Once a decision has been made, someone bringing it up for reconsideration will often be seen as irresolute or disloyal, rather than as an exemplary decision maker.

So far, we have discussed instances of active decision making: choice by **commission**. In many cases, however, decisions are made by **omission**: the organization fails to select and commit itself to a particular course of action.

The reason can be that the opportunity or necessity to take a decision was never recognized. Or the organization members were aware of the decision situation, but could not reach an acceptable outcome.

Decision by omission is in a sense the default option in every decision situation. If business as usual is continued, a particular opportunity is not seized or a particular threat is not warded off. This kind of 'choice behaviour' can be seen as the absence of strategic management. Nevertheless, it is doubtlessly of much importance for understanding the behaviour of organizations. In Chapter 3 we will focus on the relationship between deliberate choice and choice by omission, and discuss various factors that may lead to the latter process.

Implementation

Choice may imply a commitment to action, but it is the actual implementation of the choice that turns it 'from intellectual fodder into a commitment of time, energy, and resources' (Harrison, 1987: 59). This is the fundamental difference between implementation and the previous steps in the decision process. If no implementation takes place, decision processes hardly leave a trace in the organization. Mental states may have changed, and documents may have been written, but unless the decision is implemented it has no bearing on the actual processes taking place within the organization.

The kinds of issues that are relevant at the implementation stage are different from those at the earlier stages. In order to make implementation succeed, other organization members, who often have had no say in the decision process, will have to be persuaded and motivated. The decision has to be translated into concrete action programmes and budgets. Responsibilities and competencies have to be demarcated. In fact, a host of operational and administrative decisions have to be taken in order to implement a strategic decision.

Several dangers have to be warded off during the implementation phase. In the first place, top management may lose its interest in the decision. Administrating a decision is less glamorous than engineering new decisions. But if top management is known to concentrate on new issues at the expense of old problems, there is little chance that their decisions will have substantial impact on the organization.

Secondly, there may be overt or covert resistance to the implementation of the decision. Any decision of importance will inevitably go against the interests of some organization members. Pockets of resistance must be identified, preferably in advance, and dealt with. Motivating organization members to endorse the decision is a major issue here.

Thirdly, the decision may be implemented, but the situation may change so drastically that it is no longer a good solution. Once again, the time dimension has to be stressed. A decision that was good at the time it was taken may be bad at the time it is actually implemented. The implementation process should be designed in such a way as to ensure continued surveillance of the environment, and enable flexible responses to unforeseen circumstances.

Control

The last point mentioned under 'implementation' touches on the control issue. In almost every conceptual model of decision making some kind of feedback loop from the last to the first phase of the model is included. This feedback loop logically implies some kind of feedback from those implementing the decision to the original decision maker. In small firms, the decision maker may personally supervise the implementation process. But in larger organizations, some kind of more or less elaborate management information system is be put in place.

In controlling the implementation process, the actual progress is evaluated against the goals of the decision. Obviously, the same three dimensions mentioned in the discussion of goals and objectives are relevant here. That is, the results of the decision implementation are compared with the planned achievements in the real and the financial sphere, and with the adopted time schedule.

If the results of the implementation differ substantially from the expectations, two fundamentally different conclusions can be drawn, leading to radically different kinds of corrective action. In the first place, management can decide that the decision is okay, but that it has not been implemented in the right way. The corrective action in this case is to re-emphasize the original decision and the ensuing assignments, perhaps to shift responsibility to another organization member, or to change the reward system. On the other hand, management can also come to the conclusion that the decision after all was not the right one. In this case the decision-making process has to be re-entered, possibly with an adapted set of goals, or with new information about alternative courses of action.

The decision whether to take corrective action of the first or of the second kind is a momentous one. Managers sometimes stick to a plan in spite of accumulating evidence that it does not work as expected. This may lead to disaster. But managers who too often change their views and back off from their plans if resistance is met or mishaps occur are generally seen as weak, and soon lose their credibility (Staw and Ross, 1980).

2.4 Status of the conceptual scheme

One process for all decisions?

Not all situations will trigger an elaborate decision-making process as represented in Figure 2.2. Many decisions are made without much conscious thought, as illustrated by 'impulse buying' by consumers. The higher the level of involvement in the decision, the larger the chance that the decision maker will devote attention to the various steps. In the case of low involvement decisions, a short-cut may be taken, for example, from recognition directly to choice (Van Raaij, 1988).

The relevance of such low-involvement choices for strategic decision making may not be obvious. Surely, strategic decisions are 'big' decisions, and consequently a high degree of involvement may be assumed? Although this assumption makes sense, we will in the next chapter put forward that the other type of decision making (without much cognitive elaboration) is nevertheless also very important in strategic management. Largely unconscious choice behaviour often has an important bearing on the scope for cognitively elaborate decision making. Thus, it should be conceded that one model is not sufficient for describing all relevant decision-making processes.

Descriptive or normative?

Step-by-step models of decision making, such as the one in Figure 2.2, are sometimes used in a normative way. The suggestion is that if management executes a number of activities in a specified order, good strategic decisions will automatically result (see, e.g., Ansoff and McDonnel, 1990). Other process models are seen as descriptive of real decision-making processes, without immediate or obvious normative implications (see, e.g., Mintzberg et al., 1976). The model discussed in this chapter is seen as neither predominantly normative nor predominantly descriptive. As stated above, in some cases ('high involvement' decisions), it is likely that most of the activities described in the model will be performed, so that the model has descriptive relevance. In other cases, some of the steps may be skipped only to the detriment of the quality of the decision-making process. In these cases, the model has normative value.

However, the model discussed here is first of all a device for organizing our thoughts. By focusing on all the different activities and processes that can conceivably play a role in decision making the model is conducive to the identification of the mechanisms that determine decision outcomes, and points at possible bottlenecks.

Is decision making really a step-by-step process?

But even if the conceptual model is not posited as a necessarily faithful description of reality, nor as an example to be followed in all situations, the subdivision of the decision-making process in a number of phases and steps has to be justified. Doubts have been expressed concerning the step-by-step nature of decision making (Weick, 1983). Witte, in interpreting the results of documentary research into decisions concerning the purchase of electronic data-processing systems, concluded that the so-called phase theorem is not confirmed. Witte concluded instead that activities like information gathering, development of alternatives, evaluation of alternatives and choice-making are spread evenly over the time interval covered by the entire decision-making process. Moreover, he found that there was no relationship between the measure in which the various decision activities were executed in the sequence suggested by process models and the efficiency of the decision-making process. This means that the phase theorem was rejected both as a descriptive and as a normative model (Witte, 1972).

These findings, however, do not have to be taken on face value. In the first place, the reliance on document analysis only may very well have distorted the findings of the research project in question, the more so since in Witte's project only documents in the files of one of the parties concerned – the electronic data processing systems manufacturers – were used. More research into other kinds of decision situations would be necessary in order to justify a definite rejection of the phase theorem. (In other research the phase model, in spite of its limitations, has shown to be useful, for example, DIO International Research Team, 1983.)

However, the position taken here is not to defend the descriptive or the normative value of the discussed step-by-step model. Distinguishing steps or phases in the decision process makes sense for purely pragmatic reasons. Various steps or phases:

- point to essentially different activities, requiring different kinds of skills, knowledge and information;
- are associated with the division of labour within organizations, for example, top management sets goals, corporate planning generates alternatives, and so on;
- are the focus of different scientific disciplines, for example, quantitative theory focuses on evaluation, organizational theory focuses on implementation, and so on.

Thus the process model emphasizes the complexity of the phenomenon of decision making. Whether the various steps in the model are seen as taking place in a parallel fashion or sequentially is less important, as long as this complexity, and the effects of inclusion of the time dimension, are acknowledged.

The conceptual scheme points at two different kinds of barriers to full rationality in decision making as implied by logical-structural models. Even in elaborate decision-making processes, in which adequate attention is given to the various phases and the interrelationships between the different steps, there are many problems that may cause decision makers to deviate from the decision that would be taken if unlimited time and information were available. This is particularly clear in the generation and evaluation of alternatives, where steps may lead to different results depending on the mode of evaluation used.

But actual decision-making processes may also deviate more radically from the perfect rationality of the logical-structural model. As pointed out earlier, it would be wrong to suggest that decision-making processes always start with the awareness phase, after which analysis and action follow in that order. In some cases the awareness phase may be skipped, because the problem situation, rightly or wrongly, is immediately conceived as being familiar. Or the process starts and stops with action, if a routine response is triggered by a situation, and the need for more deliberate decision making is not felt.

The last case of a truncated decision-making process may also be seen as an instance of non-decision making, as the necessary ingredients of various possible options with different outcomes and/or efficiencies appear to be absent. But perhaps a substantial part of organizational 'decisions' is made in this way. In that case it would be unwise to exclude such truncated decision-making processes from a discussion of organizational strategic decision making. Rather, it appears to be our task to explain under which conditions decision-making processes will be more or less elaborate or truncated, and to spell out the consequences of various kinds of deviations from the assumptions of the logical-structural model.

In the next chapter the contrast, suggested above, between intentionally but boundedly rational decision making (elaborate decision processes) on the one hand, and non-deliberate decision making (truncated decision processes) on the other hand, is discussed more thoroughly.

Chapter summary

■ Two types of decision models can be distinguished: logical-structural models and process models.

■ In the decision-making process three broad phases can be discerned: awareness, analysis, and action. These phases do not necessarily occur in that order.

■ In the awareness phase the need to make a decision is recognized, and the problem is formulated. In the analysis phase goals are set, and options are generated and evaluated. In the action phase a choice is made, the chosen option is implemented and the implementation process is controlled.

■ Organizational goals are derived from preferences and aspiration levels of individual organization members. They can be conceived of as sets of constraints to their choice behaviour.

■ Evaluation of options can follow many different modes. The choice of an evaluation mode has an important impact on the outcome of the decision-making process.

■ Although it is difficult to recognize seperate steps in real-world decision-making processes, use of a step-by-step model makes sense for pragmatic reasons.

3

Rational decision making and programmed choice

3.1 Rational decision making and strategic management

In an important part of the literature on strategic management, strategic decision making is assumed to be a rational process. In this section three versions of the rational choice approach will be discussed: rational choice under conditions of certainty, rational choice under conditions of risk, and rational choice in situations in which the decisions of one decision maker interact with those made by identifiable other decision makers.

All these models of rational decision making are examples of logical-structural decision models as discussed in the previous chapter. This means that neither problem recognition and formulation, nor implementation of the selected solution are a theme in these approaches. (In fact, the process or procedure of coming to a choice is seen as irrelevant in these approaches, cf. Johnson-Laird and Shafir, 1993 and Shafir et al., 1993.)

Risk-free choice

Decision axioms

Rational decision makers are assumed to select the course of action that maximizes their utility. The idea of utility maximization is based on a number of axioms that indicate its limited validity. The following axioms form the foundation of the maximization hypothesis (Goodwin and Wright, 1991: 76–9; Lea et al., 1987: 109):

- **Axiom of completeness**: If a decision maker is confronted with the choice between two alternatives, A and B, he either prefers A to B, or B to A, or he is indifferent between them. This means that there will be no lack of clarity concerning preferences.
- **Axiom of greed**: Other things being equal, a decision maker always prefers more of a good over less of the same good.
- **Axiom of transitivity**: If alternative A is preferred over alternative B, and B over C, alternative A will also be preferred over alternative C.
- **Axiom of convexity**: If the quantity of a good is increased with fixed increments every next increment will be valued equal to or less than the preceding increase.
- **Axiom of continuity**: Between any two bundles of goods, A and B, always another bundle C exists that is similar to both. The utility of C lies between those of A and B.
- **Axiom of stability:** The preference orderings based on the above axioms are stable over time.

If there is no uncertainty concerning outcomes, decision making consists in 'reading' one's preferences, comparing alternatives, and selecting the alternative which yields the highest utility.

The decision situation is closed, that is, all the elements and relations are known. All this information is assumed to be taken into account in the evaluation. No matter in how many dimensions alternatives differ, the decision maker is assumed to be always able to sort out his preferences. In a complex process all possible alternatives are confronted with the decision maker's rank ordering of preferences, and the best solution is selected. Decision making as such is trivial under these assumptions, as it is known with certainty which alternative maximizes utility.

Risky choice

Approaches assuming uncertainty concerning outcomes are more relevant than the risk-free choice model in the context of strategic decision making. The dominant paradigm in the study of risky decisions is that of **subjectively expected utility theory** (SEU) (Schoemaker, 1982). According to SEU, decision makers select the alternative that is expected to yield the highest utility. An alternative that can lead to a well-defined set of outcomes with associated probabilities is called a **prospect** (Starmer, 1993).

In determining the subjectively expected utility of a prospect, both the value of the outcomes and the probability that they will materialize are taken into account. In formal notation, the subjectively expected utility of a prospect P with possible outcomes $x_1, \ldots, x_n$ and associated probabilities $p_1, \ldots, p_n$ is given by the following expression (Starmer, 1993):

$$\text{SEU}(P) = \sum_{i=1}^{n} p_i \text{U}(x_i)$$

The decision maker compares all prospects, and selects the one with the highest subjectively expected utility.

Subjectivity of decision makers is accounted for in two different ways in the SEU model. In the first place, the probabilities associated with outcomes are subjective assessments of the decision maker rather than objectively known. Secondly, utility rather than value is assumed to be maximized. In this way, the fact that a bundle of goods can have different values for different individuals is taken into account (Lea et al., 1987: 117).

On the basis of the SEU model, various other theories of decision making under uncertainty have been developed. These models attempt to explain better than the SEU model empirical observations of patterns of choice behaviour (Schoemaker, 1982; Starmer, 1993). One of these approaches, **prospect theory**, will be discussed in Chapter 4 when we take up the psychology of decision making.

Interactive decision making

Game theory

Rational decision making is even more complicated if the reactions of other decision makers to the choice made by the focal decision maker have to be taken into account. This category of decision situations is the realm of game theory. In game theory interacting decisions of two or more 'players' are analysed. In deciding on the optimal course of action, a player has to take into account possible responses of the other players.

The potential applicability of game theory to strategic management is obvious. Consider for example the situation of firms in a duopoly, which have to decide on their advertising expenses. By raising its advertising budget, a firm can increase its sales. Most of the increase, however, will come from customers lured away from its competitor, rather than from new buyers. Thus the other firm will be affected by the decision made by the first, and may be expected to react. The situation is represented schematically in the pay-off matrix in Figure 3.1.

The pay-off matrix specifies the net profits of firms A and B in the four situations that are possible in this game. If neither of the firms raises its advertising budget, both maintain their current net profit of $10 million. If only one of them increases its budget, it is able to increase its sales and its net profit rises to $12 million. However, the other firm experiences a decline in sales, leading to a drop in net profit to $7 million. If both firms increase their advertising spending, the benefits of the campaign clearly do not outweigh the costs, as both face a decline in net profits to $9 million.

A rational decision maker will systematically compare the costs and benefits of courses of action, taking into account the possible reactions of other players. Thus Firm A in the example will foresee that Firm B is likely to enhance its advertising efforts, too, and that both will be worse off as a result. The outcome of this game depends on the auxiliary assumptions that are made.

Firm B

		No increase in advertising	Increase in advertising
Firm A	No increase in advertising	10 ; 10	7 ; 12
	Increase in advertising	12 ; 7	9 ; 9

Figure 3.1 The advertising game.

If both firms can easily communicate, and are able to make credible pledges not to raise their advertising budget, the outcome will be the situation in the upper left-hand corner of the matrix. The same is true if both firms can very quickly match an unexpected advertising campaign started by their competitor (and if both firms know that this is the case). No firm will now be able to reap the benefits of luring away customers from its competitor, and the choice is between the upper left-hand corner and the lower right-hand corner of the matrix only.

However, if the firm that starts an advertising campaign gains first-mover advantages that cannot be annulled by a subsequent increase in its competitor's advertising budget, the outcome of the game will be that both firms spend more on advertising, and end up in the lower right-hand corner. Under these assumptions the strategy of raising the advertising budget dominates the strategy of not raising the budget (i.e. it yields higher outputs with every possible strategy of the competitor). This decision situation has the structure of the well-known prisoner's dilemma discussed in Chapter 1 (see also Greer, 1984).

Game theory and strategic management

In the past decade numerous applications of game theory to strategic management have been developed. These applications comprise issues such as entry deterrence and the formation and exploitation of firm reputation, but also internal strategic questions such as the choice of production capacity, and the design of the organizational structure (see, e.g., Hendrikse, 1991; Kreps and Spence, 1984; Milgrom and Roberts, 1992; Tirole, 1988; Weigelt and Camerer, 1988).

Game theory is not a theory of strategic decision making, but rather a 'toolbox' that can be used in analysing many different kinds of strategic problems. The result is a 'collage' of explanations of phenomena, identical in so far as the central place of rational choice is concerned, but differing with regard to the plethora of auxiliary assumptions (Camerer, 1991; Rumelt et al., 1991).

Game theory offers a method for analysing important aspects of strategic decision situations. However, the use of this method entails the adoption of a number of simplifying assumptions. These assumptions pertain to the availability of information and to the computational capabilities of the players (Binmore and Dasgupta, 1986). The assumptions do not appear to be in conformity with the nature of human decision makers as we know it, and with the characteristics of many real-world strategic decision situations.

Critique of the rational choice approach

The points of criticism raised in the context of the game-theoretical approach to strategy can be directed more generally at the rational choice approach. Three kinds of criticism can be levelled at rational decision theory: the applicability to truly strategic problems is limited; rational decision making is not an accurate description of actual decision-making processes; and, setting descriptive accuracy aside, the explanatory power of the approach is restricted.

Applicability of the approach

It is self-evident that the theory of risk-free choice is hardly applicable to the kinds of problems that strategic decision making is concerned with. In strategic management, decision makers always have to consider uncertain outcomes. Thus a simple comparison of known outcomes of alternative choices is not an appropriate model of strategic decision making.

Subjectively expected utility theory is more relevant in that uncertainty concerning the outcomes of strategic options is taken into account, but the kind of uncertainty differs. In strategic management a complete enumeration and evaluation of all alternatives will almost always be infeasible. (For a discussion of the shortfalls of the SEU model for describing real-world managerial decision making, see also Beach, 1993.) Furthermore, for the restricted number of options that are taken into consideration, it will mostly be impossible to draw up even an approximately accurate probability distribution. Real-world strategy-makers face uncertainty, rather than risk, to use the distinction made by Frank Knight. The concept of risk applies if the possible outcomes are known, and if the decision maker has an idea of the associated probabilities. If neither the set of possible outcomes nor (by implication) the probability distribution is known, uncertainty exists (Knight, 1965).

Game theory is most obviously applicable to strategic decision making in oligopolistic markets. Whether the game theory approach is fruitful depends chiefly on the question of the plausibility of the assumptions regarding information availability and rational behaviour. Simple situations in which clearly distinguishable alternatives have to be considered, and in which only a few players interact, lend themselves best to game-theory modelling. The assumption of full rationality is a simplifying 'as if' assumption in order to keep the complexity of the model within bounds. The conclusions of game theory reasoning are acceptable in some settings, and not in others (Saloner, 1991; Spender, 1993).

A restriction of the riskless choice and the SEU models is that they refer to single decision makers. In organizational strategy making many individuals interact in reaching a decision. If organizations are nevertheless assumed to be single decision makers, complex sets of interrelationships are anthropomorphized (Schoemaker, 1993). Even if individuals would follow the rules of the subjectively expected utility model – which, as will be argued below, they do not consistently – there is no certainty that this will also be true of organizations.

Validity of the rational choice axioms

More fundamental than the criticism pertaining to the limited applicability of rational choice theory to strategic problems, is the criticism that – even in less complex situations – people do not actually behave as assumed in the models. There is mounting evidence against a number of the axioms of rational choice described above. For instance, the psychological evidence against the insatiability assumed in the 'greed axiom' is strong and general. Also, in experiments a complete and stable ordering of preferences often appears to be absent. Preferences are 'moderately stochastic' rather than fixed and known (Lea et al., 1987: 113). Preference orderings have also been shown to be intransitive, and preferences may 'cross over' if the time frame of the decision is altered (Lea et al., 1987: 114, 126).

As far as risky choice is concerned, the SEU model does not always yield correct predictions. Here also, the basic axioms of rational choice are violated in actual decision-making processes (see Schoemaker, 1982). Not even trained economists can be relied upon to play rationally, even in a simple, structured game (Guth et al., 1982). The axiom of transitivity of preferences, for instance, was found to hold only under very restrictive conditions. The axiom of continuity was violated by nearly half the subjects in an experiment in choosing between gambles (prospects). Valuations of uncertain outcomes are consistently distorted: outcomes obtained with certainty are much more salient than uncertain outcomes; low probability–high loss events tend to be neglected. Risky choices also depend to a high degree on the context of the decision situation, and on the formulation of the problem. If the emphasis is on losses, subjects display different choice behaviour than if the emphasis is on gains (see Chapter 4).

Actual decision-making processes

Actual decision-making processes often follow evaluation modes like the disjunctive model or elimination-by-aspects rather than the holistic multi-dimensional comparison of alternatives suggested by SEU theory (Schoemaker, 1982; Van Raaij, 1988). The mode of evaluation varies with the complexity of the task and the importance of the decision: in very simple situations, and for relatively important decisions, compensatory models are more often used than in decision situations with many alternatives and many dimensions of utility – and for relatively unimportant decisions.

Attitudes towards risk varies with the perspective of the decision maker.

When a decision maker is presented with prospects that have expected values below his aspiration level, he is inclined to choose a more risky prospect. If the same decision maker is presented with prospects yielding expected values above his aspiration level, however, he will be inclined to choose a less risky prospect. This phenomenon will be discussed in detail in Chapter 4.

Subjective assessments of probabilities tend to be higher for outcomes that are seen as very desirable ('wishful thinking'). Other biases appear in the assessment of confidence intervals, and in the estimation of probabilities on the basis of available information (Schoemaker, 1982).

The kind of assumptions on which game theory is based make it unlikely that this approach yields accurate descriptions of real-world human decision making. In most game theory models, the belief systems of the players are assumed to be common knowledge, and the players are assumed to be optimizers capable of unlimited computations. Game theory is most probable as a theory of the outcome of long-run evolutionary processes (Binmore and Dasgupta, 1986: 12). Even if the assumptions with regard to human motivation and faculties are incorrect, survival of the fittest can under certain circumstances lead to optimal strategies (Camerer, 1991).

But if our goal is to understand how actual organizations go about taking actual strategic decisions, it is not very helpful to know that perhaps in the long run it is *as if* they act as perfectly rational optimizers. The upshot is that the rational decision model, in all three versions discussed here, is descriptively unsatisfactory.

Defences of rational choice theory

Descriptive accuracy is not, however, the primary aim – or even no aim at all – of the rational choice approach. A proponent of the rational choice approach could argue that individual biases and differences do not matter in aggregate behaviour. But, quite apart from the aggregate outcome, this book is based on the premise that the decision processes leading to the outcome are interesting in their own right. Thus what we need is a theory that is not bluntly at variance with the world as we know it.

A proponent of the rational choice approach could also counter that descriptive accuracy is not important, as long as the theory predicts correctly. However, there is abundant experimental evidence that, at least at the level of individuals, rational choice models frequently make the wrong predictions (Schoemaker, 1982). The models can be refined, of course, in order to enhance the predictive power. But this may in fact be a problem. Game theory, for instance, has been said to be so adaptable that virtually everything can be explained. Richard Rumelt complained that 'if a bank president was standing in the street and lighting his pants on fire, some game theorist would explain it as rational' (quoted in Postrel, 1991: 153). And, in response to this outcry, one game theorist actually did so, in a two-period game with hidden information! (Postrel, 1991). This kind of exercise does not really bring us closer to an understanding of strategic decision-making processes. To quote from a recent paper on 'frontier activities around strategy theorizing' (Spender, 1993: 19):

> Eventually the strategy theorist must abandon the game-theoretic approach with its search for that picture of possible outcomes within which rational optimization can proceed. He must focus instead on the processes by which not one but several people confront incompleteness and irrelevance under the additional uncertainty of a known but competitive interaction. Strategy becomes the set of procedures for negotiating these interactions under conditions of incomplete knowledge.

This quotation points at several crucial elements of a satisfactory approach to strategy. Strategic decision making has to do with incomplete and irrelevant information, with negotiation and with competition. It also has to do with rational deliberations but in the context of organizational strategy rational decision making will always be imperfect, and can never be more than only part of the explanation.

Therefore, we will have to employ a much more realistic concept of rationality in decision making. But first of all we will have to deal with a seemingly simple question, that is, what rationality actually *is*.

3.2 Bounded rationality

What is rationality?

In the preceding section, rationality was associated with utility maximization. Given a certain preference ordering, the decision maker is assumed to choose the optimal alternative. The choice is completely instrumental with regard to references that are assumed as given. Thus, the rationality of the decision maker is expressed in the relationship between means and ends. However, the concept of rationality can be interpreted in various ways.

In the *Oxford Dictionary of the English Language* 'rationality' is described as ['t]he quality of possessing reason; the power of being able to exercise one's reason'. The exercise of reason does not necessarily imply the maximization of utility. Reason, the faculty of thinking, does not always lead to the best choice. Reasoning may be imperfect, in that wrong inferences are drawn from the available information. But the information itself may also be imperfect or incomplete. If the decision which is objectively best in terms of a given utility function is referred to as 'substantively rational', it will be clear that reasoning will not automatically lead to substantive rationality (Lea et al., 1987; March and Simon, 1993).

Kinds of rationality

In the literature various kinds of rationality are distinguished, and different definitions have been proposed. Some of the most important are:

- **Substantive rationality**: the alternative that is objectively best – given the preference ordering of the decision maker – is chosen. No information imperfections or logical errors are assumed.
- **Instrumental rationality**: the right means are chosen in relation to an end, given the decision maker's belief system. Logical errors are not assumed, but the decision maker's belief system does not necessarily correspond to objective reality (Walliser, 1989).
- **Cognitive rationality**: all the available information about the environment is assumed to be reflected in the decision maker's belief system (Walliser, 1989). This is a special case of instrumental rationality.
- **Procedural rationality**: given the available information and cognitive faculties, a reasonable decision-making procedure is followed (March and Simon, 1993: 8).

These definitions lead to the conclusion that we have to distinguish between the rationality of the outcome of the decision-making process, and the rationality of the process itself. If imperfect information and imperfect human cognition is assumed, a rational decision-making process (procedural rationality) does not automatically lead to a rational choice (substantial rationality) (Lea et al., 1987: 105). Conversely, a substantively rational outcome may have been produced by a non-rational decision-making process (plus a stiff dose of luck). The rational choice approach has to do with substantive rationality, the approach chosen here, on the other hand, is based on the assumption that organization strategy can at best be rational in the procedural sense.

Many concepts associated with forms of rationality diverging from perfect (substantial) rationality have been introduced in the literature. The best known is Herbert Simon's concept of **bounded rationality**: 'people act *intentionally* rational, but only limitedly so' (Simon, 1957: xxiv). Many related concepts concerning decision making by individuals have been proposed in the literature (see, e.g., March, 1978).

If the focus is on decision making in the context of organizations, other departures from full rationality are also relevant. Decision making within organizations is assigned to various subunits. These subunits tend to deal only with a limited set of aspects of problems. The sales department concentrates on enhancing sales, the production department focuses on streamlining the production process, and so on. This **local rationality** has the effect that the broader implications of proposed solutions to factored problems are not explicitly taken into account (Cyert and March, 1963).

Bounded rationality and satisficing

Two aspects of rationality

In the context of decision making processes, we will take 'rationality' to denote two things (cf. Dean and Sharfman, 1993; Walliser, 1989):

1. the decision maker is open to evidence, that is, the decision is not made on the basis of prejudices;
2. the decision maker uses logical analysis in reaching a decision.

This concept of rationality marks out a rough distinction between rational behaviour, well thought out in advance, and other kinds of behaviour, based on habit, routine, or 'programmed' in some other way. In Section 3.3 these other-than-rational decision processes will be discussed under the heading of 'programmed choice'.

At this point it is important to note that with regard to openness to information, as well as to logical reasoning, an assumption of perfection seems to be unwarranted.

Barriers to full rationality

The discussion of the decision-making process in Chapter 2 showed that at all stages of the process departures from perfect rationality are likely to occur. Openness to evidence is particularly important at the awareness and the analysis phases, but the perception and interpretation of signals is distorted in many ways. People frequently decide on the basis of incomplete, irrelevant, or even plainly erroneous information. Given the cost of information and the time pressure under which many decisions have to be taken there is no simple remedy for this problem.

Logical reasoning, especially important at the analysis phase, is also characterized by imperfections. For instance, there is abundant evidence from experimental and field research that human decision makers do not use all information and draw inferences in a way compatible to the subjectively expected utility model (Schoemaker, 1982; Starmer, 1993).

To complicate things, it has been suggested that in the action phase of the decision-making process people are governed by a kind of rationality – action rationality – radically different from the decision rationality prevalent at the other phases. Organizational action is as much based on ideology and coherent culture as on thoughtful deliberation (Brunsson, 1982).

The fact that the organizational decision-making processes relevant to strategy as discussed in this book constitute a higher level of aggregation than decision making by individuals does not help. There is no good reason to believe that individual biases and imperfections will average out in the aggregate (Schoemaker, 1982). In many cases the opposite seems to be true: the aggregation of individually rational behaviour leads to 'irrational' macro phenomena (Schelling, 1978). Likewise, organizational processes and bureaucratic politics may add disturbances and departures from rationality over and above those originating at the level of the individual (cf. Allison, 1971). In many approaches to strategic management organizations are treated as if they were rational individuals (in the way in which information is used, and in the way in which means are related to ends). However, rationality on the level of individual decision makers should be questioned, and organizational processes and bureaucratic politics should be acknowledged.

Satisficing

The upshot is that if we want to understand real-world decision-making processes, a more realistic notion of human decision behaviour has to be substituted for the axiom of maximizing behaviour of the rational decision approach. That notion is that of **satisficing**: people are concerned not with the discovery and selection of optimal alternatives, but with the discovery and selection of satisfactory alternatives (March and Simon, 1993: 140–1).

Adoption of the assumption of satificing behaviour means a radical departure from the rational choice paradigm. Decision makers are no longer assumed to have a complete preference ordering against which all alternatives are tested. Instead, they set for themselves a level of aspiration, and choose an alternative that satisfies this criterion. With satisficing, the decision-making process is assumed to be sequential rather than simultaneous. Alternatives are generated and evaluated one by one, and the process stops as soon as an option exceeding the aspiration level is found (Simon, 1955).

If information becomes available in a sequential way, or if the complexity of the problem necessitates the decision maker to decompose the decision process into a number of stages, satisficing can be shown to be the optimal strategy (Kapteyn et al., 1979). The empirical evidence also clearly suggests that in complex decision situations or when information is provided sequentially rather than simultaneously, human decision makers do indeed satisfice rather than maximize (Kapteyn et al., 1979; Van Raaij, 1988).

Satisficing and organizational choice

The notion of satisficing is not only relevant in the context of decision making by individuals, it is also entirely consistent with organizational choice processes. Goals are often set in the form of acceptable levels: a minimal rate of return of investment projects, a certain percentage of sales growth, a certain number of percentage points of market share growth, and so on.

There are also important parallels between the setting of levels of aspiration at the individual and at the organizational level. The level of aspiration of an individual is influenced, among other things, by that person's earlier performance and by what is attained by 'reference groups', that is, the groups of individuals with whom the focal decision maker compares him or herself (Wärneryd, 1988: 230). This can be translated to firms, which typically take their past performance as the basis for setting strategic goals, and which compare their achievements with that of competitors in order to evaluate their performance.

All this is entirely rational, if the 'bounded' version of the rationality concept is adopted. Individual decision makers and organizations simply have to satisfice 'because they do not have the wits to maximize' (Simon, 1976: xxvii).

Where do goals come from?

Rationality has to do with the use of information and with logical analysis. Thus the behaviour of a decision maker in the pursuit of his goals can be said to be rational or not, or to be rational to a certain degree. But is it also possible to pass judgement on the rationality of the goals themselves? Presumably not.

'Rationality' shares a common root with 'ratio' in the latin verb *reri* – to reckon, to think (see *Oxford Dictionary of English Etymology*). A 'ratio' is the relation of one quantity to another. 'Rationality' can arguably be seen as pertaining to the relation of means to ends. But rationality is not a characteristic of either ends or means *per se*. If people in practical linguistic usage refer to the 'rationality' of goals, this can only be understood in the sense of the degree in which the pursuit of these goals is instrumental in the achievement of higher goals. But at the ultimate top of every ends–means pyramid there must be a goal that transcends rationality.

Goals of individuals

In rational choice theory decision makers are assumed to maximize their **utility**. What exactly utility is is left in the dark most of the time. The concept may be associated only with agreeable experiences (pleasure), or may be seen to encompass also the satisfaction derived from the pleasure of others (altruism) (Etzioni, 1986). In the most general and abstract form, utility may simply be defined as preference satisfaction.

In all cases, utility can only be conceived of as experiences or emotions. Rational behaviour is instrumental in relation to the experiences and emotions of the decision maker. David Hume was quite clear about the relationship between rationality and emotions: 'reason is, and ought only to be the slave of the passions' (cited in Suttle, 1987: 462). And self-interest is a passion, after all (cf. Suttle, 1987).

The experiences, passions and emotions governing individual behaviour may be associated with the satisfaction of feelings of hunger or sexual lust. But, as Maslow's hierarchy of needs suggests, individual behaviour is also determined by 'higher' needs, for example, needs for social acceptance and self-actualization (Maslow, 1970). Furthermore, feelings of moral obligation – originating in, for example, personal or religious norms – are also an important determinant of behaviour (Pieters, 1988). In this sense, human behaviour can be said to be value-driven (see Box 3.1).

At a supra-individual level, in the context of an evolutionary model of human behaviour, emotions may be seen as instrumental, that is, they serve

Box 3.1 Introspection for managers

Managers are increasing turning inwards to find answers that help them cope with the stress and uncertainties of their jobs. The goals of this introspection appear to be twofold. First, introspection is a way of getting to know who you are. It helps to identify the two or three key goals that really matter in life, and to focus on the core values a person wants to guide his or her actions. Secondly, introspection helps leaders to become more self-reflective, and to realize that they do not know all the answers. According to Erika Andersen, of organizational-development firm Proteus International in Boulder, Colorado, introspection by top managers leads to a 'sort of humbleness that is very charismatic, because it makes the others on their team feel useful and powerful'. This kind of charisma is becoming more and more important. According to one commentator, 'winning companies find they must engage workers' hearts as well as their minds, this increasingly emotional aspect of business is destroying the old corporate *machismo* that once allowed us to keep our feelings hidden and our inner lives mysterious, even to ourselves'.

(Source: Sherman, 1994)

the function of promoting survival and reproduction (Pieters and Van Raaij, 1988). But a function is not a purpose. In the context of intentional individual behaviour emotions are not instrumental relative to any higher purpose. This means that for a given individual, emotions (experiences, passions) are the only conceivable ultimate goal. This does not mean that rational processes do not influence emotions. Reasoning may alter a person's view of a situation, and hence his or her emotions. The relationship between cognitive appraisal and affective experience has been suggested to be a continuous loop or a circular feedback loop system (Cadland, 1977; Plutchik, 1985).

Goals of organizations

Organizations do not experience emotions. But, as indicated in the previous chapter, the goals of organizations can be conceived of as a derivative of the personal goals of the individuals concerned. Thus the goals of organizations can be seen as ultimately reducible to individual emotions and experiences.

However, the issue is more complicated than that. Organizations are not only instruments of individuals pursuing their personal goals, but also social phenomena. All organizations function within an environment which exerts pressure on it. Competition in the market forces business firms to operate efficiently, on pain of bankruptcy. Also, other types of organizations have to remain within certain bounds of efficiency in order to be viable in the long run.

Non-profit-making organizations, as well as business firms, are also exposed to environmental pressure to conform to certain norms, in order to maintain legitimacy (Meyer and Rowan, 1977).

The demands of efficiency and legitimation impose constraints on the upper level managers who make decisions on behalf of their organizations. Just like all other individuals, these managers pursue their personal goals, but the situational constraints imposed on their behaviour ensure that their decisions are – most of the time, and more or less – conducive to the survival and prosperity of the organization.

Two basic mechanisms are instrumental in this process: **incentives** and **monitoring**. Top managers face strong incentives to make their organization prosper if their personal welfare is somehow coupled to the success of their organization. This is the reason why the salary of top managers often contains a variable component (Barkema, 1988: Fama and Jensen, 1983).

As far as monitoring is concerned, every manager is closely watched by his colleagues, not only by those at the same hierarchical level, but also by his direct superiors – or outside stakeholders of the organization – and subordinates. If a manager attempts to appropriate too large a slice of the pie, others will notice, and the information will spread quickly. This kind of informal monitoring helps to keep the decisions of top managers in line with the interests of the firm at large (Simon, 1964). Conflicts between the goals of individual managers, or between different interest groups within the organization, are softened because of the inability of boundedly rational individuals to oversee all the issues and decisions. The use of acceptable-level decision rules and sequential attention to goals (satisficing) enables organization members to attain a quasi-resolution of their goal conflicts (Cyert and March, 1963).

3.3 Programmed choice in strategic management

Rational decision making and programmed choice

In the discussion above, the implicit assumption was that decision makers exercise reason – however imperfectly – in order to come to an acceptable solution. However, not all decisions within organizations are made in that way. In fact, it seems safe to assume that an overwhelming majority of decisions are not made in a rational way. According to Beach (1993: 272, 283), 'The third revolution [in behavioural decision theory], which is still in progress, comes from recognition that choices occur relatively rarely; that behaviour largely is preprogrammed', and: 'decisionmakers face far fewer real decisions than previously has been thought. Indeed, decision making in general, and choice in particular, may play a surprisingly minor role in any inclusive account of human behavior'. The reason for this is that rational decision making takes up time and attention. Both are in short supply. Consequently, many decisions are made without looking for much information, and without much deliberation. We will call this kind of decision making **programmed choice**.

Programmed choice

Rational deliberation is not the only way to make decisions. An obvious alternative, of course, is omission: simply ignore the need or opportunity for decision making. But in many cases people do make decisions (in the sense that they select a course of action and effect commitment to that course of action), but not in a way resembling rational decision making. The decision maker may follow organizational procedures, act on the basis of habit, comply with a strongly shared view of 'how things are done over here', or respond according to personal moral principles. 'Programmed choice' is used as a blanket concept here, covering various categories of relatively undeliberate choice behaviours that will be distinguished below.

The fact that not all behaviour follows the precepts of rational decision is widely recognized in the literature. What is called 'programmed choice' here, has been alluded to, among other things, as 'arational behaviour', 'routinized response behaviour', 'mindless behaviour', and 'rule-governed behaviour'. (See Lea et al., 1987: 27, 483; Van Raaij, 1988: 96; Prelec and Herrnstein, 1991: 320, respectively. For comparable distinctions geared more specifically to the field of strategic management see, e.g., Haselhoff, 1976; Spender, 1993; Steidlmeier, 1993; Thomas and Pruett, 1993.) The denomination 'programmed choice' is based on the work of James March and Herbert Simon (March and Simon, 1993).

Programmed choice is necessary, because of the limited cognitive faculties of human beings. A person simply cannot deliberate about each and every choice to be made. Programmed choice can be efficient, for habits, routines, shared beliefs, and principles often reflect seasoned wisdom and insights. But programmed choice can also be inefficient or even dangerous, for instance if a standard operating procedure is used in a situation requiring a more adaptive response.

Programmed choice and strategic management

On the face of it, programmed choice may have limited relevance for strategic management: decisions will surely be made on the basis of conscious deliberation in this context. But deliberate strategic choice in many ways interacts with programmed choice (Mazzolini, 1981).

A first observation is that programmed choice forms a constraint to rational strategic decision making. Existing organizational structures, procedures, routines and rules are a formidable barrier to the implementation of new strategies (Hall and Saias, 1980; March and Sevón, 1988) – not only at the implementation stage, but also at the formulation stage programmed choice acts as a constraint on rational strategy making. The formulation of a new strategy is based on the belief systems and mindsets of top managers. Organizational decision makers share perceptions of the characteristics of the environment and of the position of the firm in the market that tend to persist, even in the face of contrary evidence. As a result, and quite apart from structural constraints within the organization, radically new strategies often fail be formulated in the first place (Johnson, 1988; Smircich and Stubbart, 1985).

As a second observation, we could also state that programmed choice serves as the foundation for deliberate decision. Without the structures, routines, and so on, that are formed and maintained through programmed choice, the activities that constitute deliberate organizational choice would not be possible. Without programmed choice, there would be no organization to make strategy for.

Different kinds of programmed choice

Two distinctions

The concept of 'programmed choice' covers disparate phenomena. If we lift up the blanket, several categories of behaviour can usefully be distinguished. In the first place, we can distinguish between programmed choice originating primarily at the level of the individual, and that originating primarily at a supra-individual level. Secondly, we can distinguish between programmed choice originating in behavioural patterns that in the past were based on rational decision making, and programmed choice that is of an arational character. Putting these two distinctions together, we can draw a two-by-two matrix (see Figure 3.2).

The differences between the various categories of programmed choice are not always clear cut. However, the categorization offers a basis for an introductory discussion of the different kinds of behaviour. In Chapter 6, we will return to the interrelations of programmed choice and rational decision in the context of organizational strategy making.

Individual routine behaviour

In many decision situations, individuals rely on routinized responses. In the category discussed here, the routine behaviour is assumed to originate in previous rational decisions. That is, an individual has in the past deliberated about the appropriate course of action in a certain kind of situation. Subsequently, every time a like situation occurs, the same course of action is chosen without new deliberations (Heiner, 1983; March and Simon, 1993: 161; Simon, 1957). Given the dominance of rational ideology, behaviour on the basis of routines may be camouflaged as rational decision making. The rational deliberation then is a sacred ritual rather than the actual mechanism engineering choice (March and Simon, 1993: 17).

Routine behaviour makes sense, for scarce cognitive capabilities can best be focused on new problems. Thus, taking the 'cost of thinking' into account, individual routine behaviour may be construed as rational (Shugan, 1980). But

	Programmed at the level of the individual	Programmed at supra-individual level
Based on previous rational decisions	individual routine behaviour	organizational rules and procedures
Arational	habits, mindless behaviour, personal principles	shared beliefs and mindsets

Figure 3.2 Categories of programmed choice behaviour.

that does not alter the fact that the decision-making process as such is not procedurally rational.

Routine behaviour and rational decision making form no dichotomy. A continuum of decision-making styles can be drawn, from routinized response behaviour via limited problem solving to (procedurally) rational decision making (Van Raaij, 1988). Whether an individual will choose on the basis of extensive problem solving or use a routinized response depends, *inter alia*, on the level of involvement (Gensch and Javalgi, 1987). Decisions that are seen as important evoke more rational deliberation than decisions of a minor nature. The problem is of course that an important problem may not always be recognized as such.

Organizational rules and procedures

Organizations have at their disposal repertories of action programmes that serve as alternatives of choice in recurrent situations (March and Simon, 1993: 191). Thus, at the level of the organization routinized behaviour also plays an important role. Standard operating procedures and rules of thumb to a large extent determine organizational processes (Cyert and March, 1963; Etzioni, 1988; Nelson, 1991; Nelson and Winter, 1982). The choices open to individual organization members are restricted because of rules and procedures. Individuals may also voluntarily appeal to a rule, in order 'to escape the intolerable suspense of the arbitrary' (Lévi-Strauss, 1969: 87). This makes the behaviour of individuals within the organization predictable, and facilitates the coordination of processes.

On the other hand, elements of organizational structure, such as formal organization charts, also constrain (strategic) decision making. The formal division of labour has a bearing on the exposure to information of different organization members. Functionaries of organizations receive selected environmental stimuli, depending on their position. Tasks and responsibilities are formally allocated, and strategy making will be the task of a happy few rather than an activity dispersed through the organization. Consequently, the formal structure paves the way to strategic decision making on the basis of partial views of reality (March and Sevón, 1988; March and Simon, 1993). Reward systems influence the kind of strategic initiatives that are likely to be developed and to survive in the 'struggle-for-survival' of projects within the firm (Burgelman, 1983).

But organizational routines are not only functional. Over time, institutionalized patterns of behaviour are infused with value. Behaviour which originally was only instrumental in relation to some higher end may become an end in itself (Selznick, 1957). If this aspect has become dominant, the pattern of behaviour in question is part of the organizational culture, a source of programmed choice discussed below under the heading of shared beliefs and collective programming.

Habits, mindless behaviour, and personal principles

Individual choice behaviour can also be based on habits, thoughtless impulses, or moral principles. Habitual choice refers to behaviour that, however it originated, is now being repeated essentially because it has occurred before in the same context. Habits influence many kinds of behaviour (Lea et al., 1987: 482; Pieters, 1988: 179). The difference between habitual and routinized behaviour is that the latter is more clearly instrumental with regard to some end. Habitual behaviour, conversely, lacks such an instrumental feature; it can be a goal in itself, unconscious rather than conscious – although it is not always easy to draw a distinction between routine and habit.

'Mindless behaviour' is associated with a low level of cognitive and emotional involvement. The individual simply does not pay much attention to the choice that is being made (Lea et al., 1987: 483). For instance, consumers often make buying decisions on the basis of 'affect referral': a simple affective reaction – perhaps on an objectively irrelevant aspect – determines which alternative is selected (Van Raaij, 1988). Mindless behaviour comes close to decision making by omission.

This is not true of decision making on the basis of principles. A principle is a rule of behaviour which overrides the cost-benefit calculations that are typical of rational decision making. This is a fully conscious type of decision making, but in a mode radically different from the rational model (Prelec and Herrnstein, 1991). In decision making on the basis of principles, the task of the decision maker is to discover which, if any, of the prevailing principles is appropriate. In case more than one principle is applicable (e.g. the principle of loyalty to one's firm and the principle not to engage in illegal activities), the decision maker has to establish the hierarchy between the relevant principles. The main cognitive activities associated with decision making by principle are interpreting the situation and grouping comparable situations (in order to decide which principle applies).

Principles may be internally or externally imposed. Individuals may impose principles on their own choice behaviour, because they fear to be weak in the face of temptations (e.g. in the form of alcoholic beverages or cigarettes) (Prelec and Herrnstein, 1991). Moral principles, on the other hand, often originate in the social environment of the decision maker. A very general norm is that of reciprocity (Gouldner, 1960). Individuals who do not honour the principle as a personal norm may nevertheless comply with such a behavioural rule. They may do so because the (social or pecuniary) costs of non-compliance outweigh the benefits. This kind of rule-following behaviour arguably belongs to the realm of rational decision making. However, an individual may also comply with social principles because these have been internalized in a process of socialization (Wärneryd, 1988). External and internal norms merge into one another.

Shared beliefs and mindsets

The fourth category of programmed choice is the type of decision behaviour stemming from shared beliefs and mindsets. Decision makers within organizations often share a common view of the world, and more specifically of the function of their organization in the environment. This common view of reality may be a result of (self-) selection at the time of entering the organization, or of socialization processes after the individuals have entered the organization, or a combination of both.

Shared beliefs and mindsets are concepts referring to the organizational culture. The underlying idea is that people who interact closely for an extended period come to share many beliefs about reality and ways of thinking about the functioning of their organization within that perceived reality. This also helps the organization to function effectively, by giving coherence to the activities of different individuals, and in this way achieving organizational integration.

The organizational culture, while beneficial in the sense that integration and coherent action are promoted, also forms a constraint to rational decision making. If the major organizational decision makers tend to have the same view, chances are small that the existing strategy concept will be fundamentally scrutinized and challenged (see Box 3.2). Sometimes the drive for adaptation and cohesiveness is stronger than the tendency for critical reflection, and a group of decision makers gets stuck in collective *idées fixes*. This phenomenon is called 'groupthink' (see Chapter 5).

While groupthink is an extreme case, organizational culture is in all cases a source of programmed choice. Seeing one's own perception reflected in those of one's colleagues tends to numb one's capacity for self-criticism. And the desire to be a loyal member of the group may cause an individual to swallow criticism of others that would better have been voiced. The result may be that, just as in the case of individual routinized behaviour dressed up as rational decision making, decision processes become sacred rituals rather than arenas for clashing ideas.

Box 3.2 Shared beliefs at General Motors

The belief that Japanese manufacturers would not be able to produce cars that could compete with theirs, as well as the belief that Americans would never start buying small cars (in spite of the success of the Volkswagen Beetle), made General Motors slow in responding to fundamental changes in the market after the 1973 oil crisis. When GM finally awoke, it had to spend many millions of dollars in order to design and introduce smaller cars. Arriving late in the market, GM appeared not to have read customer tastes correctly, and several new cars were less than successful. Asked to explain what went wrong, Roger B. Smith, CEO from 1981 to 1990, replied: 'I don't know. It's a mysterious thing'.

(Source: Loomis, 1993)

3.4 Two spheres of strategic management

Rational decision and programmed choice are two aspects of strategic management. Both are important, and they can be integrated into a coherent view of strategic decision making.

Interaction between rational decision making and programmed choice

The processes taking place within an organization at any particular moment are always a mixture of rational decision making and programmed choice. Programmed choice determines the day-to-day routine of organizational life; rational decision making is switched on if situations occur with which existing routines cannot adequately deal. Both spheres of decision behaviour interact in many intricate ways.

Programmed choice influences rational decision

To a large extent, programmed choice constitutes the framework within which rational decision making takes place. Programmed choice is a source of inertia, and constrains the range of options that can be implemented. Programmed choice can stand in the way of strategic decision making, if responses to changing circumstances are made on the basis of habit and impulse rather than rational deliberation (Winter, 1987). But programmed choice also influences the process of rational decision making more directly. Programmed choice is instrumental in carving out organizational positions that are associated with special interests and leads to the substitution of personal or departmental goals for the goals of the organization as a whole. Programmed choice also plays a crucial role in the selection of legitimate goals for rational decision-making processes.

In many textbooks on strategic management the inertia of the existing organizational structure is seen as an important impediment to the implementation of rational strategic decisions (e.g. Hill and Jones, 1989: 318; Johnson and Scholes, 1993: 386; Rowe et al., 1994: 489). The organizational structure embodies – and tends to perpetuate – differences of interest between departments and between individuals. Any proposal for strategic change is bound to go against the interests of some departments or individuals. These individuals and departments will resist implementation of such a plan. Resistance to strategic change can take the form of denial of the necessity to change, procrastination or downright sabotage (Ansoff and McDonnel, 1990: 405). The inertia embodied in programmed choice may influence the rational decision-making process directly, in that some options are ruled out a priori because of expected resistance; or the outcome of a rational decision process may fail to get implemented because existing differences of interest have not been taken into account.

The organizational structure also determines the division of labour in rational decision processes, as well as the incentive structures individual functionaries are faced with. These incentive structures may be expected to be in line with the goals of the organization, but never perfectly so. Thus the individuals entrusted with the task of strategy formation will take decisions that are not only – or even not predominantly – to the benefit of the organization as a whole, but that are beneficial to their division, department, colleagues, and to themselves. As a consequence of this, rational decision-making processes of individual functionaries may be irrational – in the sense of substantial rationality – at the level of the organization as a whole.

Programmed choice in the sense of shared beliefs and mindsets, or the organizational culture, has a strong bearing on which organizational goals are seen as logical, legitimate and attainable. Goals that are at odds with the dominant view of the world are 'unthinkable'. Thus, of all the organizational goals that would in principle be possible, many are ruled out a priori because they are too far removed from present preoccupations (Johnson, 1988).

Rational decision making influences programmed choice

Just as programmed choice has a bearing on rational decision making, rational decision making influences programmed choice. This influence may be the result of deliberate attempts to change the existing structure. But the influence may also be unintentional, for instance if programmed choice originates in behaviour that was once based on rational decision making.

Rational decision making, even though constrained and affected by programmed choice, may nevertheless have as an outcome the intention to change the existing programming of choice. It may be a declared goal of a strategy to bring about changes in procedures, and so on. This can be the case, for example, if some important decision makers believe that the existing structure and culture are no longer functional, and have to be adapted to the changed circumstances.

On the other hand, many of the existing elements of programmed choice, rules, procedures, programmes, and so on, originate in previous rational decisions. Faced with a particular kind of problem for the first time, an organization engages in rational decision making in order to design an appropriate response. Subsequently, every time a comparable problem crops up, the same response is used. In this way organizational learning occurs, and new routines are formed. Sequences of activities that are repeated many times are subject to habitualization and institutionalization (Berger and Luckmann, 1966: 53–5). Habitualization frees the individual decision maker from a plethora of decisions, and thus provides a psychic relief.

Institutionalization occurs when in a social setting habitualized patterns of behaviour create expectations. Actor A behaved in a certain way at previous occasions, and actor B responded in a certain way. This creates expectations for future interactions in comparable situations. As a consequence, the interaction of A and B becomes predictable. In the end, these predictable sequences of interaction – or institutions – are seen as something independent of the identities of the incumbents, A and B. Institutionalized behaviour is of a routine, taken-for-granted nature. Perhaps in some distant past these behavioural patterns were the object of deliberate design, but now they are performed in an unreflective way. Institutions are 'sticky', difficult to change, as institutionalized patterns of behaviour tend to perpetuate themselves. (This is the position advocated in institutionalist theories of organizations; see, e.g., DiMaggio and Powell, 1991; Jepperson, 1991; Selznick, 1957.)

Rational decision making influences programmed choice also in yet another way: it may be instrumental in relation to goals taken as given, but in the process of rational decision making these exogenously given goals will almost inevitably become more explicit. As a result, tensions between different goals or unwanted consequences of the pursuit of certain goals may surface. This in turn may lead to a reconsideration of the principles guiding organizational action or of the dominant worldview.

The interaction between rational decision making and programmed choice is schematized in Figure 3.3. The interplay between strategy, structure and culture, touched upon in the above discussion, is taken up in more detail in Chapter 6.

Chapter summary

- Three kinds of models can be distinguished in rational choice approaches to decision making: models of risk-free choice, models of risky choice and models of interactive choice.

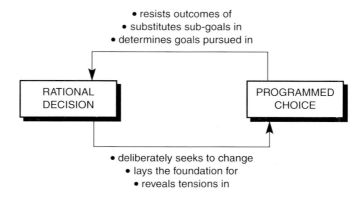

Figure 3.3 Interaction of rational decision and programmed choice.

■ Models of risk-free choice are not applicable to strategic decision making because strategic problems are characterized by uncertainty. Models of risky choice are only modestly relevant, because in real-world decision making complete enumeration and evaluation of alternatives is infeasible. Models of interactive decision making are most relevant. However, these models tell us more about possible outcomes of decision-making processes than about the decision-making process itself.

■ In analysing strategic decision making it is most fruitful to assume bounded rationality and satisficing behaviour, rather than perfect rationality and maximizing.

■ Under the assumption of bounded rationality, rationality means that the decision maker is open to evidence and uses logical analysis in making a decision.

■ Organizational goals originate in the goals of individuals, which in turn originate in emotions transcending rationality.

■ Not all decisions are made in a (boundedly) rational way: much choice behaviour is programmed by habits, routines, procedures, and so on.

■ Both boundedly rational decision making and programmed choice are important in the formation of organizational strategy. Relationships of mutual influence exist between both spheres of strategic management.

4

The psychology of decision making

In this chapter we focus on decision making at the level of the individual. Individual decision-making behaviour deviates in many ways from the prescriptions of normative-rational theory. Some of these deviations are specific to particular decision makers. We will discuss this phenomenon in the first section. Other deviations from perfect rationality can be found in the behaviour of almost all human decision makers. These deviations stem from the characteristics of human cognition, the use of heuristics, and from the way in which people tend to deal with risky choices. These phenomena are discussed in Sections 4.2–4.4.

4.1 Individual differences

Personality and decision making

Personality

It does not seem far-fetched to assume that different persons have different ways of making decisions (Hambrick and Mason, 1984; Hitt and Tyler, 1991). Individuals have distinct personalities, which influence their behaviour. The **personality** of a person refers to the total of that individual's characteristics which are stable over different situations and over time (Van Veldhoven, 1988: 54). Various dimensions of personality have been suggested in the context of decision-making analysis. We will discuss briefly a selection of these dimensions.

Locus of control

Some people are convinced that they have a strong control over their life. They feel that many of the events that occur are the result of their own efforts. These persons are of the **internal personality type**. Other individuals attribute much of what happens in their life to factors beyond their control, like fate or luck. These people are **external persons** (Rotter 1966).

The internal-external dimension has been shown to be related to various aspects of strategic decision making. General managers who have a stronger internal locus of control tend to pursue more innovative strategies. Furthermore, they display more risk-taking behaviour and have a stronger preference for proactive strategies, that is, they want their firms to lead rather than imitate the moves of competitors. Finally, more internal managers have longer planning horizons (Miller et al., 1982). All these findings correspond with what we would expect from people who believe they have a strong grasp on their fate (Wright, 1985, discusses a study with conflicting outcomes, however).

Tolerance for ambiguity

Some people prefer orderliness and familiarity, whereas others thrive on uncertainty and ambiguity. This **tolerance for ambiguity** dimension of personalities has also been associated with strategy. The findings of one empirical study indicated that managers with a high tolerance for ambiguity are more effective in implementing 'building strategies', aimed at increasing market share and improving competitive position. However, managers with a lower tolerance for ambiguity were found to be more effective in implementing 'harvest strategies', aimed at maximization of short-term earnings and cash flow, if necessary at the expense of market share and competitive position (Gupta and Govindarajan 1984).

Risk-taking propensity

Doubtlessly the **propensity to take risk** is an important variable in decision-making processes. However, it is not easy to establish a generalized personality trait of risk propensity (March and Shapira, 1988). Risk propensity varies across the decision context. Apparently, there are several sub-dimensions of risk taking, for example, monetary risk taking, physical risk taking, social risk taking, and ethical risk taking. Within similar contexts (similar sub-dimensions of risk taking) risk propensity appears to be relatively stable (Gupta and Govindarajan, 1984; Wright, 1985). In the study of effectiveness of strategy implementation referred to above, findings for risk propensity are reported which are similar to those for tolerance for ambiguity (Gupta and Govindarajan, 1984).

Cognitive style

A separate branch of personality research focuses on cognitive style as a characteristic of individuals. **Cognitive style** refers to the way of reasoning that is characteristic for a particular individual over the whole range of his or her decision-making behaviours (Goodwin and Wright, 1991: 203). In this vein, we can distinguish between decisive, flexible, hierarchic and integrative decision styles (Driver and Mock, 1975). Decision makers with a **decisive style** use only a minimal amount of information, and tend to concentrate on one option only. The **flexible style** is also characterized by parsimonious use of data, but in this style of decision making attention is spread over several alternatives. The **hierarchic style** uses a large amount of information to investigate a single option, and the **integrative style**, finally, also uses many data, but in order to investigate the pros and cons of various options. However, the empirical literature is inconclusive. Some studies indicate that these decision styles are stable characteristics of individuals, but in other research no clear difference between the 'integrative' and other decision-making styles could be identified (Wright, 1985).

Another way to categorize decision styles is to distinguish between **sensors**, who prefer to analyse isolated, concrete data, and **intuitors**, who focus on relationships between data and on the complete picture, rather than on details. In a task like predicting bankruptcy intuitors were hypothesized to do better, because accurate prediction depends on the understanding of relationships and trade-offs between financial ratios rather than on the absolute value of any of them. This prediction was confirmed (Wright, 1985).

Other personality dimensions

Many other personality dimensions may be hypothesized to have a bearing on decision behaviour. Katz and Kahn, for instance, discuss among other things ideology versus power orientation, and creativity versus common sense (Katz and Kahn, 1978: 510–13; see also Goodwin and Wright, 1991: 201–7). People driven by ideology are assumed to have internalized the values of their organization so thoroughly that any deviation is perceived as treason. Decision makers with a power orientation would be more willing to compromise in order to make use of the circumstances and to achieve their goals. Creative people are hypothesized to be strong in seeing new relations, and in imposing new structures on old facts. Others would excel in making common-sense judgements. The first type of personality may be expected to be able to generate original solutions, but may be less effective in the evaluation phase. The common-sense personality may be able to make a more realistic assessment of the applicability of solutions.

In an interesting study, Kets de Vries and Miller focused on psychotic personality types and their influence on organizational decision making (see Box 4.1). Their evidence, however, is largely anecdotal. More generally, empirical evidence pertaining to the relationship between personality traits and decision-making behaviour is scarce. Experimental findings are often difficult

Box 4.1 Psychotic decision making

Manfred Kets de Vries and Danny Miller in their book The Neurotic Organization concentrate on managers with dysfunctional personality characteristics. They distinguish five neurotic styles: the paranoid, compulsive, dramatic, depressive and schizophrenic styles. If much power is concentrated in a psychotic manager, he or she can through the interaction with other organization members exert a strong influence on the decision-making style within that organization. In this way a whole organization can become paranoid, depressive, and so on. In the compulsive organization, for instance, procedures acquire the status of rites, and become goals in themselves. In the decision-making process there is a strong emphasis on formalities. Everything has to go through the official channels, a proposal has to bear the right initials before it can be taken seriously. Strategies are planned up to the most minute details. These strategies often are variations on one and the same theme. Once the top manager has decided that this or that factor is the key to the success of the company, it becomes the basis of every conceivable future strategy.

(Source: Kets de Vries and Miller, 1984).

to interpret, and the evidence is sometimes conflicting and frequently contrary to expectations (Wright, 1985).

Demographic characteristics

Decisional variance can be associated not only with personality differences but also with differences in sex, age, formal education and career experience. See Box 4.2.

Gender

Numerous behavioural differences between men and women have been identified. For instance, males tend to be more exploitative in their social behaviour, and females more accommodative (Harrison, 1987: 313). However, with regard to decision making not many significant differences have been found. The similarities between male and female decision behaviour seem to outweigh the differences. In one study it was found that men have more confidence in their judgements than women. Another study found that women have a more participative style in group decision making (Harrison, 1987: 313). Comparative empirical studies of the cognitive abilities of males and females indicate that men are better in working with numbers and display higher activity

---

Box 4.2 The advantages of demographic diversity

Demographic diversity can be taken advantage of. Ernest H. Drew, CEO of Hoechst Celanese, realized for the first time that diversity is a strength in problem solving at a 1990 conference for Hoechst top officers. These officers, mostly white males, were joined by 50 lower-level women and minorities to consider questions regarding the way corporate culture affects the business, and how it can be changed to advantage. Those teams that were mixed by race and sex produced broader and more original solutions. Drew concluded that Hoechst needed diversity at every level of the company where decisions are made. This led to the practice of making the corporate human resource department carefully review promotion recommendations, and ensure that females and minorities are added for consideration whenever they appear to be left out. It also led to the requirement for Hoechst Celanese top officers to break out of their 'comfort zones' and become exposed to other people, by joining two organizations in which they are a minority. Drew himself is a member of the boards of black Hampton University and of SER-Jobs for Progress, a Hispanic organization.

(Source: Rice, 1994)

---

levels, whereas women score higher on verbal ability. On the whole, men perform better in laboratory experiments, in groups as well as individually, although these tasks are possibly more male-orientated (Miner, 1992: 326).

Age

Studies of the relationship between the age of top executives and organizational characteristics reveal that younger executives are associated with higher, but also more volatile, corporate growth. The existence of this correlation does not allow us to conclude on the direction of causality, however (Hambrick and Mason, 1984).

In decision-making processes, managerial age is positively associated with the tendency to seek more information and to evaluate information accurately. Consequently it is not surprising that older managers are slower in their decision making. Younger managers appear to be better able to integrate information, and have more confidence in their decisions, but are also less flexible in altering them in the face of adverse consequences (Taylor, 1975b).

Formal education

A person's education influences his or her knowledge and skill base. Presumably these differences have a bearing on strategic decision making. International comparative studies of management show considerable differences in the average educational level of managers in, for example, the United Kingdom and Germany. The same studies also suggest that German managers are more effective (Lane, 1989). However, the complexity of the issue impedes drawing conclusions from this concurrence.

One consistent finding in studies of the relationship between the educational background of managers and organizational behaviour is that a higher educational level of managers is associated with a higher degree of organizational receptivity to innovation. The type of education (administration versus non-administration) apparently is of no influence on this relationship (Hambrick and Mason, 1984).

Career experience

The specific career experience of a manager has a bearing on his or her decision making. If executives with different functional backgrounds are presented with an identical case study, they tend to define the problem in terms of their specific specialization, even when asked to consider the case from a general management point of view (Dearborn and Simon, 1958). In the study of the effectiveness of strategy implementation to which has been referred above repeatedly, an additional finding pertained to the functional background of managers. A longer experience in a marketing or sales function was found to be positively associated with effectiveness in the case of implementation of a build strategy, but negatively in the case of a harvest strategy (Gupta and Govindarajan 1984).

Individual versus situational variance

The studies referred to in this section aim to identify patterns of decision behaviour which are characteristic for a specific individual and consistent across situations. As we have seen, the evidence is mixed. What is perhaps worse, is that it is difficult to find much system in the jungle of concepts and dimensions. (For a discussion of models of personality structures see, e.g., Zuckerman et al., 1993.) Personality factors interact with environmental factors in determining behaviour, which in turn influences both the situation and cognitive and other characteristics of the acting person. A model of reciprocal determinism seems best to describe the interrelations between behaviour, personality and situation (Bandura, 1986: 22–30). All in all, individual variance should not be disregarded in explaining decision processes (cf. Hambrick and Mason, 1984).

Variations in behaviour are also associated with situational sources of variance, like the number of options available, or the formulation of the problem. Ideally, we should study individual differences and situational differences, as well as the interaction between persons and situations in the context of decision making (Wright, 1985). However, the available data do not encourage such a comprehensive exploration of the sources of decisional variance. Instead, we will now leave the discussion of individual variance and focus on more general characteristics of human decision making, as well as variations of these characteristics across situations. The reader is asked to bear in mind that at the same time individual differences remain important.

4.2 Emotions and intuition

Human decision makers are not automata that infallibly receive and process information. Human decision makers have emotions, and these emotions can interfere with the cognitive processes of decision making. Furthermore, decision makers do not rely exclusively on reasoning in making decisions. Many decisions are made on the basis of intuitive judgement. The impact on decision making of emotion and intuition will be taken up in this section of the chapter. Finally, limitations to human cognitive capabilities lead to simplifications and biases in intentionally rational decision processes. We will focus on these simplifications and biases in Section 4.3.

Emotions and rational deliberations

Emotions

In the preceding chapter we have stressed that emotions, or more generally affective experiences, are at the top of every conceivable means-ends hierarchy. But the process of rational deliberation, which is instrumental in choosing the best means in order to reach a given goal, can also be disturbed by emotions. For instance, a purchasing manager screening potential suppliers may discard a company because of a personal dislike for one of its agents. This emotion may stand in the way of reaching the ultimate goal in the manager's means-ends hierarchy, for example, the enjoyment of the social approval, status and material benefits that come with excellent task accomplishment.

Emotions also play a role in risky decisions. Risk-taking involves feelings of anxiety, fear, stimulation and joy. The satisfaction of success is augmented by the riskiness of the decision that led to it. The threat of failure and the anticipation of mastery are part of the pleasures of success (March and Shapira, 1988: 84). These feelings may lead to more risky choice behaviour than objectively warranted.

When decision makers let themselves be guided predominantly by their emotions the quality of the decision process tends to be poor. At the awareness stage, the formulation of the problem may be coloured by negative or positive emotions. Furthermore, the range of alternatives taken into consideration may be unduly restricted, the search for information biased, and the consequences of the preferred course of action not well examined (Janis, 1989: 71). Emotions are widely seen as disturbing rational decision processes (Etzioni, 1988: 103).

Emotions are strong affective reactions to persons or situations, but also milder affective experiences, such as moods, have a bearing on the decision-making process. When people are in a happy mood, they tend to see good outcomes as more likely, and bad outcomes as less likely, compared with their view in a neutral mood. Conversely, when they are sad, people view negative events as more likely and good outcomes as less likely (Etzioni, 1988: 103).

Level of emotional involvement

It would be wrong to see emotions only as a negative factor in the cognitive decision process. True enough, a high level of emotional involvement, for example, as a result of feelings of guilt, anxiety, or embarrassment, can be counterproductive (Simon, 1987). But on the other hand, emotional involvement is also a powerful motivator of human behaviour. If there is a complete lack of emotional involvement (apart from some far-removed ultimate end), a decision maker is unlikely to go through all the painstaking deliberations necessary to come to a reasoned decision. Consequently, the relationship between emotion and rational decision making is more complex.

Etzioni, on the basis of the available literature, postulates a curvilinear relationship between the level of affect and the level of rationality (Etzioni, 1988: 104). At low levels of affect or emotional involvement decision makers exert less cognitive effort than necessary for the task. Consequently, a programmed response may be given where a newly designed solution would be more appropriate, or the need for decision making may remain altogether unnoticed. At very high levels of emotional involvement, rational deliberations may be bypassed completely, and a response based on emotions only may be given (Janis, 1989: 77; Simon, 1987: 62). At intermediate levels of emotional involvement, however, there is sufficient motivation for going through the mental strains associated with elaborate thought processes. At the same time, the emotional involvement is not so strong as to override more instrumental reasoning and calculation. Consequently, the effective level of rationality in the decision-making process is assumed to be optimal in this situation (see Figure 4.1).

Stress and decision making

The level of stress, frustration, or conflict stands in the same relation to rational decision making as emotive affect. High levels of stress contribute to **cognitive strain**: the breakdown of the decison maker's cognitive processes due to information overload. But at very low levels of stress, decision makers may become bored, and pay too little attention. Or decision makers start looking for ways to make their task more interesting, in order to raise their level of emotive arousal. This may lead to excessive risk taking. Experiments indicate that the

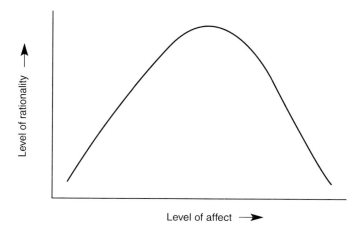

Figure 4.1 The relationship between level of affect and rationality of decision making.

optimal level of stress depends on the nature of the task. The more complex the task, the lower the optimal level of emotive arousal (Etzioni, 1988: 104; Taylor, 1975b).

Janis distinguishes five patterns of decision-making behaviour (Janis, 1989: 78–80). At very low levels of stress either **unconflicted inertia** or **unconflicted change** is to be expected. In the first case, no need for decision making is perceived, and routines that foster recommitment to the existing policy are relied upon. In the second case the need for decision making is recognized, but because of the low level of arousal simple decision rules that allow quick decisions are followed, without much deliberation. At intermediate levels of stress **vigilant decision making** takes place. In this style of decision-making policy makers, within their cognitive constraints, carry out to the best of their ability the various steps of a complete decision-making process. At very high levels of stress **defensive avoidance** or **hypervigilance** take place. Defensive avoidance occurs when a situation is seen as very threatening, while no feasible solution seems to be at hand. Problem avoidance or procrastination are the most likely outcomes. In the case of hyper-vigilance the threatening situation is escaped from as rapidly as possible by accepting the first alternative that promises to be satisfactory. The chosen option is bolstered uncritically and unfavourable aspects are ignored.

Causality of cognition and affection

We do not know very much about the causal relations between cognitive and affective aspects of (decision) behaviour (Van Veldhoven, 1988). Many models of decision making focus on cognition while neglecting affect. But psychological research suggests that affective reactions often precede cognitive deliberations (Van Raaij, 1988). In these cases the agenda for the cognitive decision-making

---

Box 4.3 Intuition and strategy in Unilever

Intuition has played an important role in the determination of the strategy of Unilever at several points in time. In the early 1980s, it was suggested that the expertise of monoclonal antibodies acquired by the company's agribusiness could also be applied to develop products for human use. At that time, the uncertainties with regard to the technical and commercial feasibility of such a project were immense. But within Unilever there was a consensus that the idea 'felt' right. On the basis of that feeling, resources were invested, and Unilever was able to launch a revolutionary home pregnancy test. A second example is Unilever's decision – as one of the first large firms – to adopt a back-to-core strategy. The move to this new strategy was triggered by the unease the executive committee felt in deciding on a large capital investment in an area in which Unilever had little expertise or experience. The realization of what was wrong with this proposal worked like a catalyst, and Unilever started to reassess its capabilities and skills in all business activities. Divestments in areas like wallpaper, floor-covering and turkey breeding were the result.

(Source: Maljers, 1990)

---

process is set by the first affective reaction. On the other hand, careful consideration of pros and cons can also alter a person's feelings. In that case cognition changes affect. As suggested in Section 3.2, it seems most fruitful to conceptualize the relationship between cognitive appraisal and affective experience as a continuous loop system (Cadland, 1977). Both spheres of the mind constantly influence one another, and it seems impossible to state which of the two is more important than, or anterior to, the other.

Intuition

What is intuition?

Strategic decision making often proceeds in a way that seems to be radically different from the conscious deliberations associated with rational behaviour. Managers not infrequently adopt or reject a solution because it does or does not 'feel right' (see Box 4.3). The founder of modern management theory, Chester Barnard, emphasized the importance of intuitive judgement in executive decision making (quoted in Simon, 1987: 57). What is intuition, and what is its role in decision-making processes?

Definitions of intuition abound (see Behling and Eckel, 1991). According to some, 'intuition is what analysis is not' (Von Winterfeldt and Edwards, 1986:

550). We will employ a more substantive definition, and define a person's intuition as the set of decision rules internalized by that individual. These decision rules are uncodified and unconscious. They enable the individual to react rapidly in problem situations, because familiar patterns of behaviour are recognized almost instantaneously, and the appropriate response surfaces automatically (cf. Simon, 1987). (According to Mintzberg, 1994: 303–18, this view of intuition is too narrow. 'Intuition' is also used to refer to other phenomena, such as creative imagination, common sense and good judgement.) The uncodified and unconscious nature of intuition differentiates it from other categories of decision rules, such as standard operating procedures and routines.

Left and right hemispheres of the brain

The mental processes associated with intuition differ fundamentally from those associated with rational deliberation or analysis. Analytical thought processes are aimed at dissecting a whole into its constituent parts. Intuition in contrast is based on synthetic thought processes, aimed at constructing a coherent whole from different pieces of information. Physiological research suggests that these two mental processes take place predominantly in the left and the right hemispheres of the brain respectively (in right-handed people; in left-handed people it is often the other way around). The left hemisphere controls language, analytic ability, logic and sequential perception; the right hemisphere controls spatial and melodic abilities, and simultaneous perception (Mintzberg, 1988; Robey and Taggart, 1981; Simon, 1987; Taggart and Robey, 1981; Taggart et al., 1985).

The left hemisphere of the brain is more active in analytic tasks like systematic reasoning; the right hemisphere in synthetic tasks like recognition of visual patterns. Intuition is based on just such a recognition process: familiar patterns of information, or *chunks*, are recognized that enable the decision maker to quickly organize a large quantity of data. As a result of this recognition process an appropriate answer emerges apparently automatically. The decision maker most of the time is unable to report how he or she attained this answer (Simon, 1987). This is not surprising, as linguistic competence is localized in the analytical left hemisphere.

Formation of intuition

How does intuition develop? The evidence indicates that experience plays a very important role. An experienced decision maker has analysed many situations before, and intuition could be described as 'distilled experience', or 'analyses frozen into habit' (Behling and Eckel, 1991: 49; Simon, 1987: 63). Furthermore, training and education is also important. Consequently, the expert may be expected to have a more effective intuition than the layman, and the experienced expert will do better than the novice.

An experiment in which business school students and experienced businessmen analysed a business policy case illustrates the working of intuition.

Although the final outcomes of the case analysis were similar, the process of reaching these outcomes differed between businessmen and students. The businessmen were very quick in identifying the key features of the case. The students took much more time, and showed many more signs of explicit analysis (Simon, 1987).

Intuition and rational thought

As we have seen, intuition can be hypothesized to originate in rational analysis. This means that the two kinds of processes are related. This is not only true with regard to the genesis of intuition, but also with regard to its use in decision-making processes. Rationality and intuition are related and complementary rather than independent and contrasting (Simon, 1987).

In the first place, in practice no decision maker will use only rational analysis or only intuition. Rather, it is to be expected that all decision makers use both rational deliberations *and* intuitive judgement in reaching a conclusion. The actual 'mix' of the two may differ from person to person. A measurement instrument exists, the Meyers–Briggs type indicator, that can be used to measure a manager's preference for using intuition in decision making (Behling and Eckel, 1991). Or, seen from the opposite end, 'need for cognition' appears to be a global personality characteristic (Pieters, 1988).

Secondly, intuitive and analytical thought processes are actually interspersed in the decision process. Between conscious steps, considerable leaps are taken on the basis of intuition (Simon, 1987). If we reasoned out all the details of our plans, the thought process would become unbearably slow.

Thirdly, even if the process of decision making is relatively conscious and rational in the awareness and analysis phases, in the final phase, when commitment to a choice has to be made, intuition typically plays an important role. In checking the results of complicated calculations, individuals – especially trained individuals – can intuitively verify the plausibility of the outcome (Von Winterfeldt and Edwards, 1986: 552). The same can be said of businessmen. If an experienced executive at the end of an elaborate decision process has negative emotional feelings, he or she often takes this as a sign that the solution that is about to be selected is not good (Janis, 1989: 72). In strategic management the conclusions of rational analysis can thus at the very last moment be overridden by top management intuition – doubtlessly often to the immense chagrin of staff specialists in strategic planning.

Intuition, cognitive biases and heuristics

It is difficult to draw a clear line between the subject of this subsection, intuition, and those of the next, cognitive biases and heuristics. All three categories can be considered 'cognitive short-cuts', but they are of a slightly different nature (Janis, 1989: 36). Building on the definition formulated above, **intuition** will be considered to be the set of all decision rules internalized by an individual pertaining to one or more specific subject areas, for example, the exploration of oil fields, or the diagnostics of pulmonary diseases (for a different view, see Mintzberg, 1994: 308–15).

Cognitive heuristics are also decision rules, but in contrast to those of intuition these rules pertain to general processes for reaching a conclusion rather than to a specific subject area. According to the definition used here, cognitive heuristics are of a processual rather than of a substantive nature. For instance, one heuristic allows decision makers to imply that if the occurrence of an event in the past can be readily called to mind it is also more likely to occur in the future. This heuristic is not specific to a particular type of event. Just like intuition, heuristics are utilized generally automatically and non-reflectively by (Janis, 1989: 43). But unlike intuition, cognitive heuristics can in principle be made explicit without essentially changing their character. In contrast, intuition made explicit is no longer intuition.

Cognitive biases are the potentially detrimental effects on the decision-making process of the use of heuristics. Heuristics often lead to adequate decisions under circumstances that impede fully rational deliberations, for example, because they allow the decision maker to draw inferences from incomplete data. However, even the most useful heuristic may, under certain circumstances, have a negative impact on the quality of the decision process (Bazerman, 1990: 41; Tversky and Kahneman, 1974). For this reason some analysts prefer to lump biases and heuristics together in one category of 'cognitive illusions' (Von Winterfeldt and Edwards, 1986: 530).

Cognitive biases and heuristics are indeed difficult to separate abstractly. Whether a certain decision rule should be placed in one category or the other depends on the way it is used, and on the nature of the problem. In the next section, therefore, cognitive biases and heuristics will be discussed as one undifferentiated category. But this should not be taken as a sign that all cognitive shortcuts are seen as unproductive. Quite the contrary, the assumption is that cognitive short-cuts are indispensable and often beneficial.

4.3 Cognitive biases and heuristics

A substantial literature deals with cognitive biases and heuristics. (For overviews see, e.g., Hogarth, 1980; Slovic et al., 1977; Tversky and Kahneman, 1974.) In this section a selection of the biases and heuristics that have been identified will be discussed, namely those that may be assumed to be of particular interest in the context of strategic decision making in organizations. In this section we will focus on biases and heuristics that in principle occur or are used in both probabilistic and in non-probabilistic decision making contexts. Biases and heuristics that are particularly relevant in the context of risky choices are discussed in Section 4.4.

In this section, the rough subdivision of decision-making processes in the phases of awareness, analysis and action will be used as an organizing principle (analogous to Schwenk 1984). The assignment of specific biases or heuristics to a particular category is always somewhat arbitrary, however. One and the same kind of cognitive shortcut can sometimes occur in various phases of the decision process.

Awareness

Perception

Before a strategic decision process can start, a need or opportunity has to be perceived. Perception is not a passive process, but an activity in which the perceiver selects, organizes and interprets information (Hambrick and Mason, 1984; Harrison, 1987: 232–5; Luthans, 1992: 55–78).

Without selection no perception would be possible. Individuals are bombarded by sensory stimuli in the form of noises, sights, smells and tactile sensations. In order to be able to concentrate on meaningful stimuli, the noise has to be shut out. Only stimuli that are above certain thresholds are consciously perceived. The level of these thresholds depends on factors like background noise and the attention of the perceiver.

Next, the selected information that enters perception is organized. This means that the perceiver unconsciously tries to construct coherent wholes of the sensorial stimuli. Four principles can be used to describe this process: closure, constancy, proximity and similarity (Luthans, 1992: 69–70). The principle of **closure** holds that people tend to construct a complete mental picture, also when the sensory stimuli are in effect incomplete. For example, when reading words with missing letters, or incomplete sentences, people close these gaps without even noticing them. The principle of **constancy** states that people tend to perceive stability in their environment. The assumption is that patterns of stimuli are continuous over time, and that the perceptions of the past can form the basis for the perceptions of the present. According to the principle of **proximity** stimuli that are close together in space or time will be perceived as belonging together. The related principle of **similarity**, finally, holds that sensual stimuli that are similar will be organized into a common group. The differences will be understated in favour of the similarities.

In the third phase of the perceptual process, coherent wholes of stimuli are interpreted. Current impressions are matched with past experiences in order to give meaning to perceptions (Harrison, 1987: 234). This is achieved by sorting familiar patterns of information into categories. These categories may be innate or reflect earlier perception, interpretation and learning (Piaget, 1970).

Perception is a basic process which doubtlessly has a profound influence on human behaviour. However, for achieving an understanding of a phenomenon like strategic decision making, higher order processes of selection, organization and interpretation of information are even more relevant. We will now turn to these higher order phenomena.

Cognitive schemata

In making sense of the information they receive, decision makers use cognitive schemata. Cognitive schemata are 'organized chunks of world knowledge that include expectations about what will occur in a given situation, what options or alternatives exist, what information is required, and how certain functions are to be performed' (Klayman and Schoemaker, 1993: 165). Put differently, they are sets of **strategic assumptions** with regard to certain contexts (Schwenk, 1988: 19). A cognitive schema of a certain type of situation reflects the decision maker's beliefs about the importance of issues, and about their cause-and-effect relations (Schwenk, 1988: 21). It enables the decision maker to select information, organize his or her thoughts and find solutions.

Cognitive schemata can be visualized using a technique called 'cognitive mapping' (Axelrod, 1973; Eden, 1989; Eden and Simpson, 1989; Klayman and Schoemaker, 1993). On the basis of a decision maker's oral or written account of a problem situation, the relevant concepts and the assumed relationships between them are identified (see Box 4.4).

A cognitive schema reflects knowledge and previous experience in a certain area. By way of analogy (parts of) schemata can be transferred from one domain to another. Experiences in one industry may be used to develop an understanding of what goes on in another industry. Alternatively, knowledge or experience from a completely different sphere of life can be used to organize one's thoughts about the business world, for example, using analogies with the military or with competitive sports (Schwenk, 1988: 23).

The drawback of reliance on existing schemata for understanding new phenomena is that the analogy always is only partial. There is never a complete correspondence between the structure of a new problem area and the cognitive scheme derived from another problem area. Moreover, even when applied in its own domain, the scheme necessarily is a simplification of reality. Out of the multitude of possible variables and relations, only a small number are selected. Individuals tend to restrict their attention to the selected variables in the subsequent thought processes (Legrenzi et al. 1993). Whereas a multitude of potentially valid schemata are possible, decision makers tend to be satisfied with a single interpretation of a problem situation (Klayman and Schoemaker, 1993: 169).

People also are reluctant to change their cognitive schemata, even when faced with powerful counter-evidence. Only if application of a schema leads to conclusions which are unbelievable (i.e. not corresponding to the decision maker's pre-existing overall belief system) will it be fully scrutinized (Evans et al., 1993: 174). Individuals tend to overestimate the importance of information which confirms their schemata, and underestimate the value of disconfirming information, and they seek out evidence which confirms rather than contradicts current beliefs (Evans et al. 1993: 174; Schwenk 1984: 116). If these beliefs are not well calibrated this tendency can be detrimental to the decision-making process.

Within organizations, the danger of uncritically accepting cognitive schemata looms particularly large when a small cohesive group or a single

Box 4.4 A cognitive map of the thinking of the director of a recruitment and employment agency

This cognitive map represents a part of the thinking of one of the directors of a small recruitment and employment agency, 'ER', specializing in providing employment opportunities for individuals, in the fields of computing and electronics, who wish to find non-defence-related work.

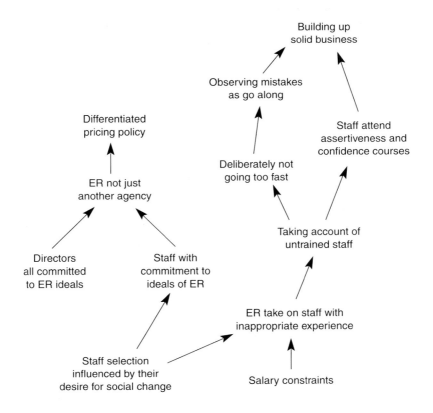

(Source: Eden and Simpson, 1989: 56)

powerful individual dominates the decision-making process (Schwenk, 1984; 1988). We will return to that problem in Chapter 5. Here I want to mention briefly that the opposite situation, with fundamental differences between the cognitive schemata employed by different decision makers within the firm, can also cause difficulties. Different cognitive schemata contain different variables and different causal relationships. As a result, the marketing manager, for instance, may just not understand what her colleague from production is talking about, and vice versa.

Correlation and causality

Relationships between variables form an important element of cognitive schemata. Unfortunately, human decision makers are not very good at judging these relationships. The expectation of a relationship between two variables often leads to a perceived correlation, even when no correlation exists (*illusory correlation*) (Barnes, 1984: 131).

A related cognitive bias is the **fallacy of causality** (Barnes, 1984; Katz and Kahn 1978: 507). People are inclined to interpret correlations as cause-and-effect relations, even when there is no evidence in this direction. In identifying causes, the importance of personal agencies is systematically overrated. Causal structures are often simplified through **linear thinking**: only a one-way sequence of cause and effect is perceived where actually a reciprocal relation between variables exists.

Context effects

Cognitive biases and heuristics, like cognitive schemata, are partly context-dependent. Every individual is positioned somewhere in (social) space and time, and is influenced by the norms and values of specific ethnic, societal, or professional groups. This position in space and time affects his or her knowledge, experience and judgements (Katz and Kahn, 1978: 502–3). An example of the effect of context on the development of cognitive schemata is provided by an analysis of public statements explaining company performance in good and bad years. Cognitive maps derived from public statements made in bad times contain significantly more external variables, while cognitive maps derived from public statements made during good times contain more elements pertaining to the effects of executive action (Schwenk, 1988: 28–9). 'Locus of control' apparently is not entirely a personality factor, but is also contingent on the decision maker's context.

Framing

The conception of problem situations is not only influenced by the decision maker's position in space and time, but also by the presentation or formulation of the problem. The way in which a problem is presented constitutes a **decision frame** which affects the decision maker's assessment of the problem and of possible solutions (Bazerman, 1990: 69; Tversky and Kahneman, 1985).

Particularly important is the question whether the decision frame emphasizes gains or losses. According to normative-rational theory, equivalent problem formulations should lead to identical decisions. Practice proves to be different. If the emphasis in the problem formulation is shifted from gains to losses or vice versa, people often come to diametrically opposite decisions (see Box 4.5).

The influence of the decision frame on the outcome of the decision process is augmented by the tendency of people to concentrate on a single important dimension when considering complex multifaceted problems. The dimension on which individuals focus may alter if the decision frame is manipulated. This is demonstrated in an experiment in which subjects were to decide on the question which of two parents involved in a divorce procedure should be given custody over the only child (Shafir et al., 1993). Parent A was described in terms that made him or her unremarkable (average income, reasonable rapport with the child, etc.). Parent B was depicted in much more vivid colours (very close relationship with the child, lots of work-related travel). If the subjects had to answer the question which parent should be awarded sole custody over the child, the majority of the subjects chose for parent B, focusing on the more pronounced positive attributes of this option. But if the subjects had to answer the question which parent should be *denied* sole custody of the child, the majority of subjects also chose for parent B, this time focusing on the more outspoken *negative* attributes of this option!

The framing phenomenon is particularly relevant in the context of risky choices. We will return to this subject in the discussion of **prospect theory** in Section 4.4.

Analysis

Preference construction

One of the activities in the phase of analysis is goal setting. Normative-rational decision theory assumes that at the level of the individual these goals are given beforehand in the form of complete and stable preference orderings. In fact, however, 'we create our wants, in part, by experiencing our choices' (March and Simon, 1993: 15). Three factors stand in the way of a direct access to preferences in decision making: conflicting values, complexity of decisions and uncertainty in values (Payne et al., 1992).

Conflict among values arises because many decisions involve options that differ in various dimensions, while there is no option that clearly dominates the others. A variety of evaluation modes is possible, as we have seen in Chapter 2. (The non-compensation evaluation modes discussed in Chapter 2 are also examples of heuristics, and they can also lead to biases.) Some of these modes are conflict confronting, such as the linear compensatory model. In this evaluation mode, the conflict between dimensions of value is confronted and resolved. Non-compensatory evaluation modes are conflict avoiding, in that trade-offs between dimensions are not made explicit (Payne et al., 1992: 93).

Box 4.5 Decision frame and epidemic control

One of the classic experiments in decision framing conducted by Amos Tversky and Daniel Kahneman concerns the choice between two possible programmes to combat an epidemic. Two groups of subjects in the experiment were given the following cover story:

> Imagine that the US is preparing for the outbreak of an unusual Asian disease, which is expected to kill 600 people. Two alternative programs to combat the disease have been proposed. Assume that the exact scientific estimates of the consequences are as follows:

The two groups of respondents were then shown two different, but formally equivalent formulations of the consequences of the programmes (in brackets are the percentages of the subjects that chose the option in question):

Group I

- If Programme A is adopted, 200 people will be saved. (72%)
- If Programme B is adopted, there is a one-third probability that 600 people will be saved, and a two-thirds probability that no people will be saved. (28%)

Group II

- If Programme C is adopted, 400 people will die. (22%)
- If Programme D is adopted, there is a one-third probability that nobody will die, two-thirds probability that 600 people will die. (78%)

A reformulation of the problem, with a shift in emphasis from gains (people saved) to losses (deaths), caused a pronounced shift in the choice of the majority of subjects.

(Source: Tversky and Kahneman, 1985)

Which mode will be chosen depends, *inter alia*, on the procedure of choice and on the decision frame.

Decisional complexity is important because it puts a strain on the cognitive abilities of individuals. Especially under time pressure, people have to use drastic simplification heuristics in order to solve a problem. Specifically, it has been shown that under time pressure people focus on the more important and/or more negative information about alternatives (Payne et al., 1992: 99).

This implies that the decision maker is unable to explore his values in dimensions that probably would have been taken into account in a simpler problem or under less time pressure.

Finally, individuals may not be sure about their values. Sometimes you know what you will get if you make a certain choice, but you do not know how much you will like that outcome. For instance, it is difficult to predict how much you will like a skiing holiday if you have never skied. People find it particularly difficult to evaluate outcomes that will materialize only in the distant future (Payne et al., 1992: 99). A feeling of disappointment seems to be endemic among those who 'have made it'.

Preference elicitation

Preferences are also sensitive to the method of elicitation. If subjects in experiments are asked to price options, they regularly reveal different preferences than if they are asked to choose one of the options. This can be explained if we assume that different elicitation procedures highlight different aspects of the options (comparable to framing effects), and thus produce different decision guidelines (Goodwin and Wright, 1991: 80; Shafir et al., 1993). Another explanation of elicitation effects is that some elicitation procedures (e.g. choice from among existing alternatives differing in several dimensions) provoke a more qualitative evaluation, whereas other elicitation procedures (e.g. determining the price that would make an incomplete option equally attractive as a given alternative) would call for more quantitative reasoning (Payne et al., 1992: 93).

Search for alternatives: how

When alternatives have to be generated, two fundamentally different processes can take place: a search for alternative solutions that already exist (but are not yet known to the decision maker), or the design of new, 'custom-made' solutions. In the first case the decision maker's memory, and subsequently his or her environment, are scanned. In the second case something new has to be created, and this entails a different kind of thought process (Mintzberg et al., 1976).

Instead of an orderly advancing process of rational thought, converging on a logical conclusion within a particular frame of reference, a divergent mode of thought is used in generating new options. The decision maker jumps from one area of application or expertise to another, using the vehicles of **analogy** and **metaphor**. A bank's branch system is not identical to the McDonald's hamburger chain, but using the analogy can help a bank executive think of solutions (e.g. standardization of branches) that may also work in his firm (Schwenk, 1988: 23). North Korea's invasion of South Korea was not identical to Hitler's invasions in Europe, but the analogy did bring United States President Harry Truman to adopting a 'no appeasement' stance (Janis, 1989:

37). A business firm is not identical to a military organization, but the metaphor can be used to suggest policy options.

Using analogies and metaphors to find new options is not a fancy management technique, but a natural thing to do. If none of the standard solutions is appropriate, the first thing to do is to search for more or less comparable cases, and look at what solution was used there (Janis, 1989: 37). Then, if still no solution is found, the cases used as analogies will be progressively more dissimilar to the case at hand. The less obvious the analogies, the more the thought process shifts from conscious reasoning to intuition. The most daring and creative analogies come to the conscious mind like a flash of lightning.

Reasoning by analogy or metaphor helps in generating creative solutions. But it may also be misleading. Decision makers may fail to realize that there are differences, perhaps critical differences between the analogy and the decision situation. Or they may fail to recognize that the analogy entails a simplification of the problem (Schwenk, 1984; 1988). The countries in southeast Asia inclining to communism were *not* dominos that could be stopped from falling by United States military intervention (cf. Steinbrunner, 1974: 116).

Search for alternatives: when

According to normative-rational models of decision making, all possible alternatives are taken into account. According to the satisficing model of decision making, often only a single solution is developed and evaluated. Only if this solution fails to be satisfactory will other options be considered.

The supposition of the satisficing model appears to be confirmed by business practice (Mazzolini, 1981; Mintzberg et al., 1976). Individuals display a tendency to focus on a single one of their goals, and then to work out a single solution that satisfies especially that particular goal. In this way possible value trade-offs are denied (Schwenk, 1984). Decision situations are often construed as the choice between carrying out a certain action or not carrying it out. Individuals focus on the action and search for more information about its consequences in order to make a decision. But they often fail to consider alternative options when these options are not explicitly stated beforehand (Legrenzi et al., 1993).

When there are already several alternatives, a decision maker has to decide whether he or she will search for even more options. Experiments show that the question whether people are willing to do so depends on how close existing alternatives are. If one of the existing alternatives clearly dominates (i.e. is superior in at least one dimension, and not worse in all other dimensions) this option is chosen, and no new solutions are searched for. But if the existing solutions are difficult to compare, for example, because one excels in one dimension and the other in another dimension, people do tend to look for alternative options. Note that it is not the attractiveness as such of the existing options which triggers search for alternatives, but the mere fact that they are difficult to evaluate (Shafir et al., 1993).

Prior belief bias

As related in the discussion of cognitive schemata, people are much less inclined to scrutinize the validity of an argumentation if the conclusion appears to be reasonable. Such an heuristic may under many circumstances be efficient, because it helps in economizing on scarce rational faculties. Furthermore, a person's beliefs form a more or less coherent whole, and it makes sense not to think lightly about challenging a part since this could undermine the entire system. Rather, one should revise beliefs only if there is a good reason to do so (Evans et al., 1993).

However, if this prior belief bias has a pronounced influence, and only a single option is evaluated (as in satisficing), it may have detrimental effects. After all, the option was initiated because it looked promising from the start, and during the process of developing it the decision maker will probably have emphasized its attractiveness (to him or herself or to other people). Laboratory experiments have demonstrated that decision makers in a process of *bolstering* develop arguments to magnify the attractiveness of an initially desired alternative (Schwenk, 1984). Therefore critical scrutiny would be in its place at the evaluation stage.

Syllogistic illusions and errors in arithmetic

Humans are victims of various kinds of syllogistic illusions. For instance, individuals have no problem with the application of the *modus ponens*:

If p then q
p
Therefore, q

However, when confronted with the *modus tollens* many people fail to draw the valid conclusion:

If p then q
Not q
Therefore, not p

Instead, many people state that no valid conclusion can be drawn from these premises (Legrenzi et al., 1993).

These failures and relative weaknesses of people in syllogistic reasoning are understandable, if we consider that human reasoners are normally not interested in deductive validity for its own sake. They want to give reasonable answers on the basis of almost always incomplete information. This forces them to go beyond the available data, and reach conclusions on the basis of induction (Legrenzi et al., 1993).

Not surprisingly, individuals make errors in arithmetic. More jolting is the observation that people systematically underestimate combinatorial possibilities and exponential growth. For instance, in an experiment in which subjects were asked to extrapolate from the early terms of a growth process, the estimates proved to be dramatically too small. This is more than just an illustrative example, for many real-world growth processes that call for human decision making are characterized by exponential growth (Von Winterfeldt and Edwards, 1986: 549).

Action

Indecision

Before implementation can take place, a choice has to be made. Here the problem can arise that with the addition of alternatives, the tendency to defer choice increases. Thomas Schelling illustrates this phenomenon by describing how, on an occasion in which he had decided to buy an encyclopaedia for his children, he went to the book store to buy one. At the book store, however, he was presented with the choice between two equally attractive encyclopaedias, and, experiencing an embarrassment of choice, ended up buying neither (related in Shafir et al., 1993: 21).

Indecision is strongest if the decision maker lacks a clear reason for choosing one option rather than the other, or when both options are satisfactory if considered independently. However, the tendency to defer choice is low when one option clearly dominates the other (Shafir et al., 1993).

Closure

Once a decision has been made, the tendency of the decision maker is to consolidate it in his or her own mind. Next, as soon as the decision is communicated to others, commitment becomes a social phenomenon. Irving Janis formulates a **bolstering rule** which captures the essence of the tendency to closure (Janis, 1989: 38–9):

> Once you have hit upon a course of action that meets fairly well the requirements you had in mind while making the decision, get your mind off its disadvantages or shortcomings; think instead about all the positive features you can.

If during the implementation information becomes available that suggests that the option chosen is not so favourable after all, a second tendency may occur which reinforces the bolstering process: selective inattention. In this process information which is inconsistent with one's thinking drops out of consciousness (White, 1971). Signals that something is wrong with the chosen solution are consequently neglected.

Both selective inattention and bolstering can be explained at the basis of the theory of **cognitive dissonance**. Once a person has made a commitment to a certain choice, he or she tends to retain thoughts that are in harmony with the selected option, and to discard other considerations (Festinger, 1957). This is achieved by unconsciously refurbishing arguments in favour of the option and suppressing bad news.

Escalation of commitment

A phenomenon related to the bolstering and selective inattention described above is that of escalation of commitment. A strategy typically is not the result of isolated decisions, but is formed by sequences of related decisions. After it has been decided first to adopt and implement a certain policy proposal, decisions to uphold or abort the policy regularly recur. Escalation of commitment implies that decision makers, when confronted with negative feedback on a policy adopted at an earlier stage, tend not to stop or mitigate that policy, but on the contrary to reinforce it.

A possible explanation for this behaviour can be found in the psychic need to justify or rationalize previous behaviour. This is what Staw calls **retrospective rationality**: the decision maker wants to appear rational in his or her decision making, to him or herself and to others (Staw, 1980). As a consequence of this need sunk costs, which in a fully rational analysis would be considered irrelevant, enter into the decision process. Losses have to be recouped, especially if the decision maker bears a clear personal responsibility for these losses. On the other hand, experiments suggest that sunk costs tend to enter into the analysis also when the decision maker does not bear personal responsibility for them (Whyte, 1986).

The degree of escalation of commitment also depends on other factors. One of these factors is the cause to which the failure is attributed. If this cause is seen to lie in external events – and not in the intrinsic merits of the policy – the escalation of commitment is strongest (Schwenk, 1984). Furthermore, factors on the super-individual level contribute to escalation of commitment, too. As we have seen, the desire to justify previous decisions towards others, for example, other members of a management team, is part of the explanation of the phenomenon. To this can be added factors on the organizational level, like procedures that have been put into effect, and that are difficult to stop or change.

A partly competitive, partly complementary explanation of escalation of commitment is based not on the need for self-justification, but on the different attitude towards risk in what are perceived by decision makers to be situations of loss and situations of gain. We will discuss this explanation in the section on risky decisions.

Illusion of control

Another cognitive bias that may affect the implementation of strategic decisions is the illusion of control. Individuals tend to overestimate their skills, and the influence they can exert on the outcome of events (Schwenk, 1988: 18). If problems occur, they assume that through additional effort they can put things right. As a result, expectancies of personal success are higher than objective circumstances justify (Schwenk, 1984: 122). This may lead to too much optimism in strategy implementation.

4.4 Risky decisions

Strategic decision making is inextricably intertwined with risk and uncertainty. Therefore the psychology of risky choice deserves special attention. Some of the phenomena discussed above, like **framing**, also play a role in the context of risky decisions. But also other biases and heuristics are important. First of all, we have to examine the question of how risk is perceived by the decision makers in whom we are particularly interested in this book, namely managers.

Managerial perceptions of risk

What is risk?

In normative-rational decision theory risk is defined in terms of the variance of the probability distribution of the outcomes associated with a particular alternative. But there are numerous indications that managers have a different definition of risk. On the basis of empirical studies, March and Shapira conclude that for managers risk is associated with the possibility of losses, rather than with the variance of the distribution of outcomes (March and Shapira, 1988). Thus the decision to start a project that may lead to losses would be considered risky, but the decision to start a project the expected pay-offs of which are all positive not, even if the variance of the outcomes of the second proposal would be larger.

Managers differentiate between risks and gambles. In gambling the odds are exogenously determined, but in risk taking as seen by managers, uncertainty can be reduced by searching for more information or good management (March and Shapira, 1988). This is an example of the illusion of control discussed above. Risk is seen as manageable. This attitude is nurtured by success: 'the experience of successful managers teaches them that the probabilities of life do not apply to them' (March and Shapira, 1988: 90). Needless to say, this attitude, if not checked by the environment of the manager, may lead to disaster.

Managerial attitudes towards risk

The attitude of managers towards risk is strongly influenced by perceptions of the managerial role and by managerial ideology. Risk taking is seen as an inherent part of the managerial role. Therefore it is not surprising that managers tend to describe themselves as risk takers. They see themselves as more willing to assume risks than their colleagues, and more so also than they really appear to be. This attitude, however, is restricted to their managerial role. Managers show a smaller risk-taking propensity when they answer questions pertaining to their personal lives (March and Shapira, 1988).

Notwithstanding managers' self-reported willingness to take risk, some data indicate that they have a tendency to search for certainty, and to reduce uncertainty in their minds by denying that it exists. Corporate managers are likely to get annoyed with advisors who point at the probability of possible events, instead of telling exactly what will happen (Barnes, 1984: 133).

Parallel to the distinction between risk taking and gambling made by the managers themselves is the tendency for managers to be judged on the basis of their success, that is, their ability to select the 'good' risks and avoid the 'bad' ones. On the basis of the success or failure of a project an evaluation of the quality of the decision is constructed *post hoc*. If the project failed, the manager should have foreseen this. The post-dictive probability of events that actually materialized is much higher than the corresponding predictive probability, a phenomenon labelled **creeping determinism** (Fischhoff and Beyth, 1975: 2). The signs of imminent failure are very salient in retrospect, indicating that the decision maker should have known better. A good manager not only takes risks, but is also lucky.

Assessment of uncertainty

Estimating probabilities

One of the reasons for managers' focusing on the magnitude of possible outcomes rather than on the moments of probabilities and outcomes may be the fact that reliable estimates of probabilities are much harder to get than reliable estimates of outcomes (March and Shapira, 1988). When trying to estimate probabilities, decision makers use two heuristic that can easily become the source of biases: the availability heuristic and the representativeness heuristic.

The **availability** heuristic implies that individuals assess the probability of the occurrence of an event by how readily they can remember it happening before. As frequently occurring events are often easier to recall than rare events, the heuristic often is reasonable. But it can also lead to sharp overreactions to decision outcomes in the recent past (Barnes, 1984; Etzioni, 1988; Schwenk, 1988; Von Winterfeldt and Edwards, 1986).

When using the **representativeness** heuristic decision makers assume that a sample is representative for the population from which it is drawn. This assumption often is unwarranted due to, for example, biases in the sampling procedure or small sample size. People more generally are markedly insensitive to sample size (Barnes, 1984; Etzioni, 1988; Luthans, 1992; Schwenk, 1984; Von Winterfeldt and Edwards, 1986). The folk wisdom of the 'law of small numbers' is expressed, for instance, in the use of anecdotes about sprightly 80-year-old grandfathers who have smoked like chimneys all their lives, to refute the statistics on the use of tobacco and mortality.

Estimating outcomes

In estimating the outcome of an alternative, decision makers tend to make an initial judgement quickly and subsequently adapt this judgement to information that becomes available or is taken into consideration later. This heuristic is called **anchoring and adjustment**. This heuristic can lead to a bias toward the initial value, for the adjustments typically are insufficient. As the initial assessment – the anchor – can easily be based on salient but not very relevant information, this is a potentially disturbing shortfall (Schwenk, 1984; Luthans, 1992; Von Winterfeldt and Edwards, 1986). To give an example, sales forecasts for a new product may mistakenly be based on a similar existing product. If information becomes available indicating that the forecasts are wide of the mark management will adjust production plans – but typically not enough.

Evaluating outcomes

Below the evaluation of risky decisions will be taken up in more detail with the discussion of 'prospect theory'. Here we will briefly discuss the phenomenon of **post-decisional regret** (Raiffa, 1991). Post-decisional regret occurs if a decision maker, after having made a risky choice that turned out badly, has a strong emotional feeling that he has taken the wrong decision. The hypothetical decision maker of normative-rational theory is not acquainted with this feeling. He maximizes expected utility, and if the whims of fortune leave him empty-handed, his confidence in having taken what was *ex ante* the best decision is not shaken.

Not so decision makers of flesh and blood. If a safe choice is discarded in favour of a risky prospect (remember that a prospect is an option that can lead to various outcomes with associated probabilities) with a much higher expected value, and the prospect turns out not to pay off, the decision maker feels that he has been too greedy, and suffers from regret. That regret is not simply a side-effect of bad outcomes is demonstrated by the fact that no (or much less) regret is felt if the decision was one between two prospects that both had blanks as possible outcomes.

Post-decisional regret, if anticipated, can lead to risk aversion. But other decision situations, not leading to regret, can foster risk seeking (see Box 4.6). This brings us to the central concern of the theory discussed in the next section: which factors determine the risk attitude of individuals in actual decision situations?

Prospect theory

An important descriptive theory of risky choice, which has received support in numerous experiments, is **prospect theory**. Prospect theory assumes that risky choices are made in two phases: editing and evaluation. In the editing phase a mental model of the decision situation is formed. Most importantly, possible outcomes are coded as gains or losses. In the evaluation phase the value of the outcomes is assessed on the basis of a value function and a weighting function, and a choice is made. Below, we will first go into the editing phase, and discuss the influence of framing. Subsequently we will focus on the evaluation phase, and discuss the **value function** and the **weighting function**. (This section is based on Payne, 1985; Tversky and Kahneman, 1985; 1992; and Weber, 1994.)

Box 4.6 Choices with and without post-decisional regret

Consider the following two prospects:

I: $1 million with certainty

II: $5 million with 10% chance
$1 million with 89% chance
$0 million with 1% chance

Given this choice, most people choose for prospect I. The reason is that the possible outcome of zero in option II would be unbearable given the fact that one could have taken $1 million with certainty. Anticipating this regret, people choose risk avoiding.

Now consider the following two prospects:

III: $1 million with 11% chance
$0 million with 89% chance

IV: $5 million with 10% chance
$0 million with 90% chance

Here the usual choice is IV. The difference is that the zero outcome in this case is not associated with regret: it could also have happened if III had been chosen. Here choice behaviour is risk seeking.

Source: Raiffa, 1991: 353)

Editing the decision situation

Consider the situation in which a decision maker has to choose between two prospects. In the editing phase, the decision maker simplifies the decision situation, in order to be able to evaluate the prospects and make a choice in the evaluation phase. This simplification is achieved by operations like cancellation – discard of components common to both prospects – and detection of dominance – finding out that one prospect is in all aspects superior to the other. Most importantly, however, the decision maker **codes** the outcomes in terms of gains and losses.

The terms 'gains' and 'losses' should not be interpreted simply as positive or negative monetary values. It is not the absolute value of an outcome which determines whether it will be coded as a loss or a gain, but rather its position relative to the **reference point** of the decision maker. This reference point can be influenced by previous decisions. Consider a person who has spent an afternoon betting on horses, and who has already lost $140. The last race is about to start, and the individual has to decide on the following prospect: either he is going to bet $10 with a chance of 1/15 of winning $150, or he is going home before the last race. If the decision on the final bet is taken independently from what has happened before, the reference point is zero: the amount the decision maker will get with certainty if he does not bet on the last race. The possible outcomes of the last bet hence are a gain of $140 and a loss of $10. But if the decision maker views his present position as a loss of $140, which appears to be a natural tendency, the outcomes are interpreted as zero (i.e., the decision maker recoups his losses) and a loss of $150. As we will see presently, this difference in interpretation can have an important impact on the individual's decision-making behaviour.

In the case discussed above the location of the reference point is determined by previous decisions (bets) of the focal individual. But this need not always be the case. The location of the reference point may also be influenced by other people. More generally, the **level of aspiration** – the goals that people set for themselves with respect to some behaviour – are determined by their own earlier performance and by comparison to reference groups, that is, those groups to which the person in question compares his or her own achievements, well-being, and so on (Wärneryd, 1988). In an organizational context, a decision maker's reference point may be determined by plans and budgets imposed from a higher hierarchical level.

In non-monetary prospects, subtle changes in wording can shift the coding from losses to gains, or vice versa. Remember the decision experiment on epidemic control related in Box 4.4. In the description of programmes A and B, the phrasing suggested the subjects to interpret the outcomes as gains. In programmes C and D, the emphasis was on losses. This rephrasing of equivalent options led to marked changes in preferences.

The value function

The coding of outcomes as gains and losses is relevant because decision makers tend to treat the two categories of outcomes differently. More specifically, prospect theory assumes that the value of an outcome is determined on the basis of a value function, the properties of which are as follows:

- the function is concave above the reference point;
- the function is convex below the reference point;
- the function is steeper for losses than for gains.

A hypothetical value functions with these properties is shown in Figure 4.2.

The fact that the value curve is concave for gains implies that there is a diminishing sensitivity for gains. This means that the difference between gains of $500 and $550 is less important for the decision maker than the difference between gains of $100 and $150. The same is true for losses: the fact that the curve below the reference point is convex implies that an increase of a loss from, say, $140 to $150 means less to the decision maker than an increase of

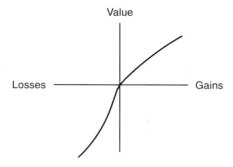

Figure 4.2 A hypothetical value function. (Source: Tversky and Kahneman, 1985.)

a loss from $10 to $20. The fact that the curve is kinked in the reference point implies that losses loom larger than gains of the same magnitude. This means that a mixed prospect with a 50 per cent chance of losing $100 and a 50 per cent chance of winning $100 will be evaluated negatively. In fact, experimental data show that subjects only accept mixed prospects with even chances to win and lose if the gain is at least twice as large as the loss (Tversky and Kahneman, 1993: 310).

The value curve hypothesized by prospect theory implies that the attitude towards risk is heavily influenced by the question of whether outcomes are interpreted as gains or losses. Individuals generally are risk averse in the domain of gains, and risk seeking in the domain of losses. This explains why the subjects in the experiment on epidemic control chose the risk-avoiding solution when the decision frame suggested them to think of the possible outcomes of gains (numbers of lives saved). Conversely, when the decision frame was manipulated as to suggest the subjects to interpret the outcomes as losses (number of people who will die), the more risk-seeking solution was favoured.

The weighting function

The attitude towards risk is not only influenced by the question of whether outcomes are interpreted as gains or losses, but also by the magnitude of the probabilities associated with these outcomes. Prospect theory assumes that different weights are associated with different probabilities. There are two natural endpoints in the evaluation of prospects: certainty and impossibility. At these endpoints, the decision weights are identical to the probabilities (1 and 0, respectively) but in between systematic deviations are assumed. Just as in the case of the value function, diminishing sensitivity is assumed. The impact of a given change in probability diminishes with the distance from the boundary (either certainty or impossibility). This means that the decision weight curve is concave near 0 and convex near 1 (see Figure 4.3).

The form of the curve in Figure 4.3, based on the results of an experiment, implies that people tend to over-weight low probabilities ($p < 0.4$), and to under-weight moderate and high probabilities ($p > 0.4$). Moreover, the curve

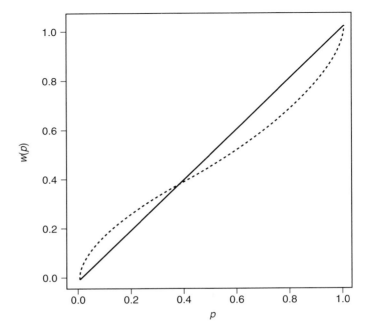

Figure 4.3 A hypothetical weighting function. (Source: Tversky and Kahneman, 1992: 313.)

is relatively flat at the middle range. This means that decision makers are relatively insensitive to changes in intermediate probabilities (for example, from $p = 0.55$ to $p = 0.60$). On the other hand, near certainty and near impossibility the curve is very steep, implying that people are very sensitive to changes in probabilities in these ranges. Thus a change in probability from $p = 0.90$ to $p = 0.95$ carries more weight than a change from $p = 0.55$ to $p = 0.60$.

All in all, a fourfold pattern of risk attitudes is to be expected on the basis of prospect theory:

■ risk aversion for gains of moderate to high probability;
■ risk seeking for gains of small probability;
■ risk seeking for losses of moderate to high probability;
■ risk aversion for losses of small probability.

This pattern is confirmed by experimental research (Tversky and Kahneman, 1992).

March and Shapira, considering studies of attitudes and behaviour of managers, confirm the general propositions of prospect theory (March and Shapira, 1988). If things are going well, managers take fewer risks than if an organization is below the mark. The managers interviewed also saw this as the right thing to do. For some this was also true in case the personal position of the manager was concerned. Managers would take riskier actions when their position is threatened. However, the interviewees had strong feelings that the survival of the firm should not be risked. If a failure could jeopardize the survival of the firm, no risk would be taken. March and Shapira interpret this as an alternative decision frame: outcomes can be framed as gains or losses relative to the aspiration level, but also as below or above the mark relative to the survival target.

Applications of prospect theory

Given the importance of decision making under uncertainty and risk in strategic management the relevance of prospect theory is evident. By way of illustration two applications of prospect theory to explain phenomena relevant to strategic decision making will be discussed. First, the explanation of the 'risk-return paradox'. Secondly, an alternative explanation of the 'escalation of commitment' phenomenon.

The risk-return paradox explained

Conventional economic wisdom as embodied, for example, in modern financial theory, suggests a positive correlation between risk and return. This expectation corresponds to the assumption that humans are uniformly risk averse. However, using a data set comprising more than 1500 firms representing 85 industries Bowman discovered that within most industries risk and return are in fact negatively related. This is the so-called 'risk-return paradox' (Bowman, 1980).

This paradox can be resolved if a target level or reference point is included as a variable in the analysis. Fiegenbaum and Thomas used the industry's median return on equity as a proxy for the target level of firms within that industry, and the variance of return on equity as a proxy for risk. They found that risk and return were negatively correlated for below-target firms and positively correlated for above-target firms (Fiegenbaum and Thomas, 1988 – their findings were largely confirmed by Jegers, 1991, who used an extended data set and additional variables). These findings are entirely consistent with prospect theory. Managers of firms who are performing below target level are inclined to adopt more risky strategies in order to improve performance. Managers of firms above target level are more cautious, and defend their position by selecting less risky strategies.

Escalation of commitment explained

Escalation of commitment was explained earlier on the basis of a hypothesized psychological need to justify or rationalize previous behaviour. However, it is also possible to explain this phenomenon on the basis of prospect theory. Decision makers who are confronted with negative feedback on earlier decisions will perceive that as a sign that they are below their point of reference. As a consequence, they will tend to display risk-seeking behaviour. One form of risk seeking would be to confirm and even to increase the commitment to the failing course of action, double or quits, so to say. From the perspective of prospect theory this option is more attractive than quitting the project, which would mean taking a sure loss (Whyte, 1986). This explanation of escalation to commitment is confirmed by an experimental study (Bateman and Zeithaml, 1989).

The escalation of commitment effect is not only caused by psychological factors, but also by social and organizational factors. We will discuss these in the next chapter.

Chapter summary

- Decision processes vary between persons and between situations; differences between persons are associated with personality characteristics, as well as with demographic characteristics.

- The rationality of most decision-making processes is optimal at intermediate levels of emotional involvement.

- Intuition, in the context of decision making, refers to the unconscious use of uncodified decision rules. Intuition is used in combination with rational analysis rather than instead of it.

- Cognitive heuristics are very general decision rules, used to alleviate the limited cognitive abilities of human decision makers. The use of them leads to biases, if compared with the hypothetical model of full rationality.

- Cognitive heuristics and biases occur in all phases of the decision-making process.

- In managerial practice, risk is often defined as the possibility of losses, rather than the variability of outcomes.

- In risky decisions, the evaluation of outcomes is influenced by the interpretation of possible outcomes as gains or losses with reference to an adopted aspiration level, and by the magnitude of the probabilities associated with outcomes. The result is that choices frequently deviate from the predictions of subjectively expected utility (SEU) theory.

5

The sociology of decision making

This chapter focuses on the implications of the fact that strategic decision making in large organizations is very much an interactive process. Strategic decisions are rarely made by a single, isolated actor. The problems that have to be solved are too complex, and the tasks of information gathering and processing too demanding, for individual decision making to be effective. Furthermore, if the strategic plans are made by one single individual, the task of implementation is presumably made more arduous, both in terms of communication and in terms of motivation.

Therefore it is not surprising that strategic decision making in organizations very often takes place in small groups (Harrison, 1987: 255; Koopman and Pool, 1990). Examples of small groups concerned with strategic decision making are boards of directors, top management teams, and strategic planning committees. The importance of group decision making can also be deduced from the observation that managers spend a substantial part of their time interacting within groups (Mintzberg, 1973). Moreover, evidence suggests that deterioration of group processes in top management teams is a central element in corporate failures (Hambrick and d'Aveni, 1992).

Group decision making has several advantages. For instance, groups can bring to bear on complex and difficult problems a number of disparate skills and talents. But groups also have disadvantages. Group decision making is more time consuming than individual decision making, particularly if all the time spent by the individual group members is added up (Luthans, 1992: 353, 356). Group processes can also lead to worse decisions than individual decision making. In this chapter basic characteristics of group decision processes will be expounded, and the advantages and disadvantages of using groups in strategy formation discussed.

A theme interwoven with the subject of this chapter is the relation between power and decision making. Strategy making implies the power to give direction to an organization. But power can have different sources and manifestations, and these differences are related to characteristics of strategic decision processes. Therefore, power and related issues will also be considered in this chapter.

Finally, the issue of leadership style, relevant to decision making as well as to power and influence relations, will be discussed briefly.

5.1 Decision groups

Groups and groups formation

What is a 'group'?

The concept of a 'group' can be defined very broadly as 'two or more individuals who influence each other through social interaction' (Forsyth, 1990: 7 – Forsyth also presents a number of examples of alternative definitions). But it is helpful to add to this definition two elements typical for groups involved in decision making. First, the individuals in a group are typically interdependent to a significant degree; the outcomes of the group process are important to the group members. Secondly, group members typically share norms and values, that is, they tend to converge in evaluations and judgements (Luthans, 1992: 347; Miner, 1992: 174). Interaction, interdependence and the sharing of norms and values are related: interaction is often triggered by interdependence and tends to increase it. Interaction also contributes to the forming of shared norms and values; people generally prefer to interact with those who share their judgements. Thus the various dimensions of 'groupness' are mutually reinforcing.

Group formation

Groups can come into being spontaneously, for instance as a result of **propinquity** (psychological or geographical proximity). Groups can also be formed more formally, because certain activities need to be coordinated. Here, too, interaction between group members is the major factor (Luthans, 1992: 347). Groups can be formed because close interaction is needed in the fulfilment of a task. But the interaction process itself, as mentioned above, has the effect of bolstering the group by promoting the development of shared sentiments. To sum up: group formation is a process of interactive social integration: it entails greater geographical proximity, a stronger interdependence, more interpersonal affection, and more extensive sharing of ideas than previously existed (Moreland, 1987).

Group characteristics

Various dimensions of group characteristics can be distinguished, the most important of which are size, structure, cohesion and stage of development (Baron et al., 1992: 5–14).

Size

The minimum number of group members according to the definition is two. Spontaneously formed groups tend to be small, between two and three members (Forsyth, 1990: 9). Many groups are larger than that, however. It is not possible to set an unambiguous upper limit to the number of group members, but if the number of individuals becomes too large, the intensive interaction that is typical for groups becomes problematic. Large groups (more than 15 members) will in practice often function as an aggregate of two or more subgroups. In other cases the **functional** group size, that is, the number of group members actively participating, is much smaller than the **nominal** group size (Baron et al., 1992: 44).

The optimal group size depends on various factors, among other things the nature of the task (see below). For many tasks a group size of between five and seven is seen as optimal, although according to some authors larger groups, up to 12 members, can also be effective (see, e.g., Harrison, 1987: 265; Miner, 1992: 210). In very small groups (up to four members) minorities of one are quite common. As we will see below, this can be a disadvantage. Very small groups are also vulnerable because *incompatibilité des humeurs* can easily paralyse the decision-making process. Larger groups, that is, 10 persons or more, tend to develop a more formal style of interaction, in which personal differences can be covered up more easily.

It is not always easy to establish the size of a group because various criteria for group membership can be used. One criterion is formal group membership: who belongs to the group in question may depend, for example, on the organization chart, formal job descriptions or minutes of meetings. Alternatively, one can look at the perception of individuals: does someone perceive him or herself to be a member of the group? Do the other group members agree, that is, do they accept him or her as a group member? On the basis of the perceptions of individuals, four kinds of group membership can be distinguished: psychological membership, preferential membership, marginal membership, and alienative membership (see Figure 5.1) (Jackson, 1959).

Psychological membership indicates the situation in which a group member feels attracted to the group, and is also accepted by the other group members. In the case of **preferential** membership the individual feels attracted to the group, but has difficulty in being accepted by the other group members. In the case of **marginal** group membership the situation is just the opposite: the other group members accept the individual, but the person in question feels little attraction to the group. In informal groups, **alienative** members can for all practical reasons be considered to be outside of the group.

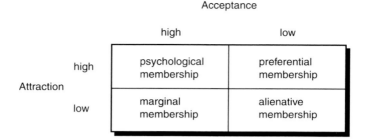

Figure 5.1 Four kinds of group membership.

But formal group membership can be of the alienative kind, a situation which is likely to cause problems in decision making.

Structure

Group structure refers to the formal or informal internal organization of the group. One dimension of group structure is **role differentiation**. Social roles are sets of behaviours that are characteristic of persons in a particular social context (Forsyth, 1990: 111). In some groups no role differentiation exists, but in most at least a distinction between the group leader or chairperson and the ordinary group members is made. Role differentiation can also be more elaborate, with specialized positions for all group members. Roles in groups can be subdivided into two categories: task roles and socio-emotional roles. Task roles are concerned with organizing the group to attain its goals. Examples of task roles are **initiator** (proposing novel ideas, approaches or possible solutions); **opinion seeker** (eliciting information from other group members); and **recorder** (taking notes and maintaining records). Socio-emotional roles are to do with the emotional needs of the group members. Examples are **encourager** (rewarding others through praise); **harmonizer** (mediating conflicts); and **group observer** (pointing out positive and negative aspects of the group's dynamics) (Forsyth, 1990: 112–13).

Some groups are subdivided into **subgroups**. For instance, an audit committee may bear special responsibility for the financial affairs of the group. Subgroups can also form spontaneously, if people of the same age, with a comparable educational background, or with other common backgrounds assemble (cf. Eisenhardt and Bourgeois, 1988).

Finally, different types of **communication networks** within groups can be distinguished. The degree of centralization is the most important feature of a communication network (Forsyth, 1990: 130). Most typical of very small groups is the situation in which every group member communicates with all the others. This type of communication network is called the **completely connected network**. In a completely connected network no centralization whatsoever has taken place. Other basic communication networks are the **wheel network** and the **chain network** (see Figure 5.2).

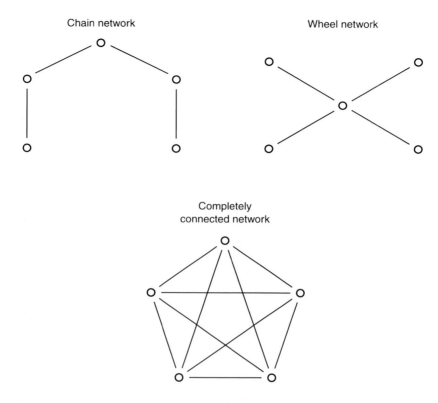

Figure 5.2 Group communication networks.

The chain network and the wheel network are more centralized, and suggest a hierarchy or at least a pronounced role differentiation within the group. These structures imply stringent restrictions to group interaction. Such communication networks are relevant if we focus on the interaction between a manager and his or her direct and indirect subordinates, for example, in the context of leadership and decision making.

Cohesion

Group cohesion can be described as the overall strength of positive relation-ships within the group (Baron et al., 1992: 8). Several factors can cause group cohesion to be high. For one thing, the group members may just like each other. Especially in informal groups, this is an almost indispensable condition of group cohesion. But group cohesion may also be bolstered by the fact that group membership provides status. In this case the desire to belong to the group is strong enough for individual members to conform to the group's norms (see below). Last but not least, group cohesion can be caused by the fact that group membership is the best way to achieve crucial individual goals, common to all group members. In this case interdependence between group members provides cohesion to the group.

Group norms are closely connected to group cohesion. The same factors that lead to a strong group cohesion also contribute to the formation and enforcement of strict group norms. Group norms are those behaviours, attitudes and perceptions that are approved of by the group and expected (or even demanded) of its members (Baron et al., 1992: 11). Group norms relate to, for example, the kind and style of interaction in the group, the level of commitment and effort of the group members and relations with outsiders. Group norms play an important facilitative role in the coordination of group activities. Norms may be written down and formally promulgated by the group, but more often norms gradually emerge and change only slowly (just like organizational culture – see Chapter 6) (Forsyth, 1990: 160).

Group norms may be internalized by an individual member to such an extent that they have become his or her own. In other cases an individual group member complies with the norms for fear of sanctions, for example, being ridiculed, or losing group membership.

Stage of development

Some groups, like formal departments or sections of an organization, have been formed in the past and live on indefinitely, although individual members come and go. These groups remain in a continual stage of maturity. In other groups, that have a more constricted lifetime, a pattern of four or five stages of development can often be distinguished (Tuckman and Jensen, 1977; see also Forsyth, 1990: 78–90).

In the first stage, **forming**, the group initially is little more than a set of individuals. The interaction is focused on establishing the precise goal of the group, the boundaries of the group, and the formal and/or informal division of roles. Group members try to convey a positive image of themselves to the others. At this stage, although the interaction is still rather inhibited, the atmosphere is cooperative. At the second stage, **storming**, the harmony is put to the test as group members get to know each other better, and begin to communicate more openly. The apparent consensus of the first stage is often undermined as the group's initial goals and role divisions are challenged. If the group survives this stage, it has developed a more realistic consensus or *modus vivendi*, based on better information about individual preferences and agendas. The group now starts building cohesion and developing shared norms and values. This stage is called **norming**. After having passed through this phase, the group can work effectively towards its goals (**performing**). Although shifts in goals and roles will still occur occasionally, the emphasis is now on task implementation. If the group is dismantled after some time, the final stage of **adjournment** is reached. Group members experience emotions of approaching separation. End-game effects may occur, in the sense that group members shift their loyalty elsewhere, and become unwilling to invest any more efforts in the group's activities.

Committees and coalitions

Primary and secondary groups

As pointed out above, groups differ in many dimensions. In some groups intensive communication, personal interaction, and strongly shared values prevail. These groups are called **primary groups**. The prime example of a primary group is the nuclear family. In organizations primary groups can also be found, for example, in the form of closely interacting peer groups. Strategic decision making will sometimes take place within a primary group, for instance if a small group of top managers has a long tradition of extensive face-to-face interaction (see Box 5.1). However, often strategic decision making will be the task of a different kind of group, the **secondary group**. In a secondary group relationships are less personal. Group members also have less direct interaction, and may see each other only occasionally. Whereas being a member of a primary group often has a certain intrinsic value, secondary groups are largely instrumental to the purposes of their members. An example is formed by management teams: the members may actually spend little time interacting with one another in the course of their daily work.

Committees

An important type of secondary group within organizations is the **committee** (Luthans, 1992: 353–8). A committee is 'a body of one or more persons appointed or elected by an assembly or society to consider, or investigate, or take action in regard to, certain matters or subjects, or to do all of these things' (Robert, 1971: 206). Thus a committee represents a larger decision-making party, of which it is a subgroup. A committee rarely bears ultimate authority: most of the time it merely advises a higher decision-making body, or its decisions are ratified by the same. But a certain degree of delegation of decision making authority is always implied by the formation of a (sub)committee (Forsyth, 1990: 291). Committees can be formed for all aspects of the management of an organization, like productivity, quality, labour relations, product or process innovation, or, most relevant for this book, strategic planning.

Coalitions

Another type of secondary group is the **coalition**. Coalitions are informal groups of actors pursuing particular shared objectives (Miner, 1992: 178). A coalition by nature is as least as instrumental as a committee. Although most coalitions are temporary, and are normally disbanded as soon as the common goal is reached (or has become clearly out of reach, or can better be reached by different means), they can be long-lived (Eisenhardt and Bourgeois, 1988). Thus coalitions can function within organizations, but, in contrast to committees, they operate outside the formal organizational structure. Coalitions tend to play an important role in political games or processes in organizations (see Section 5.4).

Box 5.1 Group decision making at AT&T

Decision-making teams play an important role at telecommunications giant AT&T. CEO Robert Allen and four other senior officers constitute a five-man presidency known as the Operations Committee. The Operations Committee is responsible for the day-to-day affairs of the company. The members meet several days a month. The idea is that for none of the four main product groups – telephone network, telecommunication network equipment, end-user products, and computers – can important decisions be made without a thorough understanding of what is going on in the other product groups. Possible synergies and trade-offs between product groups are considered carefully. Decision groups at lower levels have been formed which cut across AT&T's various businesses. In 1992 Robert Allen set up teams to explore and develop areas of opportunity, like voice recognition and processing. Each team consists of representatives of the major product groups. A specific member of the Operations Committee – most of the time not the team leader's normal boss – acts as the team's 'champion'.

(Source: Kirkpatrick, 1993).

5.2 Group decision processes

Task characteristics

One of the most important factors influencing group decision making is the nature of the task. For instance, the performance of groups relative to that of individuals depends, among other things, on the question of whether the task permits the group to pool their resources. If the task allows pooling of resources, like in a tug-of-war, groups do better than individuals. If on the other hand the task requires very precise coordination, like driving a car, individuals do better (Baron et al., 1992: 33).

Divisibility of the task

Several dimensions of task characteristics are relevant. First, some tasks are divisible, that is, they can be divided into sub-tasks that can be performed by different group members (Steiner, 1972). Groups can achieve advantages over individuals for this type of task, but only if the coordination of sub-tasks does not nullify the advantages of specialization. Other tasks are unitary, that is, they cannot effectively be subdivided into smaller tasks. Driving a car is an example of a unitary task.

Maximizing and optimizing tasks

In maximizing tasks, the performance rests on sheer quantity, the more output the better. Groups have an advantage in this kind of task. In optimizing tasks, one needs to produce the right rather than the maximum output. Solving a math problem is an example of an optimizing task (Forsyth, 1990: 262). The advantage of groups in optimizing tasks is less certain, and depends on the way in which individual inputs are combined (see below).

Combination rules required to complete the task

A third categorization of tasks concerns the way in which individual resources are linked to group productivity. Four kinds of tasks can be distinguished in this regard (Steiner, 1972). In **disjunctive** tasks, the group must select the contribution of one single group member as the group output. This is, for instance, the case in chess contests for teams. In any particular game, only one member of the team plays, and the others are not allowed to help him or her in finding the best moves. The only thing the team can do is to select the most able chess player. In **conjunctive** tasks group performance depends on the weakest group member. Examples from the world of sports are team time-trials in cycling, or mountain climbing by a team the members of which are connected to one another by ropes. At first sight a group appears to have no advantage in this kind of task, but this need not be true. In mountain climbing, team-mates can safeguard a faltering group member, and cyclists in a team can shelter each other by turns. Groups very clearly have an advantage in **additive** tasks, like tug-of-wars, in which the group output is the sum of the individual contributions. Finally, some tasks are **discretionary**, that is, the group can decide for itself in what way it will combine individual inputs. For instance, judgement tasks like estimating the height of a mountain (without measuring instruments) can be performed by averaging the estimations of all group members, by selecting the median estimate, by voting for particular estimates, by trusting the estimate of the group's 'expert', and so on. Complex mental tasks like strategic decision making are most likely of the discretionary type.

Intellective tasks and judgemental tasks

Finally, decision-making tasks differ in the degree to which they have an objectively and demonstrably right solution. **Intellective** tasks have a demonstrably correct answer: if one group member comes up with it, it will be accepted as the group solution. Other tasks are of a **judgemental** nature, that is, there is no objective basis for evaluation (Laughlin and Ellis, 1986). This distinction is particularly relevant since strategic problems are clearly of such a judgemental nature. In intellective tasks minorities or even single group members can exert a strong influence on the group's decision, if they find the objectively correct answer. Conversely, in the case of judgemental tasks the majority, or that minority that has the most power, very often wins. And although judgements are based on 'the weight of the evidence', it is by no means certain that all the relevant evidence will be taken into consideration. The option supported by the majority before group discussion tends to get selected; knowing that others have different information or opinions does not necessarily induce further discussion (Baron et al., 1992: 104; Laughlin and Adamopoulous, 1982; Stasser, 1992). The question of how individual preferences or solutions are combined into group outcomes returns repeatedly in this chapter.

Decision-making procedures

Group decision rules

The procedures by which the group comes to a decision have an important bearing on the outcome of the decision-making process. Every group uses some kind of decision rule, often implicitly. Some groups take decisions on the basis of **unanimity**. If this is the case, the group can only reach a decision if every group member agrees that the solution selected is optimal. Somewhat less demanding is the decision rule of **consensus**. Consensus is reached if each individual group member is able to accept the group's decision on the basis of logic and feasibility (Hall, 1971). This means that the chosen solution is acceptable to but not necessarily preferred by everyone. Rather, all group members agree that a certain course of action is the best that can be agreed to at the present time (Coffey et al., 1994: 343). A minority can still block the decision process. This is not the case if the decision is taken on the basis of a **majority vote**. Majority decision rules can be unqualified (i.e. half of the number of group members plus one), or qualified (e.g. a two-thirds majority). In both cases the **voting rule** used is of importance: if group members are allowed to vote for one option only a different outcome may prevail than when group members can rank order all options. In the **Borda voting system** (named after its inventor Charles de Borda), each voter's most preferred candidate gets the maximum number of points, the next more preferred one point fewer, and so on with the least preferred getting zero points (Allison and Messick, 1987: 125). More generally: if n is the number of alternatives, the most preferred gets $n - 1$ points, number two $n - 2$ points, and so on.

Voting paradoxes

Given the variety of voting procedures, one may wonder whether an optimal voting rule exists. The answer is negative; economist Kenneth Arrow has proven mathematically that the possibility can never be ruled out that a democratic group decision does not adequately represent the members' preferences (Arrow, 1963). The outcome of a vote heavily depends on the procedure followed. In the case of Borda voting, the choice can shift from alternative A to alternative B if a third alternative, inferior to A as well as B, is added or deleted. If a group has to choose by majority vote between more than two alternatives, and the alternatives are compared two-by-two, the outcome may depend on the order of comparisons (Concordet's paradox) (Allison and Messick, 1987; Goodwin and Wright, 1991: 248).

Compromising

If a majority cannot readily be achieved, or if the group strives for consensus, it may be necessary to forge a compromise. An obvious, but not always effective way of reaching a compromise is to average the various preferred solutions. This is only possible if alternative solutions are divisible, of course. An alternative for averaging is selecting the median solution.

If a compromise over an isolated issue proves to be out of reach, **logrolling** may lead to a solution. In this process factions or individuals take turns in voting for each others' preferred options. For instance, the manager of division A votes for the investment proposals of the manager of division B, and vice versa.

From individual preference to group decision

Social decision schemes

Group decision making consists in combining in some way group members' personal preferences into a single group decision. A social decision scheme (SDS) is an expedient for describing this translation process (Baron et al., 1992: 94–8; Davis, 1973). Before a group process starts, all potential group members are assumed to have a stand regarding the issue on which a decision has to be reached. If a group is formed, the number of possible starting situations prior to the group process is a function of the number of group members and the number of alternatives. This number of **initial splits** is given by the expression

$$\frac{(n + r - 1)!}{(n!(r - 1)!)}$$

in which n is the number of decision alternatives, and r is the number of group members (Kerr, 1992: 69). For instance, if two members of a management team have to decide about two strategic alternatives, A and B, three possible initial splits can be discerned: both prefer A, both prefer B, or one prefers A and the other B. An SDS is a matrix linking all possible initial splits to all possible outcomes of the group decision process (see Table 5.1).

In Table 5.1 the situation in which four group members decide on two alternatives is illustrated. There are five initial splits. The assumption is that decisions will be taken by majority rule, and that none of the group members will alter his or her opinion in the process of group discussion. In that case the probabilities associated with the three possible outcomes of the group process are those given in the table. If the initial split indicates a majority for

Table 5.1 Example of a social decision scheme

Initial splits		Group decision		
A	B	A	B	No decision
4	0	1.0	0.0	0.0
3	1	1.0	0.0	0.0
2	2	0.0	0.0	1.0
1	3	0.0	1.0	0.0
0	4	0.0	1.0	0.0

A or B, that alternative is chosen with certainty (a probability of 1.0). If the group members are equally split between A and B, it is certain that the group will not be able to reach a decision. The issue may then be referred to a higher authority.

The SDS as an hypothesis

The matrix in Table 5.1 has the character of a – very simplistic – hypothesis regarding the outcomes of the group decision process. A more sophisticated theory, allowing for the possibility that the minority in some cases influences the majority, would hypothesize a probability larger than zero for outcomes not corresponding to the majority view in the initial split. Sometimes alternatives can be expressed in a common denominator (e.g. money). In these cases, an **averaging decision scheme**, hypothesizing that the group will with certainty choose the alternative closest to the average of the members' initial preferences, appears to be reasonable (cf. Kerr, 1992). The advantage of averaging is that all group members have a voice in the decision, and individual errors or extreme opinions are cancelled out (Forsyth, 1990: 291).

Other possible hypotheses are **proportionality** (the probability that an alternative is chosen is the proportion of group members advocating that alternative); **majority-proportionality** (the group chooses the alternative advocated by the majority; if no majority exists, the proportionality principle applies); and **plurality-proportionality** (the group chooses for the alternative advocated by the plurality; if two factions are of the same size, proportionality applies) (Kerr et al., 1975). (A 'plurality' is the largest faction, but not (necessarily) a majority.) In Table 5.2 these hypotheses are illustrated in the form of sample rows from the corresponding SDSs. (Only sample rows are given in Table 5.2 since the total number of initial splits with three alternatives and seven group members is 84.)

Some of the social decision rules, for instance, plurality-proportionality, have been shown to give adequate predictions for the outcome of certain group tasks (Kerr et al., 1975). Much depends on the characteristics of the task, and on instructions concerning the decision process given to the group members.

Table 5.2 Sample rows for three social decision rules

Initial split			Proportionality			Majority-proportionality			Plurality proportionality		
A	B	C	A	B	C	A	B	C	A	B	C
5	1	1	0.71	0.14	0.14	1.00	0.00	0.00	1.00	0.00	0.00
4	2	1	0.57	0.29	0.14	1.00	0.00	0.00	1.00	0.00	0.00
3	2	2	0.43	0.29	0.29	0.43	0.29	0.29	1.00	0.00	0.00
3	3	1	0.43	0.43	0.14	0.43	0.43	0.14	0.50	0.50	0.00

The probabilities associated with possible outcomes of the group process can also be estimated on the basis of empirical data or experiments. These empirically derived SDSs can subsequently be explained on the basis of theories of group decision making (see, e.g., Kerr and MacCoun, 1985).

5.3 Efficiency and effectiveness of group decision making

Are group decisions better than decisions made by individuals?

Comparing individual and group decision making

If group decisions are prevalent in organizational (strategic) decision making, the reason presumably is that group decision making has important advantages. Indeed, it is not very difficult to think of favourable aspects of group decision making compared with individual decision making (cf. Johnson and Johnson, 1987: 87–8; Luthans, 1992: 351):

- a variety of skills and specialized knowledge can be brought to bear on a question;
- multiple and conflicting views can be aired and considered;
- beliefs and values can be transmitted and aligned;
- more organization members will be committed to decisions, since they have participated in the decision-making process.

On the other hand, group decision making also has some potential disadvantages:

- it can be more time consuming;
- it may lead to feeble compromises;
- it may, conversely, lead to more risky decisions;
- it may stifle creativity.

No general conclusion concerning the comparative advantages of group decision making can be drawn. As we have seen, much depends on the characteristics of the task. It also depends on the criterion used for comparison. If, for instance, the number of person-minutes worked on an intellective task is taken as the criterion (efficiency), individuals do better. But if the proportion of problems correctly solved is taken as the criterion (effectiveness), groups do better (Brown 1988: 127).

Below we will concentrate on the disadvantages and potential dangers of group decision making. The reason is that group decision making is a fact of life: it is impossible to imagine organizations without it. This is especially true of strategic decisions in large and medium-sized organizations. It is important to know what can go wrong in such decision-making processes. If we have a good understanding of the disadvantages and dangers of group decision making, it is easier to work on the improvement of these processes.

Efficiency and effectiveness

As suggested by the title of this section, we will consider the efficiency and effectiveness of group decision making. Efficiency has to do with the relationship between inputs and outputs; effectiveness with the quality of the output (i.e. the group decision). The efficiency of group decision-making processes is negatively affected by two kinds of **process losses**: coordination losses and motivation losses. The effectiveness of group decision-making processes is negatively affected by four phenomena: conformity, group polarization, 'groupthink', and group factors leading to escalation of commitment.

Coordination losses

What are coordination losses?

Groups have an advantage over individuals in that they can benefit from the inputs and efforts of several individuals. Consequently, for many tasks groups have a higher potential productivity. But the actual productivity of a group tends to be lower than the sum of the member resources would suggest. Two kinds of process losses may cause this: coordination losses and motivation losses (Steiner, 1972). Motivation losses occur if subjects exert less effort when working in a group than if they work individually. Motivation losses will be discussed in the next subsection. Coordination losses occur when group members are unable to combine their efforts in an optimal way. For instance, when the members of a group contesting in a tug-of-war do not pull all at the same time, the group's output is sharply restricted. We will in this subsection concentrate on coordination losses caused by imperfect pooling and use of information by groups.

Coordination losses in the analysis phase

Coordination losses may especially arise in the analysis phase, because the sharing of information is crucially important for the generation and evaluation of alternative solutions. One obvious source of coordination losses is **production blocking**: only one member of a group can talk at any one time (Baron et al., 1992: 41). On the other hand, this restriction on the emission of information is compensated in part by the fact that information can be received by group members simultaneously.

More serious than production blocking is **imperfect or biased information sampling** within groups. Groups have the potential advantage of being able to draw from the private information of all the group members. However, groups often do not pool unshared information efficiently, but tend to dwell on the information already shared by all the group members (Baron et al., 1992: 76; Stasser, 1992). As a result of self-censorship of individual group members, novel information often fails to get expressed in the group discussion. As discussion time is limited, any individual has only restricted time to contribute. Under these circumstances information fitting in with the shared information pool may be more readily accepted by the group and more readily recalled by the individual than novel information (Stasser, 1992).

Social processes may contribute to this tendency. People sometimes accede to a group decision because they think that everyone else in the group favours the decision. When no one speaks against the proposal in the belief that all others support it, the content of the discussion will be primarily positive and supportive, convincing listeners of the popularity of the idea. Each person believes him or herself to be unique in opposing the group consensus. In the extreme case, it can result in the so-called **abilene paradox**: a group decision reflecting the preferences of none of the group members (Allison and Messick, 1987: 120–1).

Even when it *is* mentioned, unshared information may have little impact on a group's decision. Experiments show that group discussions are less likely to return to previously unshared than to shared information (Stasser et al., 1989). The explanation for the relative neglect of unshared information may be that groups use a heuristic comparable to the availability heuristic discussed in Chapter 4. If groups rely on **consensual validation** a piece of information brought into the group by one individual only, without it being corroborated by any other group member, will have a low prima facie validity (Stasser, 1992).

The weight of unshared information also depends on the identity of the group member raising it. Low status group members often are less willing or able to present novel information or alternative solutions. Their view is also less likely to be accepted by the group, even if they are correct. This is shown by a study of decisions made by aircraft bomber crews. If the correct solution was proposed by the high-status pilot, it was accepted in 94 per cent of the cases. Low status tail-gunners, in contrast, failed to persuade the crew in 37 per cent of the cases, even though they were correct (see Baron et al., 1992: 39).

Table 5.3 Probability of correct group solutions under different hypothetical decision rules

Initial splits		Truth wins		Truth supported wins		Majority wins	
C	NC	C	NC	C	NC	C	NC
5	0	1.00	0.00	1.00	0.00	1.00	0.00
4	1	1.00	0.00	1.00	0.00	1.00	0.00
3	2	1.00	0.00	1.00	0.00	1.00	0.00
2	3	1.00	0.00	1.00	0.00	0.00	1.00
1	4	1.00	0.00	0.00	1.00	0.00	1.00
0	5	0.00	1.00	0.00	1.00	0.00	1.00

Notes: C = correct solution
NC = incorrect solution

Coordination losses in the action phase

In the action phase the crucial question is in which way minority views are taken into consideration in the act of choice. In illustrating this point an SDS can be helpful once more (see Table 5.3) (cf. Baron et al., 1992: 104; Brown, 1988: 137).

The initial splits in Table 5.3 indicate the number of group members that know, or are able to find, the correct solution to a problem. Whether the group will come up with the correct answer depends on the number of individual group members that are able to do so, and the social decision rule followed by the group. In the **truth wins** model the group produces the correct answer if at least one member can do so. Implicitly the truth wins model assumes an intellective task, with a demonstrably correct solution, otherwise the single group member with the correct solution would not be able to persuade the others.

The **truth supported** model assumes that the lone dissenter will indeed be overruled by the group, but that a group member with a correct solution may prevail against the majority if he or she is supported by at least one other. This model implies imperfect demonstrability of solutions.

Finally, the **majority wins** model assumes a complete absence of demonstrability (i.e. a judgemental task): a minority with the correct answer will never succeed in persuading the majority. Two kinds of mechanisms work in the favour of majorities in group decision making: (1) larger factions are able to generate more arguments for their position and to provide a more viable standard for social reality through consensual validation, and (2) larger factions are able to exert greater coercion to conformity than minorities (Baron et al., 1992: 101).

The question of which social decision rule is used is important for group performance. If we assume that five group members are drawn randomly from a population in which 50 per cent of the individuals are able to find the correct solution, groups working under the truth wins condition will produce the correct answer in 97 per cent of the cases. This figure drops to 81 per cent for the truth supported condition, but this is still much higher than that for groups working with the majority rule: only in 50 per cent of the cases will they give the correct solution, that is, they do no better than the individuals in the population! In this light it is fortunate that for intellective tasks the truth supported model appears to yield a better fit with the data.

When can minorities prevail?

From the above it is clear that coordination losses are closely associated with the characteristics of the task: the lower the demonstrability of the correct solution, the larger the coordination losses. Solutions to strategic problems may be assumed to have a very low demonstrability. This implies that majorities will very often dominate the decision-making process, even if their view is less valid than that of the minority. However, it is unlikely that the minority will *never* succeed in persuading the majority, as implied by the majority wins hypothesis. It is more realistic to assume that minorities sometimes – though not very often – are able to influence the majority. Given this assumption the question of under which circumstances a minority has the best chances of exerting influence on the group is relevant.

Minorities have to row against the current, especially in judgemental tasks. This puts considerable mental pressure on minority members. As a result minority members tend to be more nervous when defending their viewpoint, and are less likely to show personal identification with their arguments than majority members (Kerr et al., 1987). Majorities exert conformity pressures which are difficult to withstand, especially when the minority consists of one single individual. We will discuss these conformity pressures in the next section.

But, as long as reason prevails, a minority with good arguments can sometimes considerably influence the majority's judgement. Whether a minority succeeds also depends on its own behaviour. Consistency of the minority view helps, if this consistency is couched in flexible, moderate language rather than a more doctrinaire style. The majority should also be aware of this consistency, of course, and perceive it as an indication of the minority's confidence. Another factor is the extent of investment which the minority is perceived to have made in promulgating its views. Those who are seen to have made personal or material sacrifices for their cause are likely to be taken more seriously than those for whom the endorsement of minority views has been fairly painless. Finally, a minority is taken much more seriously if it is seen to be acting out of principle and not from ulterior motives (Baron et al., 1992: 82; Brown, 1988: 111; Forsyth, 1990: 152).

Conversely, persuasion of the majority is much less likely if group members have publicly expressed their commitment to an alternative at an early stage of the decision-making process. Under these circumstances compromising and yielding to the arguments of minorities is more difficult (Baron et al., 1992: 108).

Motivation losses

When people join a group, feelings of personal responsibility tend to decrease (Leary and Forsyth, 1987: 169). The motivation to contribute declines with group size. However, this **social loafing** effect does not occur if the group's task is sufficiently involving, attractive and/or intrinsically interesting, if group cohesion is high, or if the group sets its own performance goals (Baron et al., 1992: 47). Since strategic decision making may be assumed to be involving, attractive, and so on, the issue of motivation loss is relatively unimportant and we will discuss it only briefly.

The social loafing effect is strongest if individual contributions are not identifiable, or, if they are identifiable, cannot unambiguously be evaluated against those of other group members (Baron et al., 1992: 49). Social loafing is also related to the role differentiation in the group: the person who identifies a problem is more active than other group members in the analysis and action phases (Moreland and Levine, 1992). Often the group member who identifies a problem is also held responsible for solving it.

Two varieties of social loafing can be distinguished. First, the social loafer may know that the task is additive, and that his or her loafing will reduce group output, but since he or she bears only a fraction of the cost of this reduction (or of the pay-off of an extra effort), the temptation to loaf is nevertheless very real. Secondly, the individual group member may feel that his or her input is dispensable, that is, the task is not fully additive. In this case there is a temptation to free-ride on the efforts of others, even if individual contributions can be measured (Baron et al., 1992: 51).

As stated before, with intrinsically interesting and involving tasks like strategic decision making the social loafing effect is unlikely. More than that, groups may even exhibit motivation gains instead of motivation losses. This was one of the findings of the famous experiments at Western Electric's Hawthorne plant in 1927 (Forsyth, 1990: 277–80). Under certain leadership circumstances group members can encourage each other, and be motivated to work harder than individuals would.

In conclusion the social loafing effect appears to be most prominent if group members do not feel much commitment to the group, and if the group is engaged in an uninteresting task. All the same, individuals working together in, for example, a strategic planning committee will rarely all exhibit the same level of involvement and effort. Some degree of diffusion of responsibility and the concomitant social loafing are to be expected even in this kind of setting.

Conformity

The process of interaction within groups very often leads to a striking result: individual group members conform their preferences, views and judgements to those of the majority of the group. This **conformity effect** can be restricted to publicly voiced opinions, but group members may also actually change their private opinions. Conformity may have a positive effect on group performance since it promotes the regularity and predictability that is essential for coordinated and efficient group action (Baron et al., 1992: 64). But conformity can also have negative effects, when individual thought and creativity are stifled.

Factors leading to conformity

Two basic factors leading to conformity can be distinguished: **normative influence** and **informational influence**. Informational influence has been touched upon in the discussion of coordination losses. Other people are a valuable source of information, and if a majority of group members expresses a certain opinion, this may be enough for the individuals in the minority to doubt their own judgement. The majority can exert a stronger informational influence than the minority because it is able to put forth more arguments. If for instance speaking time is the same for all group members, more arguments for the majority view will be mentioned than arguments for the minority view. This may lead to the impression that the majority view is more plausible.

Normative influence can also lead to conformity, if dissent is seen as a violation of the group's norms and values. Not agreeing with the majority easily leads to conflict, especially in a group with much cohesion, and the dissenter runs the risk of loss of status, rejection or even ostracism. Holding a different opinion is often enough to trigger dislike even when it does not directly block group goals (Baron et al., 1992: 62; Forsyth, 1990: 169). To get along, you go along. But group norms are not simply external constraints. Group members also obey norms because they have internalized these standards and compliance is necessary in order to fulfil personal expectations about proper behaviour (Forsyth, 1990: 162–3).

Forms of conformity

From the discussion above it can be concluded that conformity can be a result of compliance: the individual conforms to the view of the majority solely because of the need to be accepted. The majority view as such, however, is still seen as wrong. But conformity can also be caused by internalization: the individual accepts the group view as an accurate depiction of reality (Baron et al., 1992: 67). If we make a distinction between an individual's private and public position, four different responses to conformity pressure are possible (see Figure 5.3).

An initial dissenter may express agreement with the majority view because he or she is genuinely convinced (**conversion**). But he or she may also only publicly conform, while sticking to his or her private view (**compliance**). When a group member persists in dissenting, this may be caused by **independence** of opinion, but also just by a tendency to publicly disagree with the group's majority (**counter-conformity**). Counter-conformity sometimes reflects a desire to be the centre of attention, but it may also be an artefact of the group's role differentiation. In Chapter 8 we will discuss the devil's advocate technique of group decision making, in which one individual has the explicit assignment to disagree with the majority, in order to avoid the pitfall of group conformity.

PRIVATE POSITION

		Agree	Disagree
PUBLIC POSITION	Agree	Conversion	Compliance
	Disagree	Counter-conformity	Independence

Figure 5.3 Four types of responses to conformity pressure. (Source: Forsyth, 1990: 147.)

When is conformity strongest/weakest?

The tendency to yield to conformity pressures is strongest in cases of judgement or opinion issues, when there is considerable uncertainty about the appropriate response (Baron et al., 1992: 66). In the case of a minority of one the **conformity rate**, the percentage of initial dissenters that conform to the group opinion, increases with the majority size. There is a ceiling effect, however: above a majority size of six the conformity rate hardly increases any further (Forsyth, 1990: 149). Conformity effects are undermined when the dissenter finds that he or she is not alone (see below).

Not all individuals are equally likely to conform. Independency of opinion is related to a person's personality structure. But conformity is also related to the status differentiation within the group. People who have high status or prestige in the group are more influential and therefore more likely to swing the group's opinion; low status group members are more likely to conform (Forsyth, 1990: 155). Gender is also a factor. Women appear to be more susceptible to conformity pressure, but only in situations of face-to-face interaction. Otherwise differences in conformity behaviour between men and women are almost non-existent (Forsyth, 1990: 157).

When a dissenter is not alone, it is much easier to withstand conformity pressure. The majority can dismiss a single dissenter's arguments as personal idiosyncrasies or biases, but the existence of several dissenters casts doubt on the majority's view (Forsyth, 1990: 151). Thus a minority coalition is not altogether without influence.

Group polarization

The 'risky shift' and group polarization

It may seem reasonable to assume that groups will be more cautious in decision making than individuals. Group decision making, either through consensus or through majority rule, may be expected to be less extremity-prone than individual decisions. However, an overwhelming amount of evidence suggests that this is not always the case. In particular, when individual members of a group are generally disposed toward risk, the process of group discussion will strengthen that tendency. As a result, the group's decision is more risky than the average initial tendencies of the members would make us expect (Whyte, 1989). This phenomenon is called the **risky shift**.

The risky shift is a subset of choice shift phenomena denominated **group polarization** (Kerr, 1992). The same tendency toward polarization can be seen in groups, the members of which are initially relatively cautious. After group discussion, these groups display an even stronger risk aversion. In general polarization refers to an increase in the extremity of the average response of the subject population responses. This effect has been demonstrated, not only for risk preference and risk aversion, but also for attitudes towards issues like war or capital punishment, judgements of facts and the perception of persons (Myers and Lamm, 1976).

In all cases the process of group discussion tends to intensify the opinion of group members. This is only true, however, if group members initially basically agree. The polarization effect is also confined to relatively important issues. If the issue is sufficiently unimportant group *de*polarization can occur: after group discussion the average position is less extreme than before (Kerr, 1992).

Group polarization is the intensification of a pre-existing initial group preference (Baron et al., 1992: 73). The polarization effect pertains to the average individual scores before and after group discussion. The most extreme group members may very well have become more moderate after the discussion, but on average preferences or judgements have become more extreme.

Explanations of group polarization

How can the polarization effect be explained? A first impulse may be to see it as a statistical artefact: as we have seen earlier, if the members of a group are drawn randomly from a population in which 70 per cent have a certain preference, more than 70 per cent of the group decisions will reflect that preference (assuming majority rule). However, group decision making is not an essential element of the procedure leading to polarization; a brief period of discussion followed by individual responses will also produce a shift in the group average (Myers and Lamm, 1976). This means that a shift in individual preferences occurs as a result of the group process.

More apposite explanations are based on the processes of informational and normative influence discussed in the context of conformity. As far as informational influence is concerned, the preponderance of arguments and facts put forward during group discussion will be supportive of the group members' initial inclination. This confirms the group members in their opinion. The fact that information that is consistent with one's prior belief is more likely to be noticed and taken seriously (see Chapter 4) also contributes to this phenomenon (Ferrell, 1985; Myers and Lamm, 1976).

Normative influence leads to polarization through the group members' concern for favourable self-perception and self-presentation. Subjects perceive other group members who have opinions more extremely in the direction of their own inclination as socially more desirable than group members with different inclinations. An extreme communicator of an opinion comparable to one's own stand is perceived as more sincere and competent than a moderate communicator (Myers and Lamm, 1976). The desire to be accepted by these more extreme group members, and the tendency to perceive and present oneself as a member of a favourably perceived 'in-group' both contribute to the polarization effect. The effect is reinforced by verbal commitment to a position expressed early in the group discussion: afterwards a change of position in the direction of the initial tendency (i.e. polarization) is easier to perform than a change in the opposite direction (Ferrell, 1985; Myers and Lamm, 1976).

Both forms of influence are important. Their relative importance (with regard to polarization as well as to conformity) depends on the kind of interaction and the type of task. If the interaction within the group is predominantly of a socio-emotional nature, normative influence is more important. Task-orientated interaction is more strongly associated with informational influence and persuasion. As far as the type of task is concerned, in judgemental tasks normative influence is relatively important, and in intellective tasks informational influence (Kaplan, 1987).

Groupthink

Failures of group decision making

Studies of group decision making have documented many instances of dramatic failure. Most of the examples to be found in the literature come from the sphere of public administration. The reason for this bias is not necessarily that decision making in public administration is of poorer quality than that in the private sector; researchers simply have easier access to the minutes of public decision making than to those of private corporations. Examples of disastrous group decisions that have been closely investigated are the Bay of Pigs invasion under the Kennedy administration, the failure to defend Pearl Harbor from Japanese air attack, and the Watergate cover-up under the Nixon administration. In all cases the members of small, cohesive groups of decision makers inadvertently suppressed critical thoughts in order to protect apparent unanimity, and became a victim of an illusory perception of the world. In one word, these decision-making groups fell victim to **groupthink** (Janis, 1982; 1989). Groupthink refers to 'a mode of thinking that people engage in when they are deeply involved in a cohesive in-group, when the members' striving for unanimity overrides their motivation to realistically appraise alternative courses of action' (Janis, 1982: 9). See Box 5.2.

Instances of groupthink can be diagnosed (or even prevented) by paying attention to a number of symptoms (Forsyth, 1990: 295–8). In groups where groupthink occurs strong normative pressures for conformity prevail. Dissenters must be very brave to speak up. These normative pressures are bolstered by

---

Box 5.2 Obsession with profits and groupthink

In the summer of 1994 the reputation of Jack Welch, CEO of General Electric and one of the most admired captains of industry in American business, suffered from a scandal at one of GE's subsidiaries, broker-dealer firm Kidder Peabody. One of Kidder's traders was fired and its manager replaced when it became clear that the broker-dealer firm had been reporting phony profits. One commentator notes that 'the problems at Kidder may have less to do with the fired few than with the business creed to which they subscribed, a creed whose prophet is the charismatic Welch'. This creed is that all GE businesses are supposed to show high and growing profits, always. The pressure to show profits led the management of basically unprofitable Kidder Peabody to seek business aggressively in the mortage-backed securities business, resulting in the accumulation of a large inventory of securities which wouldn't sell. It also led one Kidder Peabody trader to report profits that didn't exist at all. Groupthink may have played a role, not in the decision to brew phantom profits, but in top management's consistent failure to question Kidder's reports critically. As an internal report states: 'Time and again questions were answered incorrectly, ignored, or evaded'. Apparently, at GE meetings Jack Welch's expectations had become more important than normal business procedures.

(Source: Paré, 1994)

---

self-censorship: individuals who have doubts concerning the dominating view keep these to themselves. Sometimes **mind guards** protect group members from information which would damage the prevailing opinion. The chairperson may refuse opportunity to speak to outsiders who are critical of the group's policy. Other group members may hold back private information that contradicts the group's view. These various processes lead to an apparent unanimity, not supported by a real consensus. Furthermore, the members of groups who fall victim to groupthink share an illusion of invulnerability, the power and knowledge of the group is overestimated, and the possibility of failure played down to the point of being irrelevant. The group also develops the illusion of the inherent morality of whatever it may decide to do. Since the moral assumptions underlying the dominant view are never questioned, they appear to be above criticism. Perceptions of the **out group** (the enemy, or simply all outsiders who are potentially critical of the group) tend to be inaccurate and biased, in that they are seen as morally and intellectually inferior to the group members. As a consequence of all these factors, groupthink leads to defective decision-making strategies.

Groupthink explained

Groupthink is a complex phenomenon. An explanation can be based on a number of the issues discussed earlier in this chapter, as well as in Chapter 4. (The explanation presented here is based on Whyte, 1989.) Groups, just like individuals, have a certain aspiration level. Sometimes groups will be in the situation that due to previous decision outcomes the aspiration level is not satisfied. Under these circumstances an upcoming decision opportunity may be framed as a choice between two prospects, one relatively riskless, leading to only a slight improvement or a small deterioration of the present situation; the other more risky, with the danger of leading to a significantly worse situation, but also with the possibility of wiping out the accumulated deficit. Prospect theory predicts that, at the level of the individual, risk-seeking preferences are elicited in this situation.

Within the group, pressures for conformity will drive the group in the direction of consensus with the initial majority, especially in the case of a judgemental task like strategic decision making. Majority decision rules also add to the explanation: if a group of five members is drawn randomly from a population in which 80 per cent of individuals are risk seeking in the domain of losses (the normal inclination), 94 per cent of these five-person groups will have a majority of members who prefer the risky option over the certain loss. This means that there is a substantial chance that the consensus view of the group will be risk seeking. This effect is aggravated by the polarization effect, leading to a more extreme group decision than the initial average individual preference would suggest. In this case the group decision would be polarized in the direction of more risk-seeking behaviour. Once a risky course of action has been adopted escalation of commitment (see Chapter 4 and below) may occur, leading to the continuance of this course of action, even in the face of information disconfirming the correctness of the decision.

A major factor identifying groupthink as a group, rather than an individual phenomenon, is directive leadership. A leader who is dominant and has high prestige, such as John F. Kennedy, or Harold Geneen, former president of ITT, may paralyse the critical intelligence of his co-workers. In the time of Harold Geneen, new project proposals had to be defended in front of a very critical audience, headed by Geneen himself (Heller, 1989: 45–6). Under these circumstances the projects that will be proposed will be limited to those that are expected to please the dominant leader, and the criticism voiced restricted to an echo of his or her own opinion. Not surprisingly, directive leader behaviour has been shown to influence the frequency of groupthink symptoms significantly (Whyte, 1989).

Group factors leading to escalation of commitment

In Chapter 4 we discussed the phenomenon of escalation of commitment: the tendency to reinforce a failing policy. Besides psychological factors group factors of escalation of commitment can be distinguished, as well as organizational factors.

Box 5.3 Escalation of commitment in industrial policy

Half-way through the 1960s the large Dutch shipbuilding industry found itself in trouble as a result of dwindling demand and fierce competition, particularly from the Far East. The government, when called upon, responded with financial aid, but made this aid conditional on cooperation between individual shipyards. In the years 1967–71 this cooperation, under heavy pressure from the government, led to a merger between a number of large wharves in to the giant Rijn-Schelde-Verolme (or RSV) corporation. In the eyes of the RSV management the fact that the government had so strongly promoted this merger gave it a special responsibility for the firm's welfare. And successive Ministers of Economic Affairs seemed to respond to this responsibility, judging from the substantial sums of public money flowing to RSV throughout the 1970s. In spite of this aid the industry never really recovered, and at the beginning of 1983 RSV, at last finding the government unwilling to finance its dazzling losses any longer, applied for suspension of payment. The Dutch State at that moment had spent no less than 2 billion guilders (appr. $1.1 million) in its successive efforts to save the company. Subsequent inquiries have revealed that gradually RSV and the Ministry of Economic Affairs had become condemned to each other, as RSV could not survive without state aid, and the Ministry could not leave RSV to its own devices for fear of having its policy failures exposed. In the end the idea of RSV going bankrupt had become 'unthinkable' at the Ministry.

(Source: Noorderhaven, 1990: 5–6)

Social determinants of commitment may hold an individual to a once chosen course of action, even if he or she personally has lost faith in the possible success of the project or the utility of its purposes (Staw and Ross, 1987; see also Whyte, 1993). Four such determinants can be distinguished. First, public identification with a course of action leads to a desire not to lose face or credibility with others, and hence to continue the project. Secondly, social norms stress consistency of behaviour, and persistency is a socially valued style of leadership. Thirdly, the responsibility for failure may be put on the shoulders of the original decision maker. According to prospect theory this leads to risk-seeking behaviour. This is in itself a psychological effect, but the attribution of responsibility is a social process. Finally, escalation situations can become infused with interpersonal conflict. Not giving up the failing project can also be caused by the desire not to lose the game played against one's opponents (Bazerman, 1990: 75 speaks of 'competitive escalation of commitment' in such cases). See Box 5.3.

Four categories of organizational factors contribute to escalation of commitment (Staw and Ross, 1987). In the first place, adoption of a certain project may entail investments in plant and equipment, hiring of additional personnel, relocating existing staff, and so forth. These economic and technical side bets add costs (psychological as well as monetary) to the discontinuation of the project itself. Secondly, a project may have political support, for example, from powerful actors in the environment of the organization, that make it more difficult to stop it. Thirdly, administrative inertia may inhibit discontinuation. Budgets have been allocated, responsibilities assigned, procedures developed. One may simply have to wait until the next opportunity for organizational decision making occurs. Finally, sometimes projects have become institutionalized within the firm, that is, they are so deeply embedded in the norms and values of the firm that they are not even considered for discontinuation.

Potential problems in group decision making and phases of the decision process

Overview

In Chapter 2 a conceptual model of the decision-making process was sketched, consisting of three general phases: awareness, analysis and action. In which of these three phases should the phenomena discussed above be localized? Although all the phenomena may in some way relate to all decision phases, most of them are primarily associated with one or two of the phases (see Figure 5.4).

Awareness

Figure 5.4 shows that few of the phenomena discussed affect the awareness phase of the decision process. This is only natural: problem recognition is an important aspect of the awareness phase, and problems are always identified by individuals. Groups have no consciousness and no perceptional faculties. Of course, individual perceptions may later be shared and discussed, but we will consider this activity as part of the analysis phase. Problem formulation, the other step in the awareness phase, conceivably benefits from the joining of several viewpoints.

Two of the phenomena discussed can be assumed to have an impact on problem awareness: motivation losses and conformity. The level of motivation influences problem recognition because members who are strongly committed to the group are more likely to identify problems and threats. These problems and threats are more important to them than to marginal group members. A group member who recognizes a problem will not always feel motivated to bring it to the attention of the other group members. He or she may instead hide the problem (e.g. for fear of getting blamed), or ignore it in the hope that someone else will detect it and take responsibility. Poor problem recognition by groups may also be caused by a culture or implicit norm of complacency,

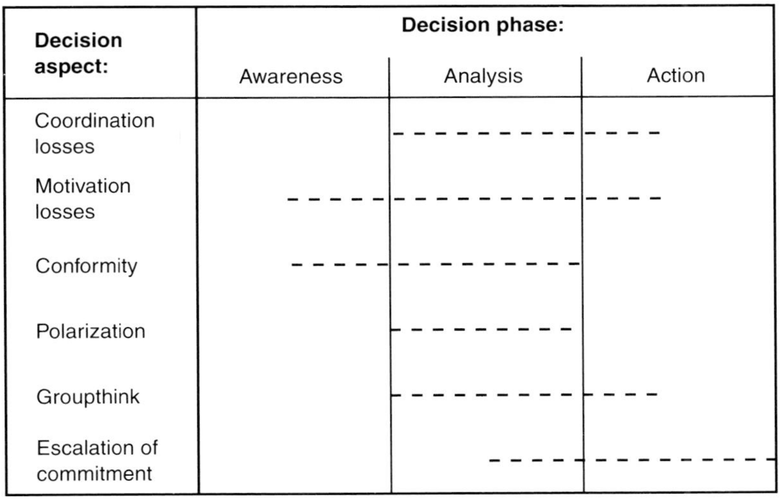

Decision aspect:	Decision phase:		
	Awareness	Analysis	Action
Coordination losses		- - - - - - - - - -	- - - -
Motivation losses	- - - - -	- - - - - - - - - -	- - - -
Conformity	- - - - -	- - - - - - - - - - -	
Polarization		- - - - - - - - -	
Groupthink		- - - - - - - - - -	- - - -
Escalation of commitment		- - - - - - - - - - - - - - -	

Figure 5.4 Phases and potential problems of group decision making.

prevailing when a group has performed very well for an extended period of time (Moreland and Levine, 1992).

The conformity tendency may influence problem awareness because our view of reality will often depend on the people with whom we communicate, and their (status) position in the group (Baron et al., 1992: 61). In the awareness phase this implies that individual group members subconsciously adapt their perceptions to the expected group view.

Analysis

With regard to the problems of group decision making discussed above, coordination losses may be assumed to play an important role in the analysis phase. In this phase information has to be generated, shared and discussed between the group members. Groups are often inefficient in pooling and using the available information. If problem analysis is time consuming or entails mental exertion, individuals may try to free-ride on the efforts of other group members. Conformity may form a problem in this phase, too, as group members may decline to advance viewpoints that deviate from the *communis opinio* within the group. This can mean that viable information is not brought into the group decision-making process. Polarization, the process through which group discussion intensifies group opinion, producing more extreme judgements among group members than existed before, pre-eminently takes place at the analysis phase. This is also true of groupthink. It is, however, a phenomenon which is also related to past and present action. Past choices leading to bad outcomes form the seed-bed for groupthink. Groupthink itself leads to the implementation of too risky and/or ill-founded decisions.

Action

If the act of choice consists in some kind of majority decision, or if the decision is made on the basis of consensus or unanimity, group decisions have the advantage of creating a more extended organizational basis for the implementation. In the implementation itself, however, responsibilities will often be divided among the group members, or delegated to non-group members. If a decision group as a whole also takes up the implementation, diffusion of responsibilities is likely. The same is true of the control of the implementation process.

The aspects of group decision making which cause or reinforce escalation of commitment are located primarily in the action phase of the decision-making process. As we have seen, public identification with a course of action, together with social norms stressing consistency, may cause a decision maker to stick to a certain decision even after he or she has stopped believing in it (Staw and Ross, 1987).

5.4 Power and influence relations and decision making

Strategic decision making is often conceptualized as an intellective process. However, it also is very much a *political* process (Eisenhardt and Bourgeois, 1988; Harrison, 1987: 338). Organization members use whatever power base they have at their disposal to bend the strategy to their own benefit or in what they see as the right direction. This means that strategic decision making is influenced by the power or political relations existing within the organization, and by the coalitions individual actors, departments and other (informal) groups build (Narayanan and Fahey, 1982). In this section we will focus on the power dimension. First, the various bases of power are discussed. Secondly, we turn to the use of power in political behaviour within organizations. Finally, the issue of leadership style is taken up. Leadership style is interwoven with power and its sources: the available power sources are an important factor in determining which leadership style can be effectively practised in a given organizational situation.

The issues of power, political behaviour and leadership style are also related to group decision making. The most common formal group in organizations is the **command group**, consisting of a manager and his or her direct subordinates (e.g. a management team or a board of directors) (Coffey et al., 1994: 320). It is within these command groups that most of the processes of the use of power, political behaviour and leadership take place. Decision making in this setting is not an activity of a single isolated individual; the influence of other individuals is always present.

Sources of power

Power and influence

Definitions of power and influence abound. Here **power** is defined as the capacity to make someone else act according to one's preferences, even if that is not in accordance with the other's own preferences. **Influence** is the process of actually changing the behaviour of the less powerful party. Influence presupposes power: power is the potential to influence, influence is the application of power. Note that power can only exist within a relationship: A can be said to have power over B, but that in itself does not imply that A has power over C.

Sources of power

Power over another person can derive from various sources. French and Raven, in their classical analysis of power, distinguished five types of power, deriving from different sources: reward, coercive, legitimate, referent and expert power (French and Raven, 1959; see also Forsyth, 1990: 182–7).

Reward power is based on the ability to distribute valuable resources. A manager with reward power can, for example, bestow financial bonuses on his subordinates, open up promotion opportunities and give social approval. **Coercive power** is like reward power, but negative: the capacity to dispense punishments, like social disapproval, ridicule, transfer to an undesirable job or even dismissal. **Legitimate power** is the socially accepted right to demand compliance. This power springs from the group structure itself – roles, status, norms – rather than from the delivery or withholding of valued resources. Yet another kind of power is possessed by people who serve as models for self-evaluation for others: **referent power**. Here obeyance is based on admiration for the leader and the desire to emulate him or her. People who serve as very important referents are said to have **charisma**. **Expert power** derives from the belief of the less powerful that the powerholder possesses superior skills and abilities. The belief in the expertise is as important as the expertise itself, but it is difficult to keep intact this belief in others if one is not really an expert in the field in question.

Legitimate, coercive and reward power are strongly linked with the organizational position of the powerholder. Expert power and and referent power, on the other hand, are closely connected to a specific person, regardless of his or her position (cf. Coffey et al., 1994: 259). Legitimate power, the socially accepted right to manage, may also be based in extraordinary personal qualities. Most powerful is an individual possessing strong personal as well as position power. Such a person is capable of exerting a dominant influence on the strategy of his or her organization.

GOALS PURSUED

Sanctioned   Not sanctioned

	Sanctioned	Not sanctioned
Legitimate	Non-political behaviour	Political behaviour II
Illegitimate	Political behaviour I	Political behaviour III

USE OF POWER

Figure 5.5 Political and non-political behaviour in organizations.

Political aspects of decision making

Political behaviour

Many textbooks on strategic management are based on the implicit assumption that managers play by the rule and pursue the promulgated organizational goals. In reality, however, managers often strive for personal interests rather than for organizational goal achievement, and use means and sanctions that do not correspond to the formal organizational rules and procedures. In other words, they engage in what is called **political behaviour**: activities aimed at obtaining ends not sanctioned by the organization or at obtaining sanctioned ends through non-sanctioned means (see Figure 5.5) (Coffey et al., 1994: 273).

According to the typology of Figure 5.5 only activities aimed at the officially sanctioned organizational goals, and remaining within the boundaries of formal authority, are examples of non-political behaviour. Some activities are aimed at the organizational goals, but the actor misuses its power or authority ('Political Behaviour I'). A departmental manager may for instance misuse his or her right to approve small expenditures by disguising a substantial capital expenditure through chopping it up into several smaller investments. In this way the necessity to ask permission of top management is avoided. This kind of political behaviour may be displayed by employees who have the best interests of the organization at heart (Coffey et al., 1994: 273).

Less benevolent is political behaviour directed at skewing organizational outcomes toward self-interest. In the case of 'Political Behaviour II', legitimate power is used in order to attain goals not sanctioned by the organization. This is for instance the case if a manager deploys his or her formal powers to achieve personal advantages, for instance, through buying a larger than necessary computer to play with, hiring attractive rather than competent co-workers, and so on. Most clear cut is 'Political Behaviour III': illegitimate use of power *and* non-sanctioned goals.

Political behaviour and strategic decision making

Political action within organizations by nature is covert. It contrasts with the open discussions and sharing of information, in settings open to all major organizational stakeholders that are the official forums for strategic decision making. Political behaviour is most prevalent where interdependence is high, goals are incompatible, and resources scarce (Coffey et al., 1994: 275). It is not surprising, therefore, that political behaviour is a way of life in organizational strategy making.

Eisenhardt and Bourgeois, in a study of eight firms from the microcomputer industry in the San Francisco Bay area, identified a wide variety of political practices (Eisenhardt and Bourgeois, 1988). Perhaps the most important form of **politicking** is the formation of alliances or coalitions. Managers with common interests (and often comparable backgrounds or personalities) build coalitions in order to increase their grip on the decision process. External actors such as management consultants may be included in these coalitions. Sometimes the coalition takes the form of an insurgency group, if a number of managers meet regularly outside the formal chain of command in order to sidetrack their superior. Another very common form of political behaviour is selectively withholding information. A manager may choose to share information in a piecemeal way, in one-on-one meetings, in order to maintain his or her privileged position. Also widespread is the practice of cooptation, defined by Eisenhardt and Bourgeois as private attempts to change the position of a key decision maker. What makes this kind of behaviour political is the fact that it is happening covertly, outside the formal meetings and information channels.

Politicking, although by no means always detrimental to the organization, can interfere with effective management (Jay, 1967). This view is corroborated by the study of Eisenhardt and Bourgeois, who found that political behaviour was associated with poor firm performance (Eisenhardt and Bourgeois, 1988). However, causality can run both ways: firms can do worse because managers engage too much in politicking, but poor performance may also reinforce the tendency to political behaviour.

Leadership and strategic decision making

What is leadership?

Leadership is another inevitable element of life in groups. In particular larger groups soon encounter problems of coordination, administration and communication. Appointing a group leader mitigates these problems. Therefore members of large groups are likely to accept leadership (Forsyth, 1990: 213, 220).

Leadership can be described as the process in which an individual is permitted to influence others in the attainment of common and private goals. This influence process consists in providing direction, energizing and obtaining commitment (Coffey et al., 1994: 289, Forsyth, 1990: 216). The role of a leader is often seen as different from that of a manager. Management has to do with efficiency and the mastering of routine; leadership with effectiveness, vision and

---

Box 5.4 The leadership style of a corporate doctor

Karl-Jozef Neukirchen is a turnaround artist. He has made it his job to assume the management of companies on the brink of bankruptcy and to prevent their collapse – mainly by cutting costs through lay-offs. In December 1993 he took on his biggest job to date: the rescue of giant German metals and engineering conglomerate Metallgesellschaft. He persuaded the banks, in particular the Deutsche Bank, to go along with a $2 billion rescue plan including the issue of new shares and the conversion of existing bank debt into equity. And he slashed jobs, some 7500 to begin with. His effectiveness is undisputed, but his leadership style evokes resistance. 'His management style is rude, to put it mildly', according to a former colleague. Management at Metallgesellschaft considered it particularly cocky when Neukirchen quoted Julius Caesar – 'I came, I saw, I conquered' – after having secured the bank bailout. However, there is also respect for his straightforwardness, and the admiration for his effective task performance seems to outweigh irritation concerning his socio-emotional leadership (or the absence thereof). The head of the works council at Metallgesellschaft comments: 'I know that our destiny as a company is completely linked to the success or failure of this man. I trust him.'

(Source: Miller, 1994)

---

change. If that is the case, an organization needs leaders as well as managers. In the context of strategic decision making, however, leadership is particularly relevant. A leader can play a dominant role in developing a vision, and is capable of passing it on to his or her colleagues and subordinates. In this way two central aspects of strategic management, setting direction and mobilization of commitment, are accomplished simultaneously (Bennis and Nanus, 1985: 21; Coffey et al., 1994: 291, 308).

Leadership styles

Strategic leadership can be exercised in different ways. Some leaders centralize decision making and try to impose their visions on the other members of the management team. Other leaders actively involve their subordinates in the development of the strategy, in order to ensure commitment from the start. Or decision making is decentralized, and the role of leadership confined largely to encouraging lower managers to come forward as champions of sound strategies (Bourgeois and Brodwin, 1984).

Elements of leadership behaviour fall into two general clusters, relationship behaviours and task behaviours. Task behaviours pertain to the

Initiating structure

		Low	High
	Low	*Laissez-faire*	Autocratic
Showing consideration			
	High	Human relations	Democratic

Figure 5.6 Four styles of leadership. (Source: Coffey et al., 1994: 296.)

establishment of patterns of organization, channels of communication and methods of procedure. Relationship behaviours address the feelings, attitudes and emotional needs of group members (Coffey et al., 1994: 295; Forsyth, 1990: 217). This categorization of leadership behaviour corresponds to the distinction between task roles (initiating structure) and socio-emotional roles (showing consideration) in role differentiation within groups. Those group members that fulfil important task and/or socio-emotional roles tend to emerge as group leaders. See Box 5.4.

If we consider both categories as independent dimensions of leadership style, and assume for the sake of simplicity that a leader can score either high or low on these dimensions, a two-by-two matrix of leadership styles can be drawn (see Figure 5.6).

Leaders that are primarily task-orientated are called **autocratic**, leaders focusing primarily on the socio-emotional aspects of the group display a **human relations** approach. Leaders scoring low or high on both dimensions have a *laissez-faire* style and a **democratic** style, respectively. (The designation 'democratic leadership' appears to be a misnomer. More adequate are Blake and Mouton's, 1964, and Graeff's, 1983, terminologies – 'team management' and 'selling', respectively.)

This figure is based on the assumption that one and the same leader can have a strong task orientation *and* a strong socio-emotional orientation. According to some, this democractic leadership style is most effective (cf. Blake and Mouton, 1964). More plausible, however, is the viewpoint that the effectiveness of the various leadership styles depends on situational characteristics. Two important factors are the ability and the motivation of the group members (subordinates). If the group members are both able and willing, *laissez-faire* leadership is effective. If the group members lack in ability or motivation, however, there is need for a stronger task-orientation and a stronger socio-emotional orientation, respectively. A leader confronted with subordinates who are both unable and unwilling can best revert to the autocratic style (Miner, 1992: 253).

Leadership style and power sources

Power, being the potential to influence, is a necessary condition of leadership (Rowe et al., 1994: 464). The power base of an effective leader will in many circumstances be more of the personal than of the positional kind. That is, a leader should have expert and/or reference power in order to be effective. The leader's power should also be accepted as legitimate. A minimum of position power (reward power and coercive power) is perhaps necessary, but in itself not sufficient for effective leadership. As expert, reference and legitimate power depend also, or even predominantly, on the group members' perception of the leader, these power bases are only imperfectly related to situational and personality characteristics. The outcomes of leadership behaviour affect the group members' perceptions, and thus the personal and legitimate power of the leader. The relationship between leadership style and sources of power is a circular one (Miner, 1992: 229).

Group processes, political behaviour and leadership styles all have a bearing on strategic decision making in organizations. Our discussion has shown that many social factors influence intendedly rational decision making. Group decision making can be more effective than individual decision making, but the opposite is also possible. Political behaviour may be rational from the viewpoint of the individual, but nevertheless lead to results that are 'irrational' if seen in the perspective of the organization as a whole. Leaders of organizations may try to influence decision processes in what they see as the right direction, but their effectiveness depends, *inter alia*, on their sources of power. All these factors have to be taken into account, if we want to understand (and improve) organizational strategy.

Chapter summary

- A group consists of two or more individuals who influence each other through social interaction.

- A committee is a (sub)group appointed or elected to perform certain (decision making) tasks on behalf of a larger decision-making party. A coalition is an informal group of actors pursuing particular shared objectives.

- The combination of individual preferences or opinions into a group decision can be described using a social decision scheme.

- Whether group decisions are better or worse than individual decisions to a large extent depends on the characteristics of the task. Groups perform relatively well on divisible, maximizing and additive tasks.

- Group decision making suffers from coordination losses (i.e. not all the information available is used efficiently) and motivation losses (i.e. not all members feel motivated to contribute to the decision-making process).

- Group decision making also suffers from pressures towards conformity and tendencies towards polarization. In combination these two pressures may lead to the phenomenon of groupthink.

- Power may stem from the ability to give rewards or administer punishment, from the formal position in the organizational hierarchy, from personal characteristics that are highly esteemed and from expert knowledge.

- Political behaviour in organizations is associated with the use of legitimate means to realize illegitimate ends and with the use of illegitimate means to reach either legitimate or illegitimate ends.

- Leadership is the process in which one individual influences others in the attainment of common and private goals. Leadership behaviour can be directed at the social relations in the group, at the accomplishment of the task, or both.

6

Strategy, structure and culture

In Chapters 6 and 7 we will focus on the organizational context within which strategic decision making takes place. The organizational setting influences decision making over and above the influences on the individual and the group level discussed in the preceding chapters. Conversely, individual and group decisions also have a bearing on the organization. An intricate interplay and mutual determination exists between decision and organization.

We will tackle this complexity by first concentrating on the interaction between strategic decision making and two important dimensions of organizations, namely structure and culture. Next, in Chapter 7, we will consider the evolution of models used to prescribe, describe and explain organizational decision making and look at the findings of empirical studies of organizational decision-making processes.

The two preceding chapters dealt with biases in and limitations to intendedly rational decision making at the level of the individual and at the level of the group. In this chapter the focus shifts to programmed choice. The organizational context of decision making can be seen as a set of restrictions within which rational decision making takes place. The organization represents the walls of a maze, and organizational decisions more often have to do with solving maze problems than with reconstructing maze walls (Katz and Kahn, 1978: 495).

We will first discuss elements of organizational structure, then consider the mutual influences between structure and strategy, and subsequently focus on the process of strategic decision making within different structural contexts. Then we will focus on organizational culture, on the relationship between culture and strategic decision-making processes and on the issue of deliberately changing the culture of an organization.

6.1 Organizational structure

In this section we will briefly discuss the concept of organizational structure, and the main variants of organizational structures. Readers acquainted with this subject matter may prefer to skip this part of the chapter.

Formal and informal organization structures

Formal structure

The concept of organizational structure refers to:

- the allocation of tasks to organizational units and individuals;
- hierarchical relationships between managers and subordinates;
- lines of communication between organization members.

The structure of an organization accommodates two basic requirements: the internal division of labour, and the integration of the contributions of the various organization members into a coherent whole (Lawrence and Lorsch, 1967: Mintzberg, 1979).

Informal structure

We have to differentiate between the formal and the informal structure. The formal structure shows the allocation of tasks, and so on, promulgated by the top of the organization. It reflects what the organization should look like according to those in power. The formal structure can be depicted in an **organization chart**: a scheme showing the organizational units and their relationships. Figure 6.1 shows the organization chart of Heras, a Dutch producer of steel fences.

The informal structure of an organization consists of the *actual* relationships and lines of communication between organizational units and individuals. This informal structure often deviates from the formal structure, sometimes strongly. To give a hypothetical example: the manager of the Purchasing Department in Figure 6.1 gives orders to the Warehouse regarding the handling of shipments, bypassing the manager of Production, or the Fabrication Department regularly performs maintenance jobs that formally are a part of the task of Technical Services. This kind of deviation of the informal from the formal structure is not necessarily bad. In some cases it is better if the formal structure is set aside temporarily, for instance because using the formal lines of communication would be too time-consuming. The informal structure contributes to the viability of the formal structure by providing additional channels of communication, and at the same time bolsters feelings of personal integrity, self-respect and independent choice, which could be hurt by a too oppressive formal structure (Barnard, 1938: 122; Mintzberg, 1979: 49).

However, if the gap between formal and informal structure becomes too large, this leads to diffusion of responsibilities and conflicts of competence,

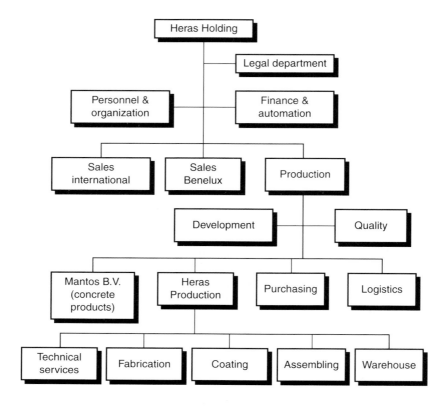

Figure 6.1 Organization chart of Heras.

and ultimately may render the organization ungovernable. As this problem area lies outside the scope of this book we will not pursue this question here. In discussing organizational structure we will assume that the formal and the informal structures largely coincide.

Elements of structure

In discussing organizational structure, several aspects can be distinguished: centralization, formalization, differentiation, integration and departmentation.

Centralization

Centralization refers to the degree to which the formal authority or the actual decision-making power is concentrated at a single point in the organization – an organizational unit (such as the management board) or an individual (such as the chief executive officer). (The discussion of centralization is based on Mintzberg, 1979: 181–213.) In a highly centralized organization, almost all decisions are referred to the highest hierarchical level. This has as an advantage that a strong coordination is achieved. But the disadvantage is that the top of the organization easily gets snowed under with issues and questions. Furthermore, all the information necessary for making the decisions has to flow through the vertical communication channels. Top managers cannot digest all that information unless it is presented in a highly aggregated form. But essential information may get lost in the aggregation process. On top of that, centralized decision-making may be too time consuming to allow rapid response to changes in the environment. Finally, centralization is not conducive to the motivation of lower managers.

For all these reasons, some degree of **decentralization** can be found in almost all organizations. Two forms of decentralization can be distinguished: vertical and horizontal decentralization. **Vertical decentralization** refers to the delegation of decision-making authority to lower (management) levels. In the context of strategic management vertical decentralization exists if departments or divisions are allowed to form their own policies (within the boundaries of the overall strategy). In the case of **horizontal decentralization**, decision-making authority is delegated to staff units. For instance, a staff department for strategic planning may be put in charge of generating and evaluating strategic options. In both forms of decentralization some degree of power is dispersed over the organization, although the ultimate authority remains in the hands of top management.

Formalization

Formalization refers to the regulation of behaviour by formal rules, procedures, and instructions (see Dessler, 1986: 192–6; Mintzberg, 1979: 81–94). Formalization reduces the variability of behaviour, and thus promotes predictability and coordination. Formalization also ensures fairness: if there are explicit rules for promotion (e.g. based on formal qualifications and/or seniority), favouritism and political manoeuvring are curtailed. In the context of strategic decision making, formalization may refer to the adoption of formal procedures for strategic planning, programming and budgeting. The disadvantage of formalization is that the relationships within the organization tend to become more rigid and impersonal, and that creativity (a particularly unpredictable form of behaviour) may be stifled.

Differentiation

The concept of differentiation is linked to the internal division of labour of the organization. The more advanced the division of labour (the more specialized the subunits), the more differentiated the organization is (Lawrence and Lorsch, 1967). Organizational subunits adapt their internal structure and culture to the characteristics of their task and to that part of the organizational environment with which they interact. As a consequence, differences between the various subunits become increasingly pronounced, and the organization becomes more complex.

Integration

As the organization becomes more differentiated, the need to integrate – coordinate – the activities of the various subunits also increases. One important mechanism for achieving integration is the formal hierarchy. However, as we have seen in the discussion of centralization, it is not efficient to refer all issues to the top of the organization. Therefore a number of other **liaison devices** are also used in order to achieve integration (Mintzberg, 1979: 162–80). One such liaison device is a functionary who mediates between two departments. For instance, in the Heras organization depicted in Figure 6.1, a member of the Logistics department could be physically located within the Heras Production offices, in order to improve the lateral contacts between both departments. A very elaborate liaison device is the **matrix structure**, in which two parallel formal hierarchies coexist. We will discuss the matrix structure below, under the heading of **departmentation**.

The achievement of organizational integration is very important for strategic decision making. If the formal hierarchy and the various other liaison devices do not succeed in coordinating the efforts of the subunits, every subunit pursues its own strategy, independent of the rest of the organization. Integration of the strategies of the various subunits can in that case, as Eigerman quipped, only be achieved with a stapler! (cf. Eigerman, 1988: 41).

Departmentation

Departmentation refers to the way the organization is split up into subunits. (Dessler, 1986: 124–41; Luthans, 1992: 525–8; Mintzberg, 1979: 104–33). Most common is departmentation on the basis of **function**. In this case organizational units are grouped according to the nature of the activities. The organizational structure of Heras (Figure 6.1) is an example of a **functional structure**. The advantage of a functional structure is that all the expertise and experience in a certain area is combined in one organizational unit. This grouping of tasks also often leads to economies of scale and of specialization.

An alternative for functional departmentation is the formation of divisions based on the product produced, or the region or type of customer served. The resulting organizational structure is called a **multidivisional structure**. Figure 6.2 gives an example of a multidivisional structure: the Hoogovens steel works.

A multidivisional structure is used if a firm produces several (groups of) products that are very different as far as production technology is concerned. Or if the company services various groups of customers, for example, industrial customers and consumers, demanding very different approaches. A third possibility is that the activities of the organization are spread out geographically. A functional grouping of tasks is often inefficient under these circumstances. A multidivisional structure has the advantage of offering a better focus on product groups, customer types, or regions. The disadvantage is the loss of economies of scale due to the fact that similar activities (e.g. with regard to purchasing) are performed in various subunits. Furthermore, functional

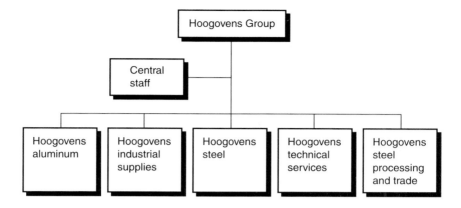

Figure 6.2 Organizational structure of Hoogovens Steel Works.

knowledge and experience are scattered over the different divisions. Within the separate divisions most of the time a functional structure prevails. Thus a multidivisional firm looks like a bundle of semi-independent functionally organized firms.

In reality organizational structures are often far more complicated than is suggested by the above. The various bases of departmentation can be combined to form a hybrid, for example, if some units are grouped on the basis of functions and other on the basis of products or regions. The structure of Heras displays such hybrid characteristics: the sales department is split up along geographical lines ('Benelux' and 'International'), and one product-based division ('Mantos B.V.') exists alongside the functional departments.

If two bases of departmentation are used simultaneously, and if both criteria carry equal weight, a **matrix organization** arises (Davis and Lawrence, 1977; Galbraith, 1977). In this structure organizational units are grouped into two separate hierarchies, for example, one on a functional basis, the other on the basis of products (see Figure 6.3).

A matrix organization can also be three dimensional, for instance if the geographical dimension is added to the two existing bases of departmentation. Of course, such a three-dimensional matrix structure is exceptionally complex. This complexity is a major source of disadvantages of the matrix structure (a high potential for conflict, time-consuming communication, excessive overhead, etc.). The major advantage of a matrix design is that it combines the specialization and economies of scale associated with a functional organization with the adaptation to technologies, markets or regions typical of multidivisional structures.

An alternative to the permanent matrix structure is a **project organization**, in which members of functional departments are assigned to project groups. Whereas the functional hierarchy is permanent, project groups are disbanded after they have completed their task, and the members are assigned

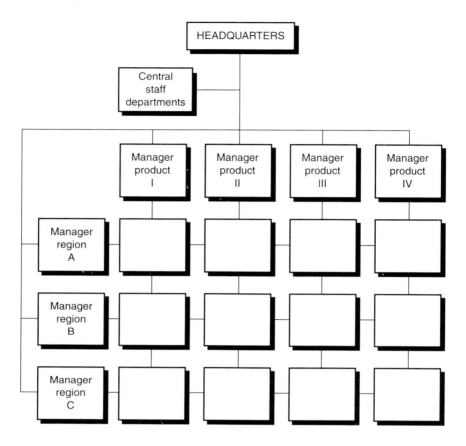

Figure 6.3 Organizational chart of a matrix organization.

to new project groups. A project organization is a matrix in a constant state of flux.

Basic configurations of structural elements

The various dimensions of structure – centralization, formalization, differentiation, integration and departmentation – are not independent, but on the contrary strongly interrelated. According to the **configuration theory** of organizational structure the various elements can be combined only in a limited number of ways to form viable organizations. These combinations form *'Gestalts'* or 'basic configurations', that are internally coherent and well adapted to certain kinds of tasks and environments. (See, e.g., Miller and Friesen, 1984; Mintzberg, 1979; 1989. The description of basic configurations below is based on Mintzberg, 1983b). Three of these basic configurations will be described briefly: the

entrepreneurial organization, the **machine organization**, and the **adhocracy organization**.

The entrepreneurial organization

This configuration is typical for small and medium-sized firms, with a top manager who in many cases also is the founder and/or owner of the firm. In this configuration virtually all the power is centralized in the hands of this top manager. It is furthermore characterized by a low degree of formalization, as the top manager rules through fiat and direct supervision rather than by means of formal rules. The degree of structural differentiation also tends to be low (for this reason this configuration is also called the 'simple structure'). No special integration devices are necessary because the top manager is able to oversee all activities, and because in a small firm informal mutual adaptation is often sufficient. Departmentation is normally based on functions.

The machine organization

The machine organization is the configuration to be found in many large production firms. It often arises if an entrepreneurial organization grows beyond the size at which a single top manager can maintain a firm grasp on everything happening within the firm, and beyond the size at which informal supervision and mutual adaptation work efficiently. In comparison with the entrepreneurial organization the machine organization is less centralized, although most decentralization is in the horizontal rather than the vertical direction. Consequently this configuration is characterized by the existence of extensive staff departments. The degree of formalization is typically very high, as this kind of organization has an obsession for control. The degree of differentiation is also high. The formal rules and procedures characterizing the machine organization also function as the chief integration device (apart from the formal hierarchy). Departmentation predominantly is on the basis of functions.

The adhocracy organization

This basic configuration is often found in high-technology industries, where firms have to be flexible and adaptive, and capable of rapid production of innovations. In order to do this, experts with divergent backgrounds (e.g. in marketing and technology) have to cooperate intensively and informally. Hence, the degree of centralization and formalization tends to be low. As the specialists are often clustered in small project groups, the degree of structural differentiation is high. Integration is achieved, apart from informal coordination, through the use of liaison devices such as project teams or a matrix structure. From this it follows that normally more than one basis for departmentation is used, for instance, products *and* functions.

6.2 The strategy–structure debate

Students of organizations have long debated the question of the causal relationship between structure and strategy. This debate is of interest because it highlights several aspects of the interrelation between the process of strategic decision making and organizational structure.

'Structure follows strategy'

Problems with the functional structure

Alfred Chandler, in a historical study of the organizational development of American industrial corporations in the first half of this century, gave the impetus to theorizing about the relationship between strategy and structure (Chandler, 1962). On the basis of his research, Chandler concluded that the structure of a firm is adapted to the strategy pursued: 'structure follows strategy'. The argument is that environmental changes compel a firm to adopt a new strategy. If the structure is not adapted to the new strategy, inefficiency results.

More specifically, Chandler observed that in a number of United States firms the adoption of a strategy of diversification brought about the need to change from a functional to a multidivisional organizational structure. A company that produces and markets more and more different products, but holds on to a functional structure, is bound to encounter two related problems. In the first place the internal coordination is hindered. Different product lines make different – sometimes opposite – demands on the production process. Logistics as well as coordination between organizational units become more complex. Changes in the production or marketing of one product may have unexpected repercussions for other products. The excessive complexity leads to delays and mistakes, and thus to inefficiency.

Moreover, the increasing complexity entails the danger of overload at the level of top management. Conflicts between organizational units are settled on the next higher organizational level, or, in case of very persistent disputes, at the level of top management. As a consequence top management risks to be overwhelmed by operational problems, and does not get around to giving sufficient attention to strategic issues. (March and Simon, 1993: 206). In this way the omission to adapt the structure to the new strategy leads to operational problems and the loss of strategic control (see Box 6.1).

The multidivisional structure as a solution

Moving from a functional to a multidivisional structure provides a solution to these problems. Within the various divisions attention can be concentrated on a limited range of products, markets or regions, and consequently complexity is reduced and coordination facilitated. Top management can leave the bulk of the decisions to the division managers, and concentrate on strategic issues. Usually, a part of the strategy making process – the formulation of 'business

Box 6.1 Introducing a multidivisional structure at Du Pont

During the First World War, America's largest producer of smokeless powder and explosives, *E.I. Du Pont de Nemours*, located in Wilmington, Delaware, experienced a tremendous growth. Prior to and during the war the company began a process of diversification into products based on nitrocellulosis, the main base material for smokeless powder. Examples of such products are imitation leather and pyroxylin, base material for, among other things, photographic film. Apart from that Du Pont also began to produce and market dyestuffs and paints, and took an interest in General Motors.

Managing these divergent lines of products proved to be difficult, particularly as far as marketing and sales were concerned. Before the war, 95% of turnover was realized selling bulk products to a small number of buyers, but now Du Pont had to learn to operate on very different markets. As a matter of fact, Du Pont made losses on all products except the traditional bulk products, although more specialized producers generated profits selling these specials. Only the profits from the powder business kept Du Pont alive.

In 1921 however, as a result of an economic depression, Du Pont went into a serious crisis. Under the pressure of circumstances a revolutionary step was made: the – at that time customary – functional organization structure was changed into a multidivisional structure. The new structure contained five product divisions: explosives, dyestuffs, synthetics, paints and chemicals, and photographic films. Thus the structure followed the strategy, albeit with a delay of 10 years. The losses soon turned into profits, and Du Pont never again experienced a crisis like that of 1921, not even in the dismal 1930s.

(Source: Chandler, 1962)

strategies' – is delegated to the divisions, and top management focuses on the strategy of the diversified firm as a whole.

'Strategy follows structure'

Chandler's generalization with regard to the relationship between strategy and structure has not remained unchallenged. At the least, the 'structure follows strategy' proposition is incomplete. The causal relationship may also be seen to be just the reverse (see Figure 6.4). (Bower, 1968; Frederickson, 1986; Hall and Saias, 1980).

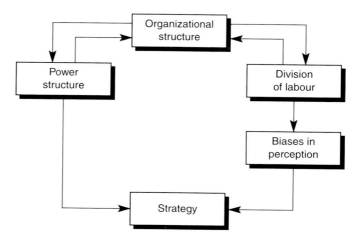

Figure 6.4 Strategy follows structure.

Political influence of subunits

Two arguments can be put forward to support the view that strategy is determined by structure. In the first place there is a strong link between the organizational structure and the distribution of power within the organization (Hickson et al., 1971; Pfeffer and Salancik, 1978). If a certain task or function is vitally important to a firm, this task or function will very likely be performed by a separate organizational unit. This unit derives power from the fact that it performs a vital task for the organization. At the same time, the formal structure itself is a source of power ('position power' or 'legitimate power', as discussed in Chapter 5).

The power that an organizational unit commands will be used, *inter alia*, to influence the strategy of the organization in the direction favourable to that unit (Horvath and MacMillan, 1979). For instance, technological innovation is likely to have a more central place in the strategy of a firm that has a separate organizational unit for research and development than in a firm in which research and development is just one of the tasks of the production department. Generally, the structuring of the organization partly determines what kind of strategic plans will be made (Mintzberg, 1994: 177).

Perception

The second argument is that the organizational structure, through the division of labour that it creates and maintains, influences the perception of the organization members. As we have seen in Chapter 4, perception is heavily dependent on past experiences and expectations. People working together in a particular organizational unit will share many of these experiences and expectations.

The effect will be strongest if units are grouped on a functional basis. The effect is also positively related to the degree of **professionalization**, that is, the extent to which the members of the organizational unit identify primarily with the norms and values of their occupational group rather than with those of the organization. Group processes leading to conformity, described in Chapter 5, boost the tendency of biased perception. Thus the structure of an organization, reflecting the importance attached to specific functions and activities, also influences the process of strategic decision-making via the perception of organization members.

Synthesis

The question remains to be answered whether the 'structure follows strategy' view and the 'strategy follows structure' view (both discussed here only in their most rudimentary form) can in some way be reconciled.

Historical background

The paradox can be resolved if we realize that Chandler's proposition is based on a historical study of a large and fundamental change, namely the adoption and diffusion of the multidivisional structure by United States companies in the first half of this century. This structural adjustment took place within the constellation of social, economic and technological factors of the second industrial revolution. The development of the railroad system allowed firms for the first time in history to serve the entire United States market from one or a few locations. At the same time producers experienced a pressure towards forward integration, in order to protect brand names and smoothen the distribution process of, for example, frozen and perishable consumables. Added to this was the policy of diversification of many firms, and that of consolidation of formerly uncoordinated activities of others. Together, these factors constituted an immense challenge to the firms concerned, and consequently the inertia of the existing structure could be overcome (albeit often only after a considerable time gap).

Hall and Saias, in expounding the 'strategy follows structure' view, discuss strategic and structural changes within a given environmental setting (Hall and Saias, 1980). Conceivably, in a relatively stable situation the influence of the structure on the strategy is stronger than vice versa. Actually, in a stable situation it may after a while be difficult to distinguish between structure and strategy, as the latter tends to coagulate into routines and programs (Miller, 1993; see also Weick, 1985).

The time dimension

The apparent contradiction between both views can be reconciled further if the time dimension is taken into consideration more explicitly. (This is also pointed out by Hall and Saias, 1980.) Today's structure has a strong influence on

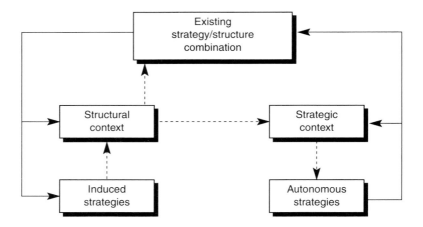

Figure 6.5 Autonomous and induced strategies.

tomorrow's strategy, but that in turn influences the structure of the day after tomorrow. As a strategy is never completely determined by the existing structure, the outcome of this process of mutual determination is not necessarily stagnation. Change, sometimes abrupt, more often gradual, is not ruled out in this explanation. The question of in which factor the change originates, structure or strategy, is like the discussion about the chicken and the egg. Or, to paraphrase Mintzberg: structure follows strategy, just like the left foot follows the right (but next step it will be the other way around) (Mintzberg, 1990a; for a slightly different view, see Amburgey and Dacin, 1994).

A multilevel view of the interaction of strategy and structure

Both influences can also coexist in one organization if the structural arrangements and incentive systems of top management determine a large part of the strategic plans of lower managers, but if some leeway for unconventional initiatives nevertheless remains. These initiatives, if successful, can *ex post* be authorized by top management, and then constitute the more fundamental changes in strategy. Probably an organization needs both, the business-as-usual plans within the promulgated strategy, and the controversial projects that are developed in the margin of the existing structure. Where one or the other is completely absent, either chaos or stagnation reigns.

Figure 6.5 shows the relationship between structure and strategy in the view of Burgelman (Burgelman, 1983; see also Mintzberg, 1994: 122–32). Instead of starting from the assumption that strategy influences structure or vice versa, Burgelman takes as his point of departure the strategy-structure combination existing at a given moment. This is in accordance with the tendency, noted above, of a strategy to become ingrained into elements of structure like procedures and routines (i.e. to become an element of programmed choice). The existing strategy-structure combination tends to nurture 'new' strategic plans amounting to more of the same thing.

Box 6.2 Autonomous strategies at Smith Kline & French and Hewlett-Packard

In the late 1960s, Philadelphia-based pharmaceutical company Smith Kline & French had a world-class researcher called James Black working at their far-away Welwyn Garden City research laboratory. Management did not really know how Black was spending their millions, but they would perhaps have protested if they had heard that Black was working in the same direction as corporate research at Philadelphia, on ulcer therapy, but following an entirely different and highly speculative route. In the end, however, Black's work resulted in Tagamet, the world's first 'billion dollar drug'.

Even at Hewlett-Packard, known for its innovative atmosphere, researchers have on some occasions been compelled to use guile in order to realize their autonomous strategies. The celebrated Dave Packard once took an on-the-spot decision that all the work on a certain electronic device should cease. The researchers ignored the order by sticking to its letter – that Packard didn't want to see the product in the lab when he came round next year. So they finished the product within twelve months, much to the profit of Hewlett-Packard.

(Source: Heller, 1989: 37, 62)

Burgelman sees strategy-making as a multi-layered process. Lower management defines (investment) opportunities and proposes projects to middle management. Middle management selects projects to be endorsed *vis-à-vis* top management. Top management defines the structural context within which middle and lower management operates. It does so by formulating general strategic aims and policies, and by the design of the incentive structure operative in the organization (the 'structural context').

Two kinds of strategies can be distinguished: **induced strategies** and **autonomous strategies**. Induced strategies consist of strategic initiatives that fit into the general strategy formulated by top management. These initiatives can be characterized as 'business as usual'. They tend to reaffirm the existing structure and strategy. The projects that embody the induced strategy have a good chance of surviving the selection process at the middle management level, because they are well aligned with the structural context. As the general strategy as well as the structural context are set by top management, the development of induced strategies is predominantly a top-down process.

Autonomous strategies do not fit in the officially promulgated strategy. They can be pet projects of local managers, who perceive an opportunity that has not been noticed by top management (see Box 6.2). Most of these strategies are weeded out, but some are likely to receive support because they appear to constitute an opportunity to change the promulgated strategy in a way opportune to middle managers. The possibilities to influence the corporate strategy by proposing unconventional but promising projects constitute the 'strategic context'. This strategic context is influenced, but not completely determined, by the structural context.

Autonomous strategies that are adopted become part of the official strategy, and therefore influence that strategy. This is a bottom-up process. Organizations need both kinds of strategies: induced strategies in order to achieve and maintain coherence; and autonomous strategies to enhance responsiveness.

6.3 Organizational structure and strategic decision making

In the preceding section the question concerning the causal relations between strategy and structure has been discussed. In this section we will look in somewhat more detail at the interplay of structure and strategic decision making. More specifically, we will focus on three elements of organizational structure, centralization, formalization and differentiation, and on the basic configurations (entrepreneurial organization, machine organization and adhocracy organization) discussed above. We will consider the effect of centralization, formalization and differentiation on the direction of strategic decision making (top-down versus bottom-up), and on the rationality and the formality of the strategic decision-making process. As there are few detailed and systematic studies of these kinds of relationships, we will in some cases in the absence of solid empirical evidence have to rely on plausible conjectures.

Centralization

In the conventional view strategy formulation is pre-eminently a task of top management (Mintzberg, 1990a). Thus little decentralization of strategic decision making would be expected, particularly in organizations that are characterized by a centralized overall structure. Whatever decentralization of strategic decision making is to be expected in a centralized organization will be horizontal rather than vertical in direction. This means that top management delegates certain steps in the decision-making process to a staff department, for example, issue recognition and the generation and evaluation of options. At the same time, the actual choice of a strategy will remain a prerogative of top management (Grayson, 1987: 59–61).

Centralization and the strategic decision process

In an empirical study of strategy-making processes and structure of 97 small and medium-sized firms to which we will refer repeatedly, Miller found a significant negative relationship between the degree of centralization and a dimension of the decision process indicated as 'interaction' (Miller, 1987). This dimension reflects the extent of bargaining in the strategic decision-making process, and an orientation towards consensus-building rather than decision making by individual managers. Thus a low score on 'interaction' can be taken to imply that the direction of the strategic decision process is top-down rather than bottom-up. This relationship was to be expected, and has been hypothesized before (Frederickson, 1986).

Miller did not find a relationship between the degree of centralization and a second dimension of the decision process, the 'decision rationality'. The rationality of the strategic decision process in Miller's study was associated, among other things, with the use of operations research techniques, the use of formalized, systematic search for and evaluation of market opportunities, a long-term orientation, explicitness of the strategy and the use of environmental scanning devices. In view of the operationalization of this dimension, it can be characterized as a measure of the procedural rationality of the strategic decision-making process and of the use of standardized procedures.

Finally, Miller did not analyse the relationship between centralization and the formalization of strategic decision making, but the raw correlations reported in his study show no significant relationships between elements of the 'rationality' dimension that are logically associated with formal decision procedures and the degree of centralization of the organizational structure. (These elements are 'analysis', 'explicitness' and 'scanning', Miller, 1987.) Other studies suggest that centralization of power tends to be associated with an informal approach (see, e.g., Horvath and MacMillan, 1979; Mintzberg and Waters, 1982).

Strategic decision making in the entrepreneurial organization

The basic structural configuration that is most strongly characterized by centralization is the entrepreneurial organization. (See Mintzberg, 1989. In earlier work, Mintzberg referred to this configuration as the 'simple structure – 1979; see also Miller, 1986.) In this type of organization a considerable degree of power is centralized in the person of the chief executive, who often also is the owner and founder of the firm. Thus it is logical to expect a strongly dominant top-down direction in strategic decision making. Strategy formation takes place more on the basis of vision and intuition than on the basis of extensive and systematic analysis. Formalization of the decision-making process will presumably be low, as formal procedures only get into the way of the creative mind of the top executive (Mintzberg, 1994: 410–11; Mintzberg and Waters, 1982, 1983). The decision-making process is characterized by a personal, intuitive and result-orientated approach (Shrivastava and Grant, 1985).

Formalization

Formalization, as mentioned earlier, refers to the regulation of behaviour by formal rules and procedures. The degree of formalization within an organization will presumably have an influence on its strategic decision-making processes.

Formalization and the strategic decision-making process

Formalization of the organization in general will almost by definition also lead to formality in strategy making. Therefore we can leave this aspect of the strategic decision-making process out of consideration here. As far as the other two aspects of strategic decision making are concerned, Miller's study revealed no influence of the degree of formalization on the dominant direction of the strategic decision-making process (top-down or bottom-up). However, we must remember that his study focused on small and medium-sized firms. In larger firms, with large specialized planning departments and extensive strategic decision procedures, the degree of formalization may reasonably be assumed to have a bearing on the direction of the decision process. Mintzberg observed that, notwithstanding all the rhetoric to the contrary, formalization of planning procedures has the effect of augmenting the role of staff departments, at the expense of the influence and involvement of line managers (Mintzberg, 1994: 30–31). This, however, does hardly amount to a shift from top-down to bottom-up.

Miller did find a significant positive relationship between formalization and the procedural rationality of the strategic decision-making process. This is not surprising: in an organization that tries to programme and control as many processes as possible, strategic decision making will be no exception. Thus the kind of techniques and procedures that form a large part of Miller's 'rationality' scale are to be expected. However, it should be stressed that this kind of rationality in the strategic decision-making process has its price. Standardized procedures may entail the gathering and processing of enormous amounts of information, but these processes in and by themselves do not necessarily lead to a good strategy. Even worse, the emphasis on procedural rationality may drive out substantive rationality. Thus the creative side of decision making, needed for setting up new and innovative strategies, tends to be discouraged by formalization (Mintzberg, 1994: 308–21; Mintzberg and Waters, 1983).

Strategic decision making in the machine organization

The basic configuration most strongly characterized by formalization is the machine organization (Miller, 1986; Mintzberg, 1979; 1989). This kind of organization is the place where the most extensive forms of formal strategic planning are to be found (Mintzberg, 1994: 399). The obsession with control in these organizations leads to an intensive analysis of problems and solutions (Shrivastava and Grant, 1985). However, the decision process tends to be reactive rather than proactive, and a machine organization rarely develops a radically new strategy. Standard 'mainline strategies', accepted in industry, are much more likely (Horvath and MacMillan, 1979; Mintzberg, 1994: 398–404; Mintzberg and Waters, 1983).

Differentiation

Differentiation refers to the division of labour within the firm. It is related to specialization and complexity: the more differentiated the organization is, the higher the degree of specialization and complexity will also be. In Miller's study differentiation *per se* was not measured. However, Miller did look at the degree of specialization, and this will be used as a proxy for differentiation.

Differentiation and the strategic decision process

Miller's findings show a strong positive relationship between specialization and 'interaction'. This indicates that in highly specialized (differentiated) organizations the strategic decision-making process tends to be less of a top-down nature. This makes sense, since complex differentiated organizations are more opaque and therefore less easy to direct from above. As top management cannot oversee and understand all processes taking place at lower levels, strategy making has to be bottom-up, at least in part.

Miller also found a strong positive relationship between specialization and the procedural rationality of the decision-making process. This is less easy to understand: standardization of strategic decision making would appear to be more difficult as the organization becomes more complex. On the other hand, greater complexity and opacity of the organization can also cause management to emphasize procedures more strongly – without necessarily achieving more rationality and control in this way. Moreover, Miller's finding can perhaps be better understood if we realize that his 'decision rationality' construct does not exclusively consist of items reflecting a strong degree of standardization. For instance, 'periodic brainstorming by senior management groups for novel solutions to problems' is also an element of 'decision rationality', but is not readily associated with the use of standardized procedures (Miller, 1987: 32). According to one study formal forms of analysis in highly differentiated organizations serve purposes of communication rather than planning and control (Langley, 1989).

Finally, although Miller provides no data on this, it seems reasonable to conjecture a negative relationship between the degree of intra-organizational differentiation and the formality of strategic decision-making. Formalization of behaviour is most often found in repetitive activities. Strategy making in highly differentiated organizations is unlikely to be such a repetitive activity.

Strategic decision making in the adhocracy organization

The epitome of a highly differentiated, and, consequently, highly complex organization is the 'adhocracy' organization (Miller, 1986; Mintzberg, 1979; 1989). An adhocracy is also characterized by a low level of formalization, and often has the structure of a matrix or of a project organization. Adhocracy organizations appear to achieve coordination by means of 'a very loose form of strategic programming, which outlines broad targets and a set of milestones while leaving considerable flexibility to adapt to dead ends and creative discoveries along what must remain a largely uncharted route' (Mintzberg, 1994: 408–9).

6.4 Organizational culture

Not only the structure of the organization influences the strategic decision-making process. The organizational culture is also relevant. The concept of 'organizational culture' is more difficult to grasp than that of organizational structure, and there has been less empirical research into its relation to strategy making. (Most of the existing studies are of the case study type, e.g. Whipp et al., 1989.) But this does not mean that the influence of organizational culture on the strategic decision process is less important. Below we will first of all concentrate on the questions of what organizational culture is, how it is formed, and which dimensions of organizational culture can be distinguished. Next we will, notwithstanding the dearth of empirical evidence, consider the relationship between organizational culture and strategic decision making. Finally the issue of deliberately changing the culture of an organization will be discussed briefly.

What is organizational culture?

The concept of **culture** has been described as 'a collective programming of the mind' (Hofstede, 1980). This description captures an essential aspect of culture, namely the fact that 'human behavior is partially prescribed by a collectively created and sustained way of life' (Van Maanen and Barley, 1985: 31). The collectivity in question can be, for example, an ethnic group, a nation, or an organization.

Elements of culture

Four groups of elements can be distinguished in the phenomena related to culture: the basic assumptions or tacit beliefs underlying one's view of the world; the values that form the evaluational basis utilized for judging situations and actions; socially shared rules and norms; and artefacts expressing these assumptions, values and norms. These groups of elements are often seen as the skins of an onion, with the basic assumptions at the core and the artefacts closest to the surface (see Figure 6.6) (Lundberg, 1985).

The basic assumptions and tacit beliefs are related to the cognitive schemata discussed in Chapter 4. Shared basic assumptions (e.g. 'prosperity is the fruit of hard work') determine the kind of explanations of reality that are socially constructed and reinforced. Shared values (for example, 'to be honest is right'; 'to steal is wrong') determine which kinds of behaviours will be approved or disapproved within a given community. They lie at the basis of rules and norms that apply to concrete situations and that may be – but not

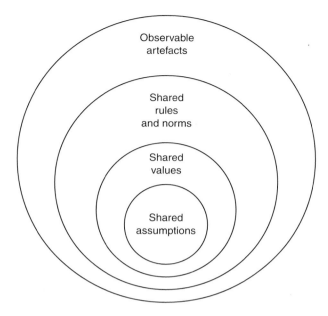

Figure 6.6 Levels of culture.

necessarily always are – codified and sanctioned. Verbal artefacts are written or oral texts, statements, or even single words or phrases that express or reflect the assumptions, values, and so on, typical of the culture. Behavioural artefacts are, for instance, rituals: 'collective activities that are technically superfluous but are socially essential within a culture – they are therefore carried out for their own sake' (Hofstede et al., 1990: 291). Physical artefacts, finally, are tangible reflections of the culture, like the outlook of housing and facilities, the style of the furnishings and decor, the way people dress, and so on.

Organizational culture

If the cultural community in question is an organization we are dealing with **organizational culture**. On this level, culture may be defined as 'the collective programming of the mind which distinguishes the members of one organization from another' (Hofstede, 1991: 180). The members of an organization also belong to other groups of course, for instance, a particular social class, a regional or an ethnic group, a nationality, and an occupational or professional group (Johnson and Scholes, 1993: 47). This means that their values, assumptions, and so on, are not only connected with the culture of the organization, but also, and in many cases predominantly, with that of the other groups they belong to. In general, organizational cultures (within a given national culture) vary predominantly with regard to rules, norms, and artefacts. National cultures also

Box 6.3 'Big Blue comes to Steve's garage'

In corporate mergers and acquisitions, as well as in joint ventures, differences between the organizational cultures of the partners are often a source of problems. Against this background, a joint venture between IBM and Apple would appear to be particularly accident-prone. All the same, such a joint venture has been set up: Taligent, a software firm that is to develop an object-oriented operating system to compete with Microsoft. On the face of it, Taligent looks much more like Apple than like IBM. Dress, for instance, is informal at Taligent. CEO Joe Guglielmi, an IBM veteran, now has to do without the elaborate support structure that used to characterize IBM. Instead of a staff consisting of a senior secretary, an assistant, and an office worker to handle the mail, Guglielmi now has to make do with one administrative assistant. And he does his own mail. The advantage of having to cope without all these assistants? 'An executive at IBM really has to work hard to stay in touch with what's going on. If you never experience the problem – but only read about it – you're so detached it's hard to imagine coming up with the solution'. In these respects, it looks like 'Big Blue comes to Steve's garage', as a commentator equipped. But on the other hand, in some ways the new venture also looks – or tries to look – somewhat more like IBM. Guglielmi likes to measure performance, and tries to impose it on the Taligent employees, most of whom come from either Apple or some small Silicon Valley firm. Although the first instinct of the Apple people is to resist, Guglielmi is confident that they will learn to like it if they see that it works. 'And if it doesn't, we try something else'.

(Source: Huey, 1993).

show important differences with regard to the core factors of basic assumptions and values (Hofstede, 1991: 182); Hofstede et al., 1990).

The elements that build an organizational culture are more situation-specific than those of a national culture. For example, an organizational culture may be characterized by norms such as 'it's not the rules that are important, but the result', or 'keeping the customer satisfied is the most important thing'. Examples of shared assumptions within an organization might be 'our product is technically superior', or 'our force lies in our relationship with our clients'. Visible features of an organizational culture are the manners of interaction, customary dress, the exterior and interior of company buildings, and so forth.

The question of whether shared assumptions or shared values lie at the ultimate core of (organizational) culture appears to be debatable. The fact that values are acquired in early childhood, and afterwards show considerable resistance to change, would seem to be an argument to place them at the deepest level of culture (cf. Hofstede et al., 1990). Assumptions, at least some categories of assumptions, may be of a more specific and variable nature. Assumptions with regard to best practices of management, for instance, are quite industry specific and often take the form of **industry recipes** (Spender, 1989; see also Gordon, 1991).

However, some authors explicitly place values at a higher (i.e. less profound) level than assumptions (e.g. Lundberg, 1985; Schein, 1985). In other cases the values that are assumed to be representative for the organizational culture appear to be those of the founder or of an influential top manager of the organization (cf. Hofstede et al., 1990: 311). These values, although perhaps partly internalized by the other organizational members, are unlikely to replace those acquired at early childhood, which presumably remain at the core of their individual psychological set-up. We do not intend to pursue this discussion any further here. Ultimately, the question of which group of elements is closer to the core, assumptions or values, is not very fruitful. Organizational culture is a dynamic system, all the elements of which are closely interrelated (Baligh, 1994; Hatch, 1993). There is hardly a point in giving a privileged position to one of the terms.

Strong and weak organizational cultures

According to the definition of organizational culture formulated above virtually every organization has its own culture. After all, there will almost always be some overlap between the assumptions, and so forth, of the individual organization members. But it is useful to distinguish between 'strong' and 'weak' organization cultures. A **strong** culture is widespread in the organization, and is shared by many of the organization members (O'Reilly, 1989). To put it differently, an organization with a strong culture is culturally homogeneous. In this case the assumptions, values and views of most of the people within the organization are by and large the same. A **weak** organization culture is shared by only a limited number of organization members; the organization is culturally heterogeneous. Strong 'subcultures' may nevertheless exist within parts of the organization, but taken as a whole, the organizational culture is incoherent. In this case the organization as a whole is no more than an 'umbrella' for a collection of subcultures (Martin et al., 1985).

An organizational culture is strongest if all its elements fit together into a seamless whole. In an internally consistent cultural system the assumptions are consistent with one another and with the basic values, which in turn are consistent with the norms and rules, and all of these are reflected in the artefacts.

An organizational culture can also be called 'strong' to indicate that it exerts an intense influence on the behaviour of organization members. (Luthans, 1992: 564). The values of such a culture are at the centre of the behavioural motivators. The rules dictated by a dominant culture cannot easily be disobeyed, because of the strong reactions evoked by such behaviour. A strong culture leaves little room for deviants. A weak culture permits greater tolerance: people have less difficulty accepting behaviour deviating from the norm if that norm is fostered less strongly.

In sum, the influence of the organizational culture on the behaviour of the organization members (and thus also on strategic decision making) is a function of the homogeneity, the consistency and the intensity of that organizational culture.

The development of organizational culture

Socialization

Two factors shape the culture of an organization. One has already been mentioned, namely the influence organization members exert on each other. This is called the **socialization** process (Pascale, 1985). A newcomer to an organization in his interaction with the other organization members gradually discovers what is seen as right and wrong behaviour. Sources of information are the reactions to his or her acts, and the moral indictments betrayed by stories and anecdotes. Eventually the newcomer comes to share, wholly or in part, the assumptions and values that form the basis of the organizational culture, and behaving in conformity with them becomes the natural thing to do.

Socialization is not only, and not even predominantly, a conscious activity. On the contrary, the person in question will often not be aware of the accommodation process, and after a while his or her values and worldview appear to have adapted spontaneously. But managers can try to manipulate or reinforce the socialization process. We will return to this point.

Selection

The second process determining the culture of an organization is that of **selection**. When hiring new personnel, those candidates that fit well into the organization naturally are preferred. 'Fitting well' into an organization is more or less synonymous with harmonizing with the dominant organizational culture. Selection is not limited to the moment of entry into the organization; later on organization members are also evaluated at key moments, for example, at the occasion of a possible promotion. One of the criteria is likely to be whether the person in question is 'a pleasurable colleague', measuring – apart from personality traits – the extent of assimilation to the organizational culture (Van Maanen and Barley, 1985).

Self-selection also plays an important role. Someone who does not feel attracted to the specific culture of the military will not apply for a job as a professional soldier. And in case the applicant was not familiar with the organization culture beforehand, self-selection may cause him or her to leave the organization at the first opportunity. The various forces shaping organizational culture are summed up in Figure 6.7.

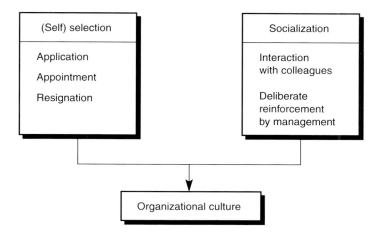

Figure 6.7 Forces shaping organizational culture.

6.5 Organizational culture and strategic decision making

Strength of culture and strategic decision making

Culture is an important factor at all stages of the decision-making process. As perception is culture-bound, the question which set of stimuli leads to problem recognition is to a large extent determined by the organizational culture. Furthermore, the norms and values emphasized by the organizational culture influence the selection of goals in the decision-making process. For every stage of the decision-making process examples of the importance of the cultural factor could be given.

However, we will avoid going into detail, and only consider the influence of the strength of the organizational culture on two broadly defined stages in the strategic decision process as discussed in Chapter 2: strategy formulation (the 'awareness' and 'analysis' modules of the decision-making process) and strategy implementation (the 'action' module).

Strategy formulation

As far as strategy formulation is concerned, a strong organizational culture will be instrumental in reaching a consensus regarding problem formulation, goals and means. But a strong organizational culture also has serious drawbacks in this phase of the decision-making process. This is most obvious with regard to problem recognition and problem formulation. In an organization with a homogeneous culture, most organization members perceive the environment in the same way. This means that only certain kinds of data are taken into consideration, and that there is a strong tendency to formulate problems in a certain pre-defined way (Johnson, 1988). For instance, in a firm with a strong technical orientation a drop in market share is likely to be defined as a problem that has to do with the technical specifications rather than with the intangible features of the product. This definition of the problem will subsequently have a strong impact on the definition of goals, the generation and evaluation of alternatives, and the choice of a solution.

In short, a very strong organizational culture may cause 'tunnel vision'. It is very useful for an organization if (moderate) divergencies continue to exist in spite of a shared culture. Our emphasis on the dangers of too strong organizational cultures seems to contrast with the popular view of strong organizational cultures as a source of success (see, e.g., Peters and Waterman's 'excellent firms') (Peters and Waterman, 1982). A strong organizational culture may be very functional in a given situation, but become a severe handicap if the organization has to adapt to changed circumstances (Coffey et al., 1994: 47). The fact that some of Peters and Waterman's 'excellent firms' ran into difficulties soon after the publication of their bestseller seems to support this view. (See 'Who's excellent now? Some of the bestseller's picks haven't been doing so well lately', *Business Week*, 5 November, 1984.)

Strategy implementation

In the strategy implementation phase the issues are somewhat different. Here the emphasis is not so much on creativity and vision, as in the assessment of a problem situation and the design of a solution, but on the loyal and intelligent execution of the plan. Loyal execution means that if not the letter at least the spirit of the strategy promulgated by top management is complied with. It will be clear that a strong organizational culture breeds loyalty. Therefore such a culture can be an important asset (cf. Bourgeois and Brodwin, 1984).

But the execution of strategic plans also has to be intelligent, of course. Strategic plans often are conceived at top management level and formulated at a high level of abstractness, and therefore inevitably contain a certain degree of vagueness. It is the task of middle management and lower managers to translate the vague formulations of the strategic plan into concrete action plans. This gives them the opportunity to adapt the strategy to local circumstances only they know in detail, and to experiment with variations within the theme of the officially promulgated strategy.

In an organization with too strong a culture, middle and lower management adopt top management's strategic decisions without question. Translation of the general strategy into concrete action plans is performed in a mechanical way in this case. This means that an important source of learning is cut off. The practical value of a strategy becomes clear only in the confrontation with reality, that is, in the day-to-day wheeling and dealing of the organization. If top management is denied feedback on strong and weak points of the strategy as it works out in practice, there is no basis for improvement (Mintzberg,

1990a). To be sure, sooner or later the success or failure of the strategy will become clear from its effect on the 'bottom line'. But if more detailed information is absent, it is impossible to say just which elements of the strategy have bred the observed success or failure.

Dimensions of culture and strategic decision making

Hofstede's research

In one of the few quantitative studies of organizational cultures, Hofstede and associates empirically identified six dimensions of perceived organizational practices (Hofstede et al., 1990). (Hofstede's findings are largely consonant with the findings of studies focusing on central values in organizational cultures; see Chatman and Jehn, 1994.) The concept of 'perceived organizational practice' refers to symbols, heroes and rituals, the three outer shells of Hofstede's model of manifestations of culture. These practices by and large correspond to what was referred to as 'observable artefacts' above. They are assumed to reflect the deeper layers of culture.

In the case of Hofstede's model, this deeper layer is assumed to consist in the values of the organization members. Hofstede found important differences in these basic values across countries, but not between organizations within one national culture (Hofstede, 1980; 1991; Hofstede et al., 1990). The general assumptions with regard to the nature of reality that apparently are also part of the core of culture in Hofstede's model are equally unlikely to vary significantly across organizations (cf. Hofstede et al., 1990: 311).

Organization-specific assumptions, however, as discussed above, are more closely tied to industries and individual organizations, and therefore may be assumed to be important variables when measuring organizational culture. We interpret Hofstede and associates' concept of 'perceived organizational practices' to reflect also these organization-specific assumptions. As we will see below, these practices are based on specific views on, for example, the type of persons to be found in the organization, the typical attitude of managers within the organization, and the key factors leading to success for the organization.

Dimensions of organizational culture

Hofstede and associates identified six dimensions of organizational culture. We will focus on two of these: process versus results-orientated organizational cultures; and employee versus job-orientated organizational cultures. **Process-orientated** organizations are very much concerned with rules and procedures; in **results-orientated** organizations it is the outcome rather than the process followed or the technique used that counts. This dimension is related to the well-known distinction between mechanistic (process-orientated) and organic (result-orientated) organizations (Hofstede et al., 1990: 302); cf. Burns and Stalker (1961). In **employee-orientated** organizations the individual well-being of the employees is seen as very important; **job-orientated** organizations focus more on the function than on the person. Here a link with group roles ('initiating structure' and 'showing consideration') and with leadership style ('autocratic', 'human relations', *laissez-faire*, and 'democratic') is obvious.

The link with strategic decision making

In the absence of empirical data with regard to the relationship between the dimensions of culture distinguished by Hofstede and associates and characteristics of strategic decision-making processes, we will have to rely on logical conjectures and indirect evidence. Schneider, in a exploratory study of the relationship between national culture and the process of strategy formulation, distinguished, among others, two dimensions of culture that seem to parallel those found by Hofstede and associates (Schneider, 1989). The process versus results orientation appears to be related to Schneider's distinction between uncertainty avoiding and uncertainty tolerating cultures. This seems to be plausible on the basis of two of the three 'key indicators' of Hofstede's results orientation – 'comfortable in unfamiliar settings' and 'each day brings new challenges' – as well as some of the other items, e.g. 'try to be pioneers' and 'mistakes are tolerated' (Hofstede et al., 1990: 303). Schneider's dimension itself is based on Hofstede's well-known study of national cultures (Hofstede 1980). The employee versus job-orientation is clearly related to Schneider's social versus task-orientation dimension. When interpreting Schneider's conclusions and conjectures, we will have to bear in mind, however, that 'national cultures and organizational cultures are phenomena of different orders' (Hofstede et al., 1990: 313). The validity of any conclusion for comparisons across organizations within a single national culture is uncertain.

As far as the uncertainty-avoiding dimension is concerned, Schneider concludes that this orientation (in contrast to an uncertainty-tolerating culture) may be assumed to be associated with more formal scanning and forecasting activities in order to identify events that may have an impact on future organizational performance. (Hofstede (1984) also hypothesizes a positive relationship between the level of uncertainty avoidance in a national culture and the degree of formalization of organizations within that culture.) Organizations with an uncertainty-avoiding culture may also be expected to search predominantly for quantitative (or quantifiable) information. Qualitative information, which is by nature more ambiguous, is more likely to be ignored. Furthermore, emerging issues are validated by means of bureaucratic rules in such organizations. This means that only issues that fit into one of the categories on the checklist used for the 'external audit' have a fair chance of being recognized (cf. Mintzberg, 1994: 54–6). An uncertainty-avoiding culture may also be assumed to be associated with the use of analytic tools in the interpretation of information. Finally, according to Schneider uncertainty-avoidance leads to more emphasis on short-term, operational plans, while organizations with a higher tolerance for uncertainty would focus on long-term, strategic plans. (This conjecture is based on Horovitz's (1980) study of top management in Europe. This study has received criticism, however, mainly because some of its findings are contradicted by several more recent studies; see Lane, 1989: 120–25.)

A culture characterized by a social orientation (in contrast to a task orientation) is associated with a preference for personal and subjective sources over impersonal sources of information. Validation of the information gathered and strategic issues identified takes place on the basis of consensus, in an interactive process between the managers concerned. An organization with a social orientation would also be more likely to give priority to issues such as job security, employee welfare, health and safety, and product quality, than an organization with a task orientation. (Hofstede, 1984, assumes that the task orientation versus social orientation is associated with the level of individualism of the national culture; in individualist cultures the task orientation would be expected to dominate.)

On the basis of various cultural dimensions and related aspects of strategic decision-making processes, Schneider constructed two broad models of strategy formulation, the **controlling model** and the **adapting model**. The controlling model, expected in cultures that are characterized, among other things, by uncertainty reduction and a task orientation, is described as (Schneider, 1989: 160):

> a top-down process, controlled by the dominant elite, involving formal long-term planning, with reliance on quantitative information and analytical techniques so that strategies are arrived at 'objectively'. This model represents a strategic planning approach.

The adapting model is expected in uncertainty tolerating, social-orientated cultures. This model is characterized as (Schneider, 1989: 160):

> a more bottom-up activity, involving people at multiple levels, with more reliance on qualitative information and intuition. Here, strategies evolve or emerge in the form of adaptive and reactive behaviours, constrained by the organizational and environmental context. This model represents a more emergent, incremental, adjustment orientated, or evolutionary approach.

Schneider suggests that these two models are representative for 'stereotypic views' of the United States and Japan (Schneider, 1989: 162). However, on the basis of the study of Hofstede and associates discussed above a point can be made that they also form the extremes of dimensions that lie at the heart of cultural differences of organizations within one particular national culture. The controlling strategy described by Schneider bears a strong resemblance to an approach to planning that in the next chapter will be discussed under the heading of **synoptical planning**. This model is indeed very typical for the mainstream normative approach to business strategy in United States management theory. (Mintzberg, 1990a, b; 1994). The adapting approach bears resemblance to **logical incrementalism**, also to be discussed in the next chapter, an approach which aims to reflect actual decision-making practices found in United States firms. Thus, it is all but clear that the controlling strategy is indeed typical for the actual decision-making processes within United States firms. In analysing organizational culture (national) stereotypes should be kept at bay.

6.6 Changing organizational culture

Can organizational culture be changed?

Functionality of organization culture

The importance of cultural factors to organizational effectiveness is stressed in the popular management press. Peters and Waterman, for instance, in their book on 'excellent companies' mention several characteristics of successful companies, but the special importance of culture is underlined: 'Without exception, the dominance and coherence of culture proved to be an essential quality of the excellent companies' (Peters and Waterman, 1982; 75). Note that both elements of a strong culture discussed above are mentioned in this quotation: dominance and coherence.

However, an organizational culture should not only be strong, but also functional. A culture stressing the importance of low-cost production is dysfunctional when the product in question is (no longer) seen as a commodity. The classic example is Henry Ford's stubborn pursuit of cost-effectiveness and persistence in producing only one type of car, the T-model. The managers at General Motors realized much earlier that the United States customer desired a differentiated product. On the other hand, a too strong orientation to customers may be dysfunctional in a firm that threatens to lose control over the production process as a result of excessive customization.

Given the importance of the functionality of a culture the question arises whether organizational culture, or at least of the dysfunctional elements of it, can be deliberately changed (Hassard and Sharifi, 1989).

A time-consuming process

A first observation is that a change in culture may be expected to be a much more time-consuming process than a change in an organization's strategy or structure. Deep-rooted values and worldviews are at issue. It is not possible simply to order someone to look at the world in a different way, or to make different value judgements. This means that the existing organizational culture, however functional it may have been in the past, can be a major obstacle in case of a change in the strategy pursued (Johnson, 1988; 1992). Moreover, neither culture nor strategy or structure can be changed drastically without also adapting the other elements.

Culture is more correctly depicted as something an organization *is* rather than something an organization *has* (Smircich, 1983). Managers are influenced by the existing culture, just like other organization members. Consequently, a manager wanting to bring about a planned change of culture has to perform an act like that of Baron Munchausen who pulled himself and his horse out of the quicksand by his own ponytail. However, under some circumstances it will be less difficult to change culture. For instance, if a firm is taken over by another corporation, new management is often installed, not yet imbued with the existing culture (Martin et al., 1985).

Studies of efforts to change organizational cultures suggest that total culture changes are extremely difficult to perform (Beer et al., 1990; Mirvis and Berg, 1977). Support from top management is essential, but a top-down planned change programme has little chance of success. The most effective cultural change programmes start from a relatively small basis, and gradually spread throughout the organization. Changes in the organizational structure should follow, rather than precede cultural change.

We will assume that deliberately influencing an organizational culture is difficult, but not altogether impossible (cf. Luthans, 1992: 573; Whipp et al., 1989; for a different view see, e.g., Robbins, 1990; 456–7).

Instruments

Assuming that cultural change can be managed, what instruments are available? Presumably the two processes that give shape to an organizational culture, socialization and selection, can to some extent be manipulated consciously.

Achieving cultural change through socialization

Socialization normally takes places through the interaction with colleagues, but it can be reinforced and directed with special programmes (see Box 6.4). Various instruments can be used: information dissemination through the company magazine, talks by top managers, group discussions, training seminars, and so on.

The cost of such programmes can be substantial. At the same time, the effect is uncertain. The chances of accomplishing a transformation of culture are best if there is a clear necessity for change, and if top management has sufficient credibility within the organization. If the top has announced changes before, but has not been able to realize these intentions, it will be difficult to convince the employees once more. And even if changes in the organizational culture have been achieved, it is very difficult to let them take root. People often slip back into the old patterns. After all, norms, values and assumptions are also influenced by factors outside of the grasp of management: man is more than just an employee.

Achieving cultural change through selection

The second instrument that can be used to change a culture is that of selection. The policy with regard to hiring and promotion can be geared to populate the

Box 6.4 Managing organizational culture in the Japanese firm

Organizational culture also has a prominent place in many explanations of the success of Japanese enterprises. The personnel policy of many Japanese firms emphasizes norms geared to cooperation and harmony. Selection and training of organization members establishes and reinforces these norms. In the selection of prospective managers, not necessarily the most brilliant candidates succeed, but those that are assumed to fit well into the company's culture. The selected candidates enter a commitment with the firm that in principle spans their entire career ('lifetime employment'). Before actually entering the firm the new employees go through a socialization programme often referred to as 'spiritual education'. Such a programme may encompass, for example, military drilling, volunteer work on farms, Zen meditation, and endurance walks. The goal of these activities is to teach moral values through experience rather than words. Early in their career young managers frequently change posts, so that they learn to know all parts of the company. A too strong bond with any specific department or division is also avoided in this way. Every time the young manager gets another assignment a new socialization programme has to be followed. In the selection for promotion to higher management levels individual achievements are less important than the ability to function well in groups. The result of this policy is a very strong loyalty of the Japanese manager to his company as a whole.

(Sources: Rohlen, 1973; Terpstra and David, 1991)

organization with individuals with the desired mental characteristics. But this is also a time-consuming process, as it is mostly impossible to replace a sizeable part of the workforce in a short time. In the case of a change of strategy triggered by a crisis it may be necessary to lay off many employees. This necessity may be used to bring about a shift in culture by sending away the employees with unwanted norms and values. It will be wise not to make explicit such a policy, otherwise strong opposition, for instance from the side of the trade unions, is to be expected. In most cases the replacement of personnel is a step-by-step process, and consequently will not yield quick results.

And then there is always the danger that the socialization process undoes the effects of a careful selection procedure, if new organization members adapt to the existing culture. This is especially true for blue-collar workers, who are much more remote from the norms and values of top management than for instance middle managers. All in all, influencing the organizational culture is one of the most difficult tasks in strategic management.

Chapter summary

- Important elements of organizational structures are centralization, formalization, differentiation, integration and the basis of departmentation.

- Organizational structure follows organizational strategy in so far as management adapts the structure to the requirements arising from the adoption of a new strategy.

- Strategy follows structure in so far as the existing structure influences the formation of strategy, via the perception of the organization members and via the existing power relations.

- Induced strategies arise in the organization in response to the overall strategy and structure set by top management; autonomous strategies arise in the margin, and in spite of the existing strategy and structure, but can change both if successful.

- Structural centralization is associated with top-down strategic decision making. Structural formalization is associated with a formalized and procedurally rational strategic decision-making process. Structural differentiation is associated with a bottom-up strategic decision-making process.

- Organizational culture is the collective programming of the minds of organization members, expressed in shared assumptions, values, rules and norms and artefacts.

- Strong organizational cultures are homogeneous, consistent, and intense.

- Organizational culture is developed and maintained through processes of socialization and (self-) selection.

- In cultures characterized by uncertainty reduction and a strong task orientation a controlling mode of strategic decision making is to be expected; in cultures characterized by tolerance for uncertainty and a strong social orientation an adapting mode of strategic decision making.

- Organizational culture can to a certain degree be changed through a conscious manipulation of the processes of socialization and selection. This is a difficult and time-consuming process.

7

Organizational decision-making processes

In this chapter we will discuss various conceptual models of organizational decision making. We will roughly follow the chronological order in which the models have been developed. The various approaches are also compared, and their applicability under different circumstances is assessed. After that, a large-scale empirical study of organizational decision making is discussed, and the outcomes of this study are compared with the conceptual models.

7.1 Four conceptual models of organizational decision making

Many – if not most – of the approaches to organizational decision making are based on theoretical considerations or preconceived conceptions about how organizations do or should make decisions, rather than on systematic empirical research. These conceptual models can be grouped into four categories: **synoptical planning models**, **disjointed incrementalism**, **logical incrementalism** and the **interpretative approach**.

Synoptical planning

The synoptical planning model is a prescriptive model, rooted in endeavours to formulate guidelines for practical management. According to this model, top management should periodically reconsider all aspects and functions of the organization. In this way, a strategy and a plan for realizing that strategy should be formulated in a systematic way. The approach is 'synoptical' in that the strategic decision process is all-embracing: all relevant aspects of an organization's activities should be dealt with in a single comprehensive procedure.

Two variants of the synoptical planning school can be distinguished: the 'design school' and the 'strategic planning school'. (The denominations are taken from Mintzberg, 1990b; 1994.) Both approaches share many characteristics. We will first discuss the design school; then we focus on the strategic planning school.

The design school

The design school approach is characterized by a strong emphasis on top-down decision making. (The discussion of the design school is based on Mintzberg, 1990a, 1994: 36–9. Authors associated with this approach are, e.g., Andrews, 1971, 1980; Learned et al., 1965; Christensen et al., 1987.) The top manager or chief executive officer is assumed to be *the* strategist. The possibility – and in many cases necessity – of support by lower managers and staff specialists is acknowledged, but their role is seen as largely constricted to information gathering in the service of the CEO, and to the loyal implementation of the strategy once it has been formulated. The actual design of that strategy is assumed to take place inside the brain of the top manager.

The strategic decision process prescribed by the design school is akin to the prototypical model of the normative-rational approach depicted in Figure 2.4: a linear sequence of discrete steps. Adoption of this model implies that strategy formulation and strategy implementation are separate activities, with formulation preceding implementation. This order may appear self-evident, but, in combination with the presumption that the CEO is *the* strategist, it also implies that strategies must come out of the design process fully developed, ready to be implemented. Consequently, there is little leeway for adapting the strategy to unforeseen circumstances.

The emphasis on the CEO as the key strategy designer also implies that the strategy must be made explicit: it has to be communicated to other members of the organization who have not been involved in the formulation of the strategy, but who are assumed to implement it. Another consequence of the key role of the CEO is that the process of strategy formulation should be kept simple and informal: the complexity should be limited to what can be contained in the mind of a single individual; and no formal procedures are necessary if all decisions are taken by the CEO.

The characteristics of the design school form a hermetical and consistent whole, built around the principles of strategy formation as a controlled and conscious process and of the CEO as *the* strategist (see Box 7.1).

The most important drawback of a strategic decision process following the design school approach is that by separating formulation from implementation the possibility of learning is severely hampered (Mintzberg, 1990a). Only when a strategy is actually implemented can management find out if its assessment of strengths, weaknesses, opportunities and threats has been realistic, and if its plans work out the way expected. But if strategy formulation is isolated from strategy implementation – both in time because one follows the other, and in

---

Box 7.1 Principal prescriptions of the design school approach to strategy making

- Strategy making should be a controlled and conscious process.
- The CEO should be *the* strategist.
- The strategy-making process should be kept simple and informal.
- Strategies must come out of the design process fully developed.
- Strategies should be made explicit.

(Source: Mintzberg, 1994: 38–9)

---

the organization because different people are responsible for both processes – the process of trial-and-error that leads to organizational learning is impeded (Argyris, 1984).

In complex situations not all the relevant information can be digested by the small number of managers at the top. For this reason, the information that they receive will be filtered in its way up the hierarchy. The analysis based on this second-hand and incomplete information is doubtful. For instance, can top managers ever hope to get as good a grasp of the specific details of internal strengths and external opportunities as, respectively, a foreman at the shop-floor or a sales agent?

The strategic plans that are based on the kind of second-hand, incomplete and aggregated data top managers typically get at their desks may very well be detached from reality and be based on hopes and aspirations instead. Consequently these plans often need revision soon after they are formulated, but the top-down decision making suggested by the design school approach inhibits a flexible learning-by-doing (Mintzberg, 1990a). For fear of being blamed, lower managers may be tempted to postpone the communication of the bad news (Argyris, 1984). It is doubtful, therefore, that top management will get an honest feedback if its pet plan fails to bring the expected success. Lower managers are assumed to implement loyally the strategy designed by the CEO, and not to question its validity. If the strategy does not work out as expected, that is bound to be perceived as a problem of implementation rather than as a problem of formulation (Mintzberg, 1994: 25).

The strategic planning school

The strategic planning school of strategy making developed at approximately the same time as the design school but differs from it in one important respect: the strategic decision process is not kept as simple and informal as possible, but is elaborated and formalized. (This discussion of the strategic planning school is based on Mintzberg, 1990b, 1994. Authors associated with this approach are, e.g., Ansoff, 1965, Hofer and Schendel, 1978, Lorange, 1980, and Steiner, 1969.) This literature is rooted in a strong belief in the controllability of the long-term development of organizations, coinciding with the conviction that the future can be forecasted. The emphasis is on rational deduction of the best strategy on the basis of all the information available. Box 7.2 shows an example of a synoptical strategic planning system.

On the face of it, there is a compelling logic in this approach. Of course, one first has to know where one wants to go, otherwise it makes no difference which direction you take, as the Cat said to Alice. And only if a long-term plan is made first, can the medium-term and operational plans be formulated so that they contribute to the realization of the strategy. To give an example: if a firm decides that its long-term goal is to grow through in-house development of new products, the strategic plan should indicate the direction and magnitude of research and development efforts. The medium-term plan should be geared to generating the means necessary for realizing the plan, and the various operational plans should with adequate precision point out which activities are to take place in order to realize the medium-term plan. Thus Marketing and Sales may be instructed to 'milk' the existing mature products, Production to dedicate capacity to pilot lines for experimental products, and Purchasing to establish contacts with suppliers commanding vital technological capabilities. Characteristic of the synoptic planning model is the use of flow charts, depicting the strategic decision-making process as a computer program. Many examples can be found in the work of Igor Ansoff (e.g. Ansoff, 1965; Ansoff and McDonnell, 1990), one of the founding fathers of this school of thought.

Box 7.2 Synoptical planning at Texas Instruments around 1980

The OST (Objectives, Strategies, Tactics) system, developed at Texas Instruments in the 1960s, is an example of synoptical, top-down strategy making. A company officer described the OST system as 'an attempt to make explicit the company's longer range goals, strategic objectives, and shorter term tactics to achieve them'.

The corporate objective stated the reason of existence of the organization. It was supported by a set of business objectives, expressing the boundaries of a business and the main potential opportunities in it. For every business, a strategy was worked out which described the business environment in detail. Each strategy was assigned to a strategy manager.

Within every strategy, a number of more concrete tactical action programmes was formulated. Every tactical action programme, covering 6–18 months, described in detail the steps necessary to reach the goals of a specific strategy. For each tactical action programme a responsible individual was designated. The strong top-down character of the OST system is expressed graphically in the figure below.

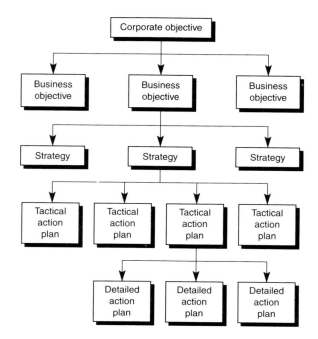

(Source: Quinn et al., 1988: 262–9. A further adaption of Figure A, originally published in Richard F. Vancil and Ronald Hall, Texas Instruments Incorporated: Management Systems, 1972. Case 172-054. Boston: Harvard Business School, 1972, p. 3. Copyright © 1972 by the President and Fellows of Harvard College. Used with permission.)

The strategic planning school, just like the design school, prescribes a mode of strategy formation with a strong emphasis on top-down decision making, and in which strategy formulation is separated from strategy implementation. Therefore, the criticism of the design school applies to this school of thought as well. There are a number of additional criticisms of the strategic planning school.

In the first place, this approach appears to assume virtually unbounded rationality. Many, if not all possible options should be taken into consideration, all the consequences of options systematically analysed; and a strict separation between goals and means maintained (Braybrooke and Lindblom, 1963). The preceding chapters of this book go to show the inadequacy of such an approach from a descriptive point of view.

Secondly, if the prescriptions of this school of thought are followed, strategic decision making to a large extent becomes a task of staff specialists rather than top management. The reason for this is that most top managers do not have the time (and otherwise do not feel inclined) to perform the elaborate planning tasks themselves. Therefore important parts of this task will be delegated to staff specialists, typically placed in a strategic planning department. It is one of the 'cardinal principles' of the strategic planning school that strategy making should be a task of line managers (Schwendiman, 1973: 43). But in practice top managers will only be involved in the process at certain key points, and given the information advantage of the planning specialists it is doubtful whether they will have an overriding influence on the direction of the strategy (Mintzberg, 1994: 30–1).

Finally, an underlying premise of the strategic planning approach appears to be that analysis breeds synthesis. All the analytical steps and techniques for forecasting future developments, for performing the SWOT analysis, and for evaluating possible strategies are carefully spelled out, but there is 'one missing detail': it is unclear where these strategies are assumed to come from (Mintzberg, 1994: 33). The emphasis on decomposition obfuscates the integration and creativity necessary to come up with a strategy.

Contemporary synoptical planning

In spite of the descriptive and prescriptive shortcomings of the underlying model, the synoptical planning approach is anything but dead. In fact, the design school and the strategic planning school are still dominant in the normative, practitioner-orientated literature on strategy making (Stacey, 1990). About a decade ago, the vast majority of practitioners were deemed to be proponents of the synoptical planning approach (Walter, 1980). It is doubtful whether that proportion will have decreased dramatically by now.

The design school approach originally developed at Harvard Business School is still in use, with only minor alterations. The original 1965 textbook has been succeeded by a number of new editions, with new co-authors, but the basic approach is the same. (The most recent edition is Christensen et al., 1987. For a description of the minimal alterations in this text compared to Learned et al., 1965, see Mintzberg, 1990a.) The strategic planning approach is also still very much alive. Ansoff's writings provide an example (e.g. Ansoff and McDonnell, 1990; other examples are Godet, 1987, and Hax and Majluf, 1984).

But perhaps most importantly, the synoptical planning approach still predominates in educational textbooks on strategic management (see for example Hill and Jones, 1989, and Rowe et al., 1994). This means that generations of future strategy makers are imbued with this heroic model of decision making in organizations. Far from dismissing the synoptical planning approach altogether, the point we want to make in this chapter is that the underlying model of organizational decision making is of limited applicability. In Section 7.2 we will determine in which situations the approach can best be used. First we will discuss a number of other approaches. The first of these, the disjointed incrementalist model, shows a marked contrast with the synoptical planning approach.

Disjointed incrementalism

Incremental decision making

The model of disjointed incrementalism is in more than one respect a reaction to the idealized picture of organizational decision making underlying the synoptical planning approach (Braybrooke and Lindblom, 1963; Lindblom, 1959). Instead of being prescriptive, the disjointed incrementalism model is predominantly descriptive. Instead of unbounded rationality, severe limits to rational decision making are assumed.

Managers are assumed to command only restricted rational faculties in the disjointed incrementalist view, and consequently they are not able to oversee all aspects of a strategy, nor to foresee all consequences of a chosen line of action. The strategy of an organization is seldom if ever completely reconsidered. Rather, managers decide on small changes in the existing situation. As a result changes of strategy are most of the time only marginal or 'incremental'.

The organizational decision-making process is incoherent ('disjointed') in two respects: in time, and over issues. According to the proponents of disjointed incrementalism decision makers do not even try to look far ahead (ostensive attempts to do so are mere rituals). Instead they concentrate on goals that are proximate in time. Thus, rather than trying to formulate a strategy for the coming decade, decision makers prefer to try to achieve an advantage next month, or next year at the latest. The distant future is heavily discounted.

Negative coordination

In the synoptic model decisions pertaining to all kinds of disparate issues are related to one another, and all decisions contribute to the realization of one overall strategy. According to the disjointed incrementalist model real-world organizational decision making is fragmented. Different agents are entrusted with different issues. All agents have their own perceptions of reality, and pursue their own goals. Coordination with other policy makers, if existent, is negative rather than positive. **Negative coordination** means that preventions are being taken to ensure that the decisions of various managers or parts of the organization are not in flat contradiction. **Positive coordination** is the orchestration of all decisions within one strategy, as prescribed by the synoptical model. Fragmented negatively coordinated decisions can result in a patchwork strategy at best.

Although the disjointed incrementalist approach is mainly descriptive, it also formulates rules of behaviour that are assumed to have prescriptive value. The main prescriptions of the disjointed incrementalist approach are summarized in Box 7.3.

The model of disjointed incrementalism has been developed to describe decision making in the context of public administration. It does not fit in with the picture of efficient organizations pushed to the limit by the unrelenting

---

Box 7.3 The main rules of incrementalist decision making

- Choose as relevant objectives only those worth considering in view of the means actually at hand or likely to become available.
- When contemplating means, continue at the same time to contemplate objectives, and vice versa.
- Limit attention to alternatives that differ only incrementally between themselves.
- Limit attention to alternatives that differ only incrementally from the present situation or policy.
- Evaluate alternatives only through a comparison of their incremental effects on the present situation or of their incremental difference from the present policy.

(Source: Braybrooke and Lindblom, 1963)

---

pressures of the market. Nevertheless, if the assumptions of disjointed incrementalism are productive in the public sector, there is no a priori ground to dismiss the model for application in the private sector. We see the model as a useful correction to the synoptical approach, but in its over-simplified negation of any form of long-term planning it may be almost as unrealistic as the contested model.

The garbage can model

A variant of the disjointed planning approach is the 'garbage can' model of organizational choice developed by Cohen, March and Olsen (Cohen et al., 1988; March and Olsen, 1976). The model is developed to describe decision making within 'organized anarchies'. An **organized anarchy** is an organization without a clear set of central goals, using a technology unclear to itself, that is, it does not very well understand its primary processes. Furthermore, organized anarchies are characterized by fluid participation: 'the boundaries of the organization are uncertain and changing; the audiences and decision-makers for any particular kind of choice change capriciously'. (Cohen et al., 1988: 295). Universities are examples of organized anarchies (the model was in fact developed on the basis of empirical studies of decision making at universities).

In an organized anarchy decision making does not look at all like the orderly process prescribed by the synoptical planning approach. The decision making context can best be described as a 'garbage can' in which problems, solutions, and decision makers are dumped more or less at random. Thus the process in many cases is not driven by the urge to solve a problem, but by the desire to use a particular solution, or by the fact that a decision maker is looking for something to do. If a problem, a solution, and a decision maker with certain goals happen to match, a decision is made. On the other hand, many decisions are made by oversight, because no solution and/or motivated decision maker happens to be available at the right time.

Garbage can decision processes may appear to be pathological, but only if the inappropriate standards of rational choice are used. In spite of its limitations, garbage can decision making 'does enable choices to be made and problems resolved, even when the organization is plagued with goal ambiguity and conflict, with poorly-understood problems that wander in and out of the system, with a variable environment, and with decision-makers who may have other things on their minds' (Cohen et al., 1988: 323). An organization trying to emulate synoptical planning procedures under these circumstances could easily become paralysed.

Logical incrementalism

Intuitive, evolutionary, fragmented yet logical

In contrast to the model of disjointed incrementalism and the garbage can model, the logical incrementalist model is developed explicitly for the description of strategic decision-making processes within private sector firms. James Brian Quinn (Quinn, 1978–79; 1980) attempts to demonstrate that incrementalist decision making, if applied in the right manner ('logically'), may be efficient also for business firms, whereas synoptical decision making would be too difficult or risky.

According to the logical incrementalist model, strategic decision making in organizations is an intuitive, evolutionary and fragmented process. Intuition is important because there are no clear criteria as to what is the best strategy in a given situation. Many consequences have to be taken into account, most of which are uncertain, and there is no common denominator to which all pros and cons can be reduced (i.e. compensatory evaluation of alternatives is impossible). In the absence of a completely rational procedure, the manager has always to some extent to rely on his or her gut feelings in choosing a strategy. Restrictions to the rational faculties of human decision makers and scarcity of information make strategic decision making an evolutionary process. Rather than rushing head-on into a completely new strategy, managers will first experiment on a smaller scale with various alternatives, progressively changing policies and goals as more information becomes available. Differences in views and interests and dispersion of power over the organization cause decision making to be fragmented.

Logical and disjointed incrementalism

In these respects logical incrementalism resembles the disjointed incrementalist model. But logical incrementalism also diverges from the purely incrementalist approach. In Quinn's view managers do pursue long-term strategic goals, but

---

Box 7.4 The main points of logical incrementalism

■ Effective strategies for the organization as a whole emerge from the partial strategies of subsystems.
■ The decision-making processes within the various subsystems follow a logic and tempo of their own.
■ Within each subsystem specific restrictions with regard to information availability, cognitive constraints and process characteristics apply.
■ Strategic decision making is strongly influenced by unexpected major events.

(Source: Quinn, 1980)

---

they are smart enough to realize that formal synoptic planning is not the best way to attain these goals. In other words, the absence of the comprehensive logic of a strategic master plan does not mean that managers are muddling through in a completely 'disjointed' way. A good manager keeps an eye on his or her long-term goals, but also on the political and cognitive restrictions with which he or she has to cope (cf. Wrapp, 1984).

Quinn does not consider the practice of his version of incrementalism poor management. On the contrary, logical incrementalism is an adequate response to the complex problems managers are confronted with. Accordingly, Quinn claims that logical incrementalism is both descriptively accurate and prescriptively valid. It is assumed to give not only a better description of what real-world organizational decision making is about, but also to offer better directions for practice than both the disjointed incrementalist and the synoptic planning model.

The outlines of the logical incrementalist model are summarized in Box 7.4. We will discuss these main points seriatim. But first we will have to make clear what in the context of logical incrementalism is to be understood with a 'subsystem'.

A **subsystem**, as the concept is used by Quinn, should not automatically be identified with an organizational unit like a department or a division. A subsystem is a group of organization members that in a particular problem area formally or informally has the competence to make decisions on behalf of the entire organization. These subsystems, consisting of the key decision makers in the area in question, often cut through several organizational units. Quinn distinguishes subsystems for, among other things, innovation, diversification, divestments, reorganizations and external relations. Other possible subsystems are those for internationalization, production optimization and personnel.

In many cases a subsystem will be made up from one or more members of the executive board, plus managers from the departments or divisions most concerned. The manager of the research and development department is likely to be a member of the innovation subsystem, the marketing manager of the diversification subsystem, the personnel manager of the reorganization subsystem, and so on. It is also very likely, and for the coordination of strategic decision making desirable, that the various subsystems overlap.

Characteristics of logical incrementalism

The first characteristic of logical incrementalism mentioned in Box 7.4 is the proposition that effective strategies for the organization as a whole emerge from the partial strategies of subsystems. This flies in the face of the conventional wisdom codified in the synoptical planning approach. According to Quinn, however, it is not effective to design an overall strategy at the top and subsequently have that strategy elaborated into plans for the shorter term and for various parts of the organization. Top management lacks the detailed knowledge and information necessary to make these more concrete plans. But how could top management be able to design a realistic overall strategy without this information and knowledge? In short, strategic decision making should be more of a 'bottom-up' and less of a 'top-down' activity.

The second proposition of the logical incrementalist model is that the decision-making process within every subsystem has its own peculiar 'logic' and tempo. For instance, when starting up a new plant at a new location a firm does not have to worry about existing personnel practices, commitments to the local community, and so on. But these things are critically important if an organization wants to discontinue or radically change activities at an existing plant.

The 'logic' of diversification is primarily of a financial-economic and technical nature, as the questions to be answered pertain to the market offering the highest growth potential, and to possible synergies between the activities to be performed. On the other hand, in the 'logic' of divestments psychological and juridical-institutional aspects are also crucially important: one has to cast off emotional commitments to an activity or location, examine the legal conditions for laying off redundant workers, assess the impact of such lay-offs on the relationship with trade unions, and so on.

Thirdly, within each subsystem specific restrictions with regard to information availability, cognitive constraints and process characteristics apply. In some subsystems 'hard' data and objective information are relatively abundant. For instance, it is possible to attain information about the cost of capital, or about the effects of promotional campaigns. But it is much harder to judge the comparative effectiveness of several possible organizational structures, or to evaluate possible programmes for boosting employee motivation. In the absence of 'hard' data, a different decision-making process is called for, employing small-scale experimentation and trial-and-error to yield additional information. It is for this reason that organizational decision-making processes according to the logical incrementalist model are often of an evolutionary nature.

The fourth and final major characteristic of logical incrementalism is that strategic decision making is seen as strongly influenced by unexpected major events. Such events can be things like technological breakthroughs, political landslides, or the sudden death of a key executive. Unanticipated events are a source of irreducible uncertainty, and often put much pressure on the decision-making process because of limited response time. Under these circumstances top managers try to gain time by taking broad and flexible decisions, and by avoiding irrevocable commitments (see also Ghemawat, 1991). As the situation unfolds and initial assumptions are put to the test, the new strategy can be given shape: strategic decision making following major unanticipated events tends to be evolutionary.

Achieving overall coordination

Although strategic decision making according to the logical incrementalist model can best take place within the various subsystems, a danger of this procedure is that these decisions drift too far apart, and the achievement of general purposes is obstructed. Top management should not try to fine-tune all subsystems, but rather give global directions that leave enough room for the decision-making processes in the subsystems to unfold in their own way and at their own speed.

The (partial) integration of the decision-making processes of the subsystems can be achieved in three ways:

1. The top manager can personally try to maintain a broad overview of the various decision-making processes, and in the case of major developments in one subsystem work out the consequences for other subsystems.
2. The existence of personal overlaps between subsystems can achieve the same goal. If several managers play the role of 'linking pins' between subsystems, the risk of overstraining the rational faculties of individuals is less than if one top manager tries to do so on his own. The disadvantage of this system, is, of course, that no individual manager has a complete overview.
3. Formal planning procedures can play an important role in integrating visions and strategies. In this case the formal planning system is not seen as the *source* of corporate strategies, but rather as a device for forging one corporate strategy from the several subsystem strategies. The formal planning system forces managers to look ahead and stimulates communication about goals, strategies and resources across subsystem boundaries (cf. Langley, 1988).

Logical incrementalism as a model of organizational learning

The most important difference between logical incrementalism and the synoptical planning approach is that the latter does not really allow for **organizational learning**. To be sure, most of the synoptical models of strategic decision making are equipped with some kind of feedback from outcomes of actions to the decision-making process (cf. Figure 2.4). But as strategy formulation is supposed to be a comprehensive and top-down process, the implication seems to be that the function of the feedback loop is to detect deviations in the implementation process that demand corrective action *vis-à-vis* the implementors rather than adjustment of the strategy.

In the logical incrementalist model decision, cycles are deliberately kept short in order to gather information in small-scale experiments. As a consequence there is much more opportunity to learn from the experience gained in the implementation. The much stronger bottom-up orientation of logical incrementalism also helps to enable this kind of organizational learning, of course.

The synoptical model appears to allow only 'single-loop learning': on the basis of information on the outcomes of the implementation process corrective actions can be taken in order to attain the pre-specified goals. Logical incrementalism on the other hand allows 'double loop learning' to take place: information gathered in small-scale experiments may be used not only to change the means used for pursuing given goals, but also to alter these goals (see also Chapter 8) (Argyris, 1984).

The interpretative approach

Organizations as paradigms

The interpretative approach to strategic decision making takes issue with the 'logical' aspect of Quinn's model. According to the interpretative approach – also called the 'organizational action approach' – accounts of strategic decision-making processes given by managers should not be taken at face value (Johnson 1987, 1988; Johnson and Scholes, 1993 – other authors associated with this school of thought are Donaldson and Lorsch, 1983; Pfeffer, 1981; Sheldon, 1980; Shrivastava et al., 1987; and Weick, 1983). *Post hoc*, managers rationalize decision making to a process closely resembling logical incrementalism or even synoptical planning. But in reality these decision-making processes are much less 'logical'.

In the interpretative approach strategic decision making is seen as a semi-closed system. Managers are often assumed to react to signals from the environment, but in fact their response is triggered by their *perception* of these signals. As we have seen in Chapter 4, decision makers interpret changes in the environment using simplifying cognitive schemata. These schemata will often be more closely connected with the history than with the present situation of the organization. For instance, managers who in the past have successfully pursued a strategy of cost minimization and low selling prices may interpret a decline of sales as a signal that prices should be lowered and costs reduced even more. In this way the very success of a given strategy may carry in it the seeds of future disaster. Success breeds simplicity: all minds are set at continuing a given successful policy. Organizational structures and procedures, as well as power relations, perpetuate this state of things (Miller, 1993).

Perceptual filters and cognitive heuristics at the level of the individual manager have a bearing on organizational decision-making processes. But the interpretative approach does not stop there. If the belief sets of individual

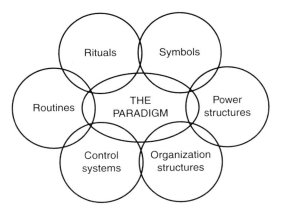

Figure 7.1 The organizational paradigm. (Source: Johnson, 1988: 85.)

managers are relatively persistent and homogeneous within the organization an 'organizational paradigm' may be said to exist. This paradigm is the prevalent model of reality in the organization, and conditions the way in which environmental stimuli are perceived. Thus a kind of 'groupthink' – as discussed in Chapter 5 – is occurring at the level of the organization as a whole.

The organizational paradigm derives its persistency from the fact that individual belief systems are relatively stable, as well as from reinforcement mechanisms at the level of the group and of the organization. The organizational paradigm will among other things be reflected in the organizational power structure (e.g. if serving the client's needs is seen as most important, marketing and sales will be powerful departments). The same is true of the organizational structure, control systems, and routines for accomplishing tasks. Likewise the organizational culture, reflected in rituals, myths, and symbols in force in the organization, will tend to reinforce the organizational paradigm (see Figure 7.1).

The interpretative approach and logical incrementalism

The most important difference between the interpretative approach and the, closely related, logical incrementalist model has to do with the scope for rational choice that is believed to exist if barriers to rationality on the level of the individual, the group and the organization are taken into account. The interpretative approach is much more pessimistic in this respect than the logical incrementalist model. The difference is depicted graphically in Figure 7.2.

On the left side of Figure 7.2, the process of strategic adjustment as assumed in the logical incrementalist model is shown. Changes in the environment, represented by a shift along the vertical axis, are followed, imperfectly and with some delay, by corresponding changes in the organizational strategy. On the right-hand side of the diagram, the process of strategic adjustment according to the interpretative approach is shown. Here the direction of strategic

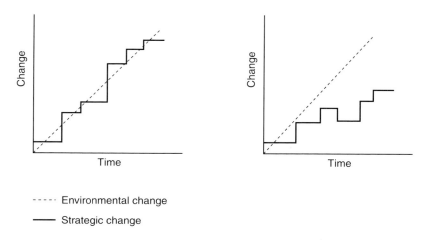

----- Environmental change

——— Strategic change

Figure 7.2 Logical incrementalism and the interpretative approach. (Source: adapted from Johnson, 1988: 88.)

adjustments corresponds only roughly to the rate and direction of environmental change. Occasionally a shift in the environment is misinterpreted completely, and the strategic adjustment actually leads to a worse 'fit'. Over time, the strategic adjustments cannot prevent the organization from getting out of tune with the environment. This phenomenon is called 'strategic drift'.

Of course, an organization – specifically a business firm – cannot neglect or misinterpret environmental changes with impunity for a very long time. Gradually, the signs that something is fundamentally wrong will become more salient. In the terminology of the interpretative approach there is a growing 'dissonance' between the signals from the environment and the expectations of the organization members. Some individuals will start doubting the generally accepted model of reality, and challenge the established strategy. After a while, when several attempts to restore organizational effectiveness using the accepted model have failed, the environmental pressure and internal dissidence may grow strong enough to tilt the balance, and the until then dominant paradigm is replaced by a new one.

This kind of change is revolutionary if compared with the normal pattern of incremental adjustments, and will in many cases be accompanied by changes in staff (Starbuck et al., 1978).

Normative implications of the interpretative model

Although the interpretative approach to organizational strategic decision making is predominantly descriptive, two normative implications can be deduced from the model (Johnson, 1988: 89–90). In the first place, in order to avoid being caught in a self-perpetuating paradigm, a constructive tension must be maintained between forces preserving what exists and forces of renewal. This constructive tension should exist at the level of individual perceptions as well as at the level of organizational structure and culture.

At the level of individual perception the view of outsiders may at times be helpful in order to remove perceptual blinders. This may in fact be a more important function of management consultants than the application of the latest analytical tools (Kiechel, 1982). At the organizational level, structures may be designed so that initiatives from lower management levels and corporate entrepreneurs are not hewn down prematurely. At top management level, decision-making procedures may be adopted that, by institutionalizing conflict, help avoid premature consensus. We will return to these points in Chapter 8.

The second normative implication of the interpretative approach is that in managing strategic change one should not neglect paraphernalia of the organizational paradigm (rituals, myths, symbols), that may otherwise preserve the integrity of the existing paradigm, and block change. Organizations are successful at managing strategic change not in the first place because of superior analytical capacities, but because of the ability to use the mechanism of symbolic manipulation (Deal and Kennedy, 1982).

7.2 Conceptual models of organizational decision making in perspective

Historical development

The four approaches discussed above are roughly representative of the developments in the conceptualization of organizational strategic decision making in the last three decades. As every new approach was to a certain extent a reaction to its predecessor, a kind of oscillating movement between the extremes of perfect rationality and pure prescription on the one side, and non-rationality and pure description on the other, characterizes the evolution of models of organizational decision making (see Figure 7.3).

The synoptical planning approach is close to the rationalist-prescriptive extreme. Managers are assumed to be (extremely) farsighted, and restrictions to rational behaviour or biases stemming from group processes are not taken into account. With disjointed incrementalism and the garbage can model the pendulum swings to the other extreme, as managers are assumed to be entirely myopic, and only very modest prescriptive pretensions are left.

Logical incrementalism takes us back in the direction of the other pole, although by no means as far as the synoptical planning approach. Here the descriptive and the prescriptive objectives are more in balance. Quinn describes strategic decision making in large companies, explains why the processes discovered should be considered logical, and uses these insights as a basis for more general prescriptions with regard to strategy making.

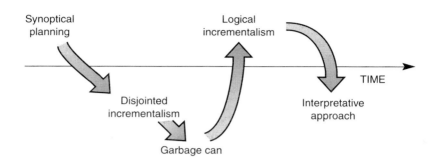

Figure 7.3 Schools of thought in organizational decision making.

The interpretative view, finally, constitutes a move back to the non-rational and descriptive pole. But the difference between logical incrementalism and the interpretative approach is not nearly as dramatic as that between synoptical planning and disjointed incrementalism. The interpretative approach is predominantly descriptive, but normative statements can also be derived.

Applicability of the models

The fact that the various models of organizational decision making have been presented as a historical sequence should not be taken as a suggestion that the 'older' models are by now completely obsolete. Whereas in general terms our view of organizational decision-making processes has over time gained in sophistication, some of the older models still have descriptive and normative validity under specific circumstances.

Power and relative cognitive capabilities of top managers

The conditions of applicability of the various models can be explored by distinguishing two dimensions: the power (top) managers have to impose their strategic plans on the rest of the organization; and the strength of the cognitive abilities of top managers, relative to the requirements of the situation. If we assume a continuum from 'weak' to 'strong' on both axes, the situations in which the various models are most applicable can be illustrated (Figure 7.4). It should be noted, however, that Figure 7.4 is a simplification of the complex issue of comparing schools of thought and approaches to organizational decision making that differ in many respects.

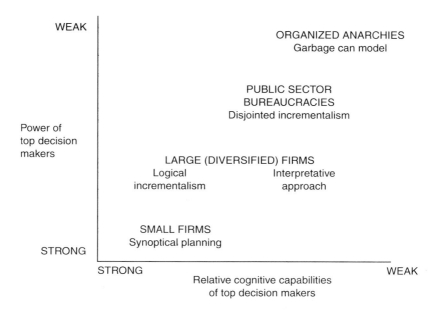

Figure 7.4 Applicability of organizational decision-making models.

Applicability of the synoptical approach

The synoptical model, in particular the design school variant, is of most use in small firms. These firms are often characterized by simple organizational structures, with short communication lines from top to bottom. The top manager, often the founder-owner of the firm, is in many cases intimately acquainted with what is going on the shop-floor (Mintzberg, 1979: 305–13). As small firms tend to focus on a limited number of products or services, they face a less diverse and complex environment than the large diversified firm. Consequently, cognitive limitations do not necessarily preclude comprehensive planning, and top-down implementation is possible. In many small firms the synoptic planning model also has normative validity, as these organizations are managed top-down anyway. If this is the case, the model can help the manager-owner to avoid myopic concentration on day-to-day problems. The more formalized versions of synoptical planning as prescribed by the strategic planning school, on the other hand, will meet considerable resistance in small firms, because they get in the way of the informal management processes typical for these organizations (Mintzberg, 1994: 410).

Applicability of logical incrementalism and the interpretative approach

Both the interpretative approach and the logical incrementalist approach seem to be most applicable to large firms. These firms are internally complex and often also face complex environments, especially if they are diversified. This means that the cognitive capabilities of top managers are relatively weak, compared with the complexity of the problems. Logical incrementalism, however, assumes that top management will nevertheless be able to manage strategically in a more or less rational way, providing enough decisions are delegated to the relevant subsystems.

The interpretative approach is less sanguine with regard to the rational faculties of top decision makers. The organizational paradigm may function as a blinder making managers only see part of the reality, and this through a particular set of lenses. This situation may persist, as large firms normally have enough slack and are sufficiently inert to allow managers to respond to a mistaken view of reality for a considerable time. Consequently, both the interpretative model and the logical incrementalist model may be assumed to give useful descriptions of, and prescriptions for, strategic decision making within large firms.

On the other hand, large firms, especially if they are not strongly diversified, often use rather formalized planning procedures akin to those prescribed by the strategic planning school (Fredrickson and Iaquinto, 1989). These procedures, according to Henry Mintzberg, keep the organization in the desired direction, but are unfit to bring about strategic change. Mintzberg describes the tension between strategic change and the status quo in words that are reminiscent of the interpretative approach (Mintzberg, 1994: 402):

> [S]omeone had better worry about change, about forces that can upset the given direction – new technologies, shifting customer tastes, the advent of unforeseen competition, etc. – and about the need for creative strategic response to them. The senior managers may not be so inclined. They, after all, have had to be the guardians of the (hitherto) successful strategic direction, not to mention possibly having been the creators of it.

Thus, although the formal procedures prescribed by the strategic planning school may ostensibly be used for strategic decision making, the real strategic decisions – those that change the future shape of the firm – are likely to be made outside this framework, by those not blinded by the dominating view of reality (Mintzberg, 1994: 394, speaks of left-handed planners, to refer to individuals 'inclined towards the intuitive processes identified with the brain's right hemisphere' – see also Chapter 4). There is also evidence that rational decision procedures like those advocated by the strategic planning school are used predominantly when the organization perceives little environmental threat and faces well-understood issues (Dean and Sharfman, 1993).

Applicability of disjointed incrementalism

Disjointed incrementalism is most applicable to strategic decision making in public sector bureaucracies. In these organizations the power of top managers to impose strategic changes on the organization is limited by the rigidity of organizational structures and systems. On top of that, the complexity and uncertainty of the environment preclude synoptical decision making. Under these conditions, managers can best advance step by step, and issue by issue, that is, in a disjointed incrementalist way.

Applicability of the garbage can model

If the situation is extremely complex, and consequently top managers' rationality very inadequate, and if there is hardly any effective centralization of power, the garbage can model may be most applicable. This may be the case in organized anarchies like universities. In fact, empirical research suggests that the garbage can model may be somewhat more widely applicable. In a study of 73 organizations involved in service delivery (hospitals, governmental agencies, insurance companies, consulting firms, and so on) processes similar to the garbage can model were found to be quite common in decision making stimulated by opportunities. Many of these cases could be characterized as solutions and/or decision makers in search of a problem (Nutt, 1984).

Conclusion

Over time, approaches to organizational strategic decision making have become more sophisticated. But the concomitant conceptual models, although arguably more accurate descriptively, have also become more complex. At the same time, prescriptions for strategic decision making have become more equivocal and hedged with added provisos. The picture may look confused now that intervening variables at the level of the individual, the group, and the organization have been added to the once simple model of decision making.

In order to increase the transparency of an admittedly complicated conceptual whole, we will in the next sections describe three broad categories of organizational strategic decision-making processes emanating from empirical research, and link these categories to the conceptual models of organizational decision making discussed above.

7.3 An empirical view of organizational decision making

Although empirical research into organizational decision-making processes is – apart from in-depth studies of single cases – far from abundant, by now a number of seminal studies are available. In the preceding sections of this chapter, as well as in the preceding chapters of the book, some of these studies have been referred to (e.g. DIO International Research Team, 1983; Dean and Sharfman, 1993; Eisenhardt and Bourgeois, 1988; Fredrickson and Iaquinto, 1989; Hauschildt, 1986; Horvath and MacMillan, 1979; Miller, 1987; 1993; Mintzberg et al., 1976; Nutt, 1984; Witte, 1972). In this section we will concentrate on the most comprehensive empirical research project to date, the

Bradford studies of organizational decision making (Cray et al., 1988; 1991; Hickson et al., 1986; Wilson, 1980; 1982; Wilson et al., 1986 – this section is based on the publications by Cray et al. and Hickson et al.). These studies, performed by a group of British scholars around David Hickson of the University of Bradford, have yielded a general typology of three categories of organizational decision-making processes, and have linked these categories to crucial dimensions of decision situations.

Three types of organizational decision processes

Aspects of decision processes

The Bradford studies consist of detailed case studies of organizational decisions and the analysis of data from 136 strategic decisions in 30 British organizations. The sample includes a diversity of institutions, for example, privately owned as well as state-owned manufacturing and services firms. The organizations on which the studies focused could be independent, or part of a larger whole.

The aspects of the decision-making process on which the Bradford studies focused were information collection, interaction between decision makers, the flow of the decision-making process, the duration of the decision-making process, and the level at which the final decision was authorized. With regard to **information collection** the number of sources of information, the variance in the decision maker's confidence in different sources, the use of external (in contrast to internal) information, and the effort expended in gathering information were considered. As far as the **interaction process** was concerned the amount of formal and informal interaction, and the scope for negotiation were looked at. Dimensions of the **decision flow** were the length and occurrence of disruptions in the decision-making process, and the causes of these disruptions (from less serious causes, such as awaiting priority in the order of attention, to more serious causes, such as active internal or external resistance). The aspects of **process duration** considered were the gestation time (the interval from the first mention of the issue until the beginning of decision-making activities) and process time (the interval from the initiation of decision-making activities to the moment of final authorization). The **level of authorization**, finally, ranged from 'below the divisional level or equivalent' to 'outside and above the organization'. This level of authorization was seen as a measure of the centrality to the organization of the decision-making issue.

The 136 cases were investigated using cluster analysis and discriminant analysis in order to discover empirical patterns of decision-making processes. Two dimensions appeared to capture much of the variance on all variables. The first dimension is **discontinuity**, reflecting the extent to which many different decision makers are involved and many different sources of information used, and the process is characterized by disruptions with relatively serious causes. The second dimension is **dispersion**, reflecting the distribution of decision making through the organization (and its environment).

This procedure yielded three clusters of decision-making processes, baptized **sporadic, fluid** and **constricted** decision processes. (Two variables, the use of external information and the gestation time were found not to contribute significantly to the differences between the clusters. The remaining 10 variables were used to interpret the three clusters of decision processes.) The most important characteristics of these three types of processes are summarized in Box 7.5.

Decision-making processes, discontinuity and dispersion

Sporadic decision making scores high on both the discontinuity and the dispersion dimensions. These processes are characterized by a large number of serious delays, resulting in a long duration. There is much informal interaction and some negotiation. Many sources of information, with disparate confidence levels attached to them, are used. Although different managerial levels may be involved in a sporadic decision-making process, final authorization tends to take place at a high level within (or even outside of) the focal organization. It should be noted that the denomination 'sporadic' refers to the lack of continuity in the decision-making process, and not to the frequency with which this type of decision occurs within organizations.

Fluid decision processes are the opposite of sporadic decisions in that they score low on discontinuity, but they resemble sporadic processes as far as the relatively wide dispersion is concerned. Fluid decision processes are characterized by a smooth process. There are fewer delays, and with more innocent causes. Also, fewer sources of information are used. The interaction tends to be more formal than in sporadic decision-making processes, although there is some scope for negotiation in fluid processes as well. The duration of the decision-making process is shorter, and final authorization, just like in the case of sporadic processes, takes place at a relatively high level.

The third group, constricted decision-making processes, is characterized by a low degree of dispersion, and stands midway between sporadic and fluid processes as far as discontinuity is concerned. The decision-making process is narrowly channelled, and although there are many sources of information, this information tends to be easily accessible, its validity is not doubted, and there is little effort to acquire additional information. Interaction is limited, mainly because only few individuals are involved. Where coordination is needed the procedures prevailing in the organization are used. Authorization takes place at a somewhat lower level than in both other types of decision-making processes, but still very near the top of the organization (this is understandable since the Bradford studies looked only at strategic decisions).

Explaining decision-making processes

Three groups of explanatory variables were included in the Bradford studies: the matter for decision or decision topic; the kind of organization in which the decision process takes place; and the characteristics of the decision situation.

Box 7.5 Sporadic, fluid and constricted decision processes

Sporadic decision processes

Discontinuous and dispersed:
- more delays
- more serious causes of delays
- more sources of information
- more variability of confidence in information
- more informal interaction
- some scope for negotiation
- more time to reach a decision
- decision authorized at highest level

Fluid decision processes

Continuous and dispersed:
- fewer delays
- less serious causes of delays
- less variability of confidence in information
- some scope for negotiation
- more formal interaction
- less time to reach a decision
- decision authorized at highest level

Constricted decision processes

Narrowly channelled and fairly continuous:
- more sources of information
- less effort to acquire information
- little scope for negotiation
- less formal interaction
- decision authorized below highest level

(Source: Cray et al., 1991: 229)

Decision topic

As far as the decision topics are concerned, 10 categories were distinguished. Some of these seem to be linked to the type of decision-making process, in that a certain type of process is unlikely to arise in connection with these topics. For example, decisions concerning new products, or concerning personnel matters, were either of the sporadic or of the constricted type, but in no case fluid. If the new product decision is weighty and novel, the process is likely to be sporadic. More routine product decisions are processed in a constricted fashion. Likewise with personnel decisions: these are most often processed in a constricted manner, but if strong resistance is met, for instance from trade unions, a sporadic process results. Other decision topics, such as those pertaining to investment in new machinery or buildings, can lead to any of the three types of decision processes (Hickson et al., 1986: 131–64). All in all, the decision topic does not appear to be an important factor in explaining decision-making processes.

Type of organization

The same can be said of the type of organization. In the Bradford studies, a distinction was made between public and privately owned organizations, commercial and non-commercial organizations and manufacturing and services organizations. These distinctions were hypothesized to have a bearing on the type of decision processes to be found most frequently within the organization. For instance, it was hypothesized that in commercial organizations fluid decision processes would be more common, whereas public ownership would lead to a higher proportion of sporadic processes. The first hypothesis was not confirmed by the data, the second was. However, contrary to expectations, sporadic decision-making processes are also more common in manufacturing organizations, where constricted processes were expected (Hickson et al., 1986: 189–233).

Unfortunately, the Bradford studies did not measure organizational variables pertaining to structure and culture like those discussed in Chapter 6. Two observations can be made. In the first place, larger organizations, which are assumed to be more bureaucratic, do indeed show more formal interaction, but no particular tendency towards one of the three types of decision processes. Secondly, in organizations with a very dominant CEO constricted processes occur more frequently. This finding is more likely to be associated with the personality of the CEO than with a variable at the organizational level, such as structural centralization, however (Hickson et al., 1986: 230).

Characteristics of the decision situation

The most important explanatory variables used in the Bradford studies refer to characteristics of the decision situation. Two dimensions of decision situations were found to be important: complexity and politicality. (This discussion is based on Cray et al., 1991.)

The **complexity** of a decision situation is determined by a number of factors. Issues that occur infrequently lead to more complex decision situations, because there are no ready-made procedures for such problems. Some decisions follow logically from earlier choices, but other decisions are precursive, that is, they set the parameters for later decisions. The latter kind of decision situation is arguably more complex. Situations are also more complex if more different criteria are used for evaluating decisions (cf. Chapter 2). Finally, the more diverse the functional backgrounds of the decision makers involved, the more complex the decision situation.

The **politicality** of a decision situation is determined, among other things, by the degree of contention between different interests that develops around a decision topic. Another factor contributing to the politicality of an issue is the imbalance between the various interests. If one individual or group is able to impose a decision, the degree of politicality is lower than if the interests have roughly the same amount of power, and an agreement has to be reached through bargaining and negotiation. Finally, intervention from outside the focal organization is seen as intensifying the politicality of a decision situation (Cray et al., 1991).

Relating process types and decision situations

Sporadic decision processes were found to be most common with complex and political issues. These decision situations were called **vortex matters**, because they tended to suck many decision makers into swirls of activity. Less complex and non-political issues tend to lead to fluid decision-making processes. These decision situations, called **tractable matters**, are unusual, but also non-controversial, making them more malleable. Constricted decision processes, finally, were found to be associated with decision situations that were the least complex and only mildly political. The politicality of these issues is mitigated because only internal interests are involved (in vortex matters also external interests), and because there is a clear imbalance, in that one of the parties (normally the CEO) is much more powerful than the others. These decisions situations were called **familiar matters**, because they were normal and recurrent (Hickson et al., 1986: 172–86). The relationship between decision situations and decision-making processes is summarized in Figure 7.5.

7.4 Comparison of empirical and conceptual views

In this last section we will map the findings of the Bradford studies on the different views of organizational decision making discussed in the first section of this chapter. This mapping will inevitably be somewhat speculative, as the

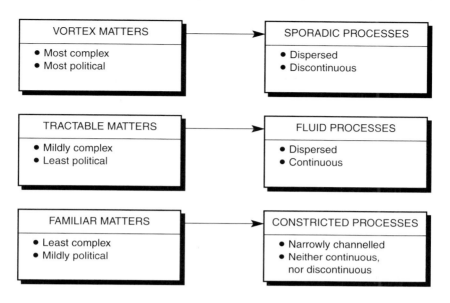

Figure 7.5 Decision situations and decision processes. (Source: adapted from Hickson et al., 1986: 175.)

various conceptual approaches to organizational decision making are not expressed in terms that can readily be translated to the variables measured in the Bradford studies.

Politicality and complexity

The dimensions of politicality and complexity, discussed above, can be helpful in building a bridge between the Bradford typology and the various conceptual models.

The politicality dimension in the Bradford studies is reminiscent of the relative power of the top manager, which was one of the dimensions used in Section 7.2 to compare the conceptual approaches. If an issue is strongly contested, if there is a balance of power between various divergent interests, and if there is intervention from outside the organization, the power of top managers to have it their way is severely restricted.

The complexity dimension from the Bradford studies is clearly related – if not identical – to the cognitive capabilities of top managers, relative to the requirements of the situation. Thus we can map the Bradford typology on a two-dimensional field akin to that in Figure 7.4 (see Figure 7.6).

The important difference between Figures 7.4 and 7.6 is that in the latter decision-making processes are related to decision situations, and not to types of organizations. The decision-making processes analysed in the Bradford studies proved to be much more strongly related to decision issues, than to types of organizations (Hickson et al., 1986: 244).

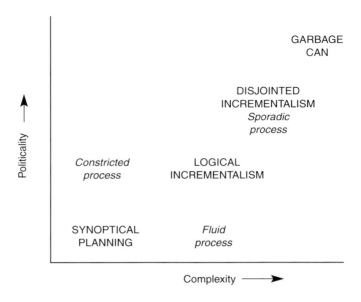

Figure 7.6 Empirical and conceptual types of organizational decision processes.

Synoptical planning – constricted decision-making processes

A first observation is that the Bradford studies found constricted decision-making processes in the situation where synoptical planning processes would logically seem to be most applicable. At the face of it, there is a contradiction between the *synoptical* aspirations of the conceptual approach and the *constricted* characteristics of the empirical class of decisions. But if we take a better look, there is a clear similarity. In the decision procedures prescribed by the synoptical planning approach, few organization members are assumed to be directly involved in the decision-making process – only top managers in the design school approach and top managers and strategic planners in the strategic planning school approach. This corresponds to the narrow channelling that is characteristic of constricted decision processes.

The fact that constricted decision-making processes are found in situations which are 'mildly political' may seem to contrast with the synoptical planning approach, which is apolitical if anything. But the situations invoking constricted processes are political only in the sense that there is one party which has an overriding power, even in the face of opposing interests. This kind of unilateral power of top managers is not at all in contrast with the synoptical approach, but is in fact implicitly assumed by the authors in this school of thought.

Finally, the correspondence between the synoptical planning approach and constricted decision-making processes is partly confirmed by the finding that these constricted processes are more frequent in organizations with a very dominant CEO. This corresponds to the role of the CEO in the view of the design school, but not necessarily to that in the view of the strategic-planning school, which reserves a more important role for staff specialists.

Disjointed incrementalism – sporadic decision-making processes

A second observation is that the sporadic processes of the Bradford studies were found where disjointed incrementalism was to be expected. This makes sense, as the processes described by Lindblom and others bear a strong similarity to the characteristics of the sporadic process.

Sporadic decision-making processes may be assumed to be incremental, because possible solutions are confronted with information from disparate sources and with diverging interests. Non-incremental solutions, leading to a radical departure from the status quo, are less likely to survive in such a decision process than incremental solutions calling only for small changes. Therefore the identification of sporadic processes with disjointed incrementalism is natural (Cray et al., 1988).

Logical incrementalism, garbage can and interaction approach

The place in the two-dimensional field at which the logical incrementalist approach is located is conspicuously empty in the Bradford typology. That could be taken as a sign that this type of decision-making process, identified by James Brian Quinn in nine United States corporations, is not as widespread as he assumes (Quinn, 1980). On the other hand, the findings of the Bradford studies should not be taken as the last word in organizational decision research. It is very well possible that future research will identify new types of decision-making processes, combining elements of the sporadic and the fluid processes from the Bradford studies. Both of these types contain elements that bear resemblance to aspects of logical incrementalism.

The garbage can model as such has also not been identified by the Bradford studies. This could mean that Cohen, March and Olsen are too pessimistic, and that organizational decision making in practice is more rational than the garbage can model suggests. On the other hand, the data used in the Bradford studies were based on *post hoc* accounts given by key protagonists. Doubtlessly these stories are somewhat rationalized, meaning that garbage can decisions may pass under the guise of sporadic decision processes.

For a comparable reason it is understandable that nothing resembling decision making according to the interpretative approach was found in the Bradford studies. The methodology used in the project implied that the researchers took the organizational members' worldview for granted, as there was no attempt to validate this view through sources outside the organization. According to the interpretative approach although all the decision behaviour measured and classified in the Bradford studies may very well have actually taken place, much of it may have had only a marginal impact on the strategy of the organizations. Real strategic decisions arise only when the accepted worldview is challenged.

Conclusion

The possibility of identifying most of the conceptual models with empirically derived types of decision-making processes endorses the view that the various conceptual models all have their value if used in the appropriate context. At the same time, the Bradford studies show the inordinate complexity of organizational decision processes. No single model will ever be sufficient for all types of organizations and all types of problems. In trying to understand organizational strategic decision-making processes, choosing the right conceptual tool to do the job is of crucial importance.

Chapter summary

- The synoptical planning approach to organizational strategic decision making is strongly prescriptive, emphasizes top-down decision making and a separation of strategy formulation and implementation. The design school variant rejects formalization of the strategic decision process; the strategic planning school variant recommends formalization.

- The disjointed incrementalism approach is predominantly of a descriptive nature. The limitations to human rationality are emphasized. Strategic decision making is depicted as a continuous process of marginal changes.

- Logical incrementalism is a mixed descriptive/prescriptive approach to organizational strategic decision making. Strategy formation is seen as an intuitive, evolutionary and fragmented process. Nevertheless, this process is also logical, in the sense that various sub-decision processes follow their own logic, and that integration of sub-decision processes is achieved through various means.

- According to the interpretative approach managers' perceptions of the environment are strongly biased by their past experiences and expectations. These biases are maintained and reinforced by the organizational paradigm, that is, the prevalent model of reality in the organization.

- In the Bradford studies, three types of decision-making processes are distinguished: sporadic, fluid and constricted decision-making processes, varying in the degree of discontinuity and dispersion of the process. The associated decision situations, varying in the degree of complexity and politicality, are vortex, tractable and familiar matters, respectively.

- Synoptical planning corresponds largely to the category of constricted decision-making processes and disjointed incrementalism to that of sporadic decision-making processes. Logical incrementalism and the interaction approach can be less easily associated with one of the decision-making processes identified by the Bradford studies.

8

Improving strategic decision making

This final chapter, in contrast to the preceding chapters, is predominantly prescriptive in nature. We will discuss various techniques and procedures that can be used to improve strategic decision making at the level of the individual, the group and the organization.

In the previous chapters we have seen how real-world decision makers and decision-making situations in many ways deviate from what is assumed in the model of perfect rationality. It would therefore not be very productive to use the rules of perfect rationality as a yardstick, and advise decision makers to emulate this model. A distinction between 'normative' and 'prescriptive' approaches is useful. **Normative** approaches to decision making spell out what would be perfectly rational behaviour under various circumstances. **Prescriptive** approaches, on the other hand, seek to formulate recommendations that lead to better decisions, given the complexity and uncertainty characteristic of real-world situations and given the true nature of decision makers as we know it (Johnson-Laird and Shafir, 1993).

8.1 Revitalizing strategic decision making

As discussed in Chapter 3 programmed choice in the form of routine behaviour, habits, organizational procedures and shared beliefs and mindsets, in many ways moulds and constrains decision making. Therefore activities to improve strategic decision making almost inevitably involve attempts to de-programme behaviour. Routines and habits of individual organization members are questioned and if necessary changed, organizational procedures are adapted to newly formed strategies, shared mindsets are confronted with divergent perspectives. We will call this process of de-programming **revitalizing** strategic decision making.

The thrust of much of the prescriptive literature on strategic management goes in the opposite direction. The procedures prescribed by the normative-rational school of strategy formulation, for instance, can be seen as methods for programming formerly unprogrammed thinking. The assumption pervading this literature is that in order to get better strategies, the process of decision making should be formalized and divided into a number of well-described steps (Mintzberg, 1994). In a way, this appears to be the proper thing to do. After all, March and Simon observed that highly programmed tasks tend to take precedence over highly unprogrammed ones (March and Simon, 1993: 206). Programming strategic decision making may be a way to avoid the fact that daily worries drive out systematic attention to the problems of the future. In Jelinek's words: innovation should be 'institutionalized' (Jelinek, 1979).

However, this solution may backfire. If strategic decision making is programmed, this also inevitably means that rational deliberations become constrained by routines and procedures. We simply cannot have our cake and eat it, that is, programme strategic decision making and avoid the conditioning that comes with programming. The upshot is that programming strategic decision making always, to some extent, stifles creativity and constrains the type of strategies an organization will be able to form. It is a fallacy to think that innovation can be institutionalized (Mintzberg, 1994: 294).

De-programming and re-programming

On the other hand we should realize that institutionalization and programming of behaviour within organizations is not only unavoidable but also necessary. Without some degree of it coherent action would be impossible, because man's limited cognitive capabilities become overwhelmed by the complexity of the decisions that have to be made. Formalized decision procedures may also serve other goals than rational decision making. They may, for instance be used to justify decisions already taken on other grounds (Langley, 1989). We will in the last section of this chapter return to the question of the advantages and disadvantages of programmed choice, and the need to strike a balance between conscious, deliberate, intentionally rational decision making and habitual, routinized and rule-guided choice behaviour.

Because of the inevitability and necessity of programming choice, in revitalization of strategic decision making de-programming is always followed by re-programming. In the terminology of Lewin: it is possible to 'unfreeze' programmed behaviour, but after some time it must be 'refrozen' (Lewin, 1947). Adoption of a new way of thinking or of a new decision procedure will for a while make the decision process more conscious and deliberate (Mintzberg and Waters', 1983, distinction between convergent thinking (programming) and divergent thinking (de-programming) is apposite). But after some time the new approach becomes ingrained in the organization, and no longer is an object of critical reflection. This means that after a while revitalization will be necessary once again. No method or procedure will do forever. This is illustrated by the observation in the context of the use of the nominal group technique (to be discussed in Section 8.3) that 'repeated use may have a dampening effect on a participant' (Moore, 1987: 35).

Programming and de-programming of decision making should not be seen too simplistically in terms of a clear opposition. Procedures that to a considerable extent programme the behaviour of organization members may paradoxically be instrumental to the stimulation of creativity. This can be the case if the prescribed procedures rule out certain kinds of behaviour that tend to block creativity, such as virulent criticism of unconventional ideas or of ideas coming from low-status organization members. On the other hand, decision-making processes may on the surface seem unprogrammed, because no (formal) rules or procedures appear to apply, but in reality be determined by habits and mindless behaviour, and characterized by very low levels of conscious deliberation.

The question of whether the adoption of a certain technique constitutes a programming or a de-programming move depends not only on the technique itself, but also on the organization in which it is used. If the new technique is radically different from what the organization members were used to, this will lead to a heightened level of conscious attention to the decision-making process. But if the new procedure is similar to those used before, the impact will be much more limited. And after some time even the radically new technique will have become part of the accepted way of doing things, and will be performed routinely.

8.2 Improving decision making by individuals

In the next three sections we will focus on methods and techniques to improve decision making. In this section ways to improve decision-making processes at the level of the individual will be discussed. In Sections 8.3 and 8.4 we will consider methods at the level of the group and the organization, respectively. The distinction between these two levels is not always very clear, and sometimes arbitrary. Some of the group techniques may have a major impact on the organizational decision processes, if all the important decision makers are included in the group. On the other hand, methods for improving organizational decision-making processes rarely draw in all organization members.

As far as methods on the level of the individual decision maker are concerned, two broad categories can be discerned: methods to make the decision process more rational (grouped under the heading of **decision analysis**), and methods to promote creativity. We will discuss examples of each category, without any claim to be exhaustive. The discussion of decision analysis will be more voluminous than that of creativity, simply because less is known about the latter.

Decision analysis

Decision analysis is a group of techniques that can be used to promote rational decision making in complex problem situations. The techniques of decision analysis are based on the assumption that complex problems can be broken down into smaller problems which can be dealt with separately, after which the results can be integrated into a solution for the entire problem. Decision analysis techniques may be used to solve all or some of the parts of the problem (Goodwin and Wright, 1991: 3–4).

The assumption that problems can usefully be subdivided into smaller problems which can be solved independently is by no means undisputed. One could ask whether it is really possible to decompose strategic problems into meaningful parts that can be solved separately. It is equally doubtful whether the solutions to partial problems can really be integrated into one overall strategy. To quote Mintzberg: 'Humpty Dumpty taught us that not everything that comes apart can be put back together' (Mintzberg, 1994: 303). We will nevertheless assume that partial problem solving with the help of decision analysis techniques can in many instances be useful.

It is vital, however, that the analytical approach does not completely dominate or replace more holistic approaches, based on intuition, judgement and experience. The results of decision analysis will often conflict with intuitive insights. How should these conflicts be dealt with? One possible reaction would be to dismiss the intuitive insights. However, it is much more productive to explore the causes of the differences between the outcomes of analysis and intuition. Possibly the representation of the problem on which the decision analysis has been brought to bear was not a faithful representation of the real problem (as perceived by the decision maker). Relevant variables may have been omitted, or preferences of the decision maker not adequately incorporated. But, on the other hand, the rational analysis may also reveal genuine inconsistencies in the mental model or the preferences of the decision maker. In this case the analysis rightly leads to a questioning of intuitive insights, and a deeper understanding of the problem is obtained (Goodwin and Wright, 1991: 29–31). It is the interaction between analysis and intuition that leads to the best results.

Decision trees

Strategic problems often involve many possible actions, of the organization itself as well as of actors in its environment, and many probabilistic outcomes. The complexity of these situations is frequently increased by the fact that uncertain outcomes call for subsequent decisions to be made, the outcomes of which are again uncertain. Because of the complexity of such multi-stage decision problems, it can be very difficult to keep track of the various options and their possible outcomes. A tool which can be very helpful in gaining an understanding of the structure of the problem is the decision tree. (The discussion of decision trees is based on Goodwin and Wright, 1991. See also Nutt, 1989: ch. 18.)

A decision tree is a graphic representation of a decision problem, showing the options that can be chosen at various stages, chance events that may occur and the probabilities associated with these events, and possible outcomes (see, e.g. Figure 8.1). In a decision tree two symbols are used: squares to indicate decisions, and circles to indicate chance events. Lines departing from a square represent the various possible choices. Lines departing from a circle represent the possible outcomes of a probabilistic event.

An example may be used to clarify the use of decision trees. Assume that a firm has received an order for a product that can be manufactured either with general purpose equipment, or with specialized equipment. In the first case, the firm has to invest $800,000, in the second case $1 million. There is a 70 per cent chance that the firm will next year receive a repeat order for the same product. If a repeat order is received, there is a 70 per cent chance that the year after a second repeat order will also be obtained. However, if no repeat order is obtained next year, the chance that there will be a repeat order the year after is only 10 per cent. After two years, no further repeat orders are to be expected. The special purpose equipment allows the firm to produce more economically and yields an operating profit of $500,000 on every order, against only $300,000 for the general purpose equipment. The salvage value of the special purpose equipment is $400,000 after having been used for the production of one order, $200,000 after having produced two orders, and nil after the production of three orders. The corresponding figures for the general purpose equipment are $600,000, $400,000, and $200,000, respectively. It is assumed that the special purpose equipment will be economically obsolete at the end of the three year period, and, regardless of its use, will have no salvage value. The general purpose equipment, on the other hand, will have a minimal salvage value of $200,000 at the end of the decision period, even if used intensely. This decision problem, although extremely simple if compared to real-world investment problems, can be confusing because many different sequences of decisions and chance events are possible. The various possible outcomes are conveniently arranged in a decision tree (see Figure 8.1).

The rolling-back technique

On the basis of the problem representation in a decision tree, an optimal policy can be selected. This is done through a technique known as **rolling back** the decision tree. The analyst starts at the right-hand side of the decision tree, and works back to the left. For every chance node the expected value of the outcome is computed (see Chapter 3). This value is written above the chance node in question. For every decision node, the choice leading to the highest (expected) outcome is selected and written above the node. Choices leading to lower outcomes are eliminated by placing a double bar over the inferior branches.

In Figure 8.2, the decision tree for the investment problem is 'rolled back'. The value of the 12 possible outcomes can be computed by taking all associated

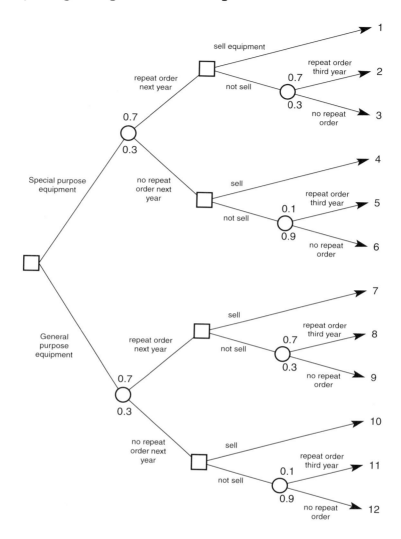

Figure 8.1 Decision tree for an investment problem.

costs and benefits into consideration. For instance, in case of outcome number 8, the firm earns three times $300;000 with three orders, plus $200,000 salvage value of the general purpose equipment. From this we have to deduct the initial investment of $800,000, making the net outcome $300,000. In the same way the outcomes associated with the other chains of decisions and chance events can be computed. The value associated with the chance nodes can now easily be computed. The optimal decision (assuming that the probabilities and the values of outcomes are correctly assessed) is to invest in special purpose equipment, and to sell this equipment in the case that no repeat order is received in the second year.

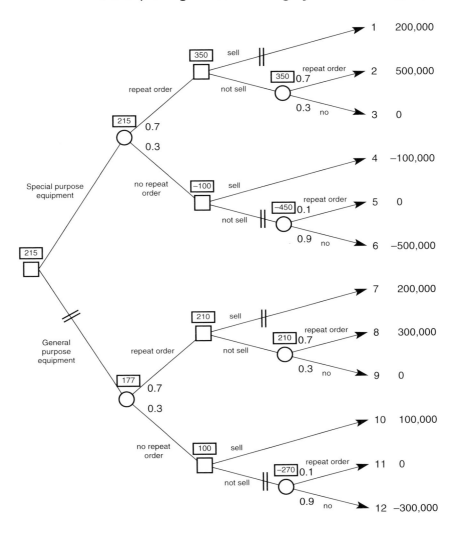

Figure 8.2 Rolling back the investment decision tree.

Decision trees help decision makers to get a clear perception of complex choices, especially multi-stage choices under circumstances of uncertainty. It allows decision makers to interconnect decisions that have to be taken at different points in time, while taking into consideration the various possible outcomes of chance events.

The technique should not be taken to provide the ultimate answer to complex problems, but rather as a device for decision makers to structure their thoughts. Building a decision tree is an iterative process: preliminary thoughts about the problem lead to a first rough representation, which is subsequently refined while the decision maker thinks through the problem in more detail.

It is counter-productive to try to construct very large and complex trees, however (Goodwin and Wright, 1991: 103). Every decision tree always remains a simplification of reality, but very complex simplifications convey a false impression of accuracy.

The decision-tree technique, in the form presented above, has various limitations. One limitation is that only the expected monetary value of outcomes is taken into consideration. This implies that the decision maker is risk-neutral, and that attributes of decisions that cannot be expressed in monetary outcomes are irrelevant. Both assumptions are questionable, if not downright incorrect. Furthermore, the probabilities associated with the outcomes of chance events are almost always the result of subjective assessment. As human decision makers are notoriously bad at probability assessments (see Chapter 4), the outcomes of decision-tree analyses should be taken with a pinch of salt. Some of these shortfalls of decision trees can be remedied, for instance by substituting the decision maker's subjective utility for the monetary value of outcomes (Goodwin and Wright, 1991: 107–11). However, these remedies come at the price of making the approach much more complicated, while simplicity is one of its virtues. It therefore seems wise to take the decision tree technique exactly for what it is, a possibly useful tool for understanding complex decision situations.

Influence diagrams

Influence diagrams are related to decision trees, but they offer a more flexible and often more intuitively appealing way of specifying decision problems. (The discussion of influence diagrams is based on Goodwin and Wright, 1991: 118–22.) An influence diagram summarizes the interdependencies that are believed to exist among events and choices in a decision situation. As in the case of decision trees, event nodes are represented by circles and choice nodes by squares. Arrows between nodes indicate the direction of influence. An arrow pointing to an event node indicates that the probabilities associated with different outcomes of the event represented by the node are influenced by prior decisions or events. An arrow pointing to a choice node indicates that the decision in question is influenced (constrained) by a prior decision, or that the decision is influenced by prior events. Figure 8.3 shows an influence diagram of the investment problem discussed above.

Influence diagrams visualize the structure of a decision situation. The activity of specifying them can help a decision maker to realize which partial choices are implicated in the decision problem, and to take stock of relevant chance events that can influence the outcomes of these decisions.

Stimulating creativity

Creativity may be one of the most crucial aspects of strategic decision making; it is also certainly one of the most enigmatic. For the many predominantly analytical approaches to strategic decision-making creativity is an elusive and

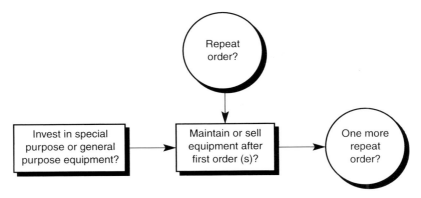

Figure 8.3 Influence diagram of an investment problem.

perhaps even troublesome phenomenon, not unlike intuition. It is not surprising that this aspect of strategic decision making is all but neglected in the normative-rational approach. Mintzberg points at a text in which two of the boxes in the flow diagram bear the labels 'Apprehend Inputs' and 'Add Insights' (Mintzberg, 1994: 66 the example cited by Mintzberg is from Malmlow, 1972). It is only a small step to appeals to 'Use Intuition', and to 'Be Creative'.

The incapacity of the normative-rational approach to come to grips with creativity may be understandable, but it is not without danger. The unbalanced emphasis on and formalization of those aspects and phases of the decision-making process that are more susceptible to rational analysis may very well in many organizational strategic decision-making processes stifle the creativity that is a natural characteristic of humans (Cf. Mintzberg, 1994: 180–2).

What is creativity?

Creativity is an assumption-breaking process (Bazerman, 1990: 86). New ideas often fail to be developed or are blocked from consciousness because we unwittingly apply assumptions that constrain our thought processes. Tacit assumptions constrain the perception of a problem, preventing aspects that are obviously unimportant from becoming part of the problem definition. Tacit assumptions also exclude options from (further) consideration, and restrict the development of new alternatives. Finally, our evaluation of those alternatives that are developed is guided by tacit assumptions regarding the relative importance of certain aspects or criteria. The use of assumptions is inevitable, for one needs a focus in order to be able to see anything, but the assumptions that are actually used by a given individual in a given situation may very well be false, that is, they may restrict our view in an unproductive manner or bias our decisions in the wrong direction.

Creativity-limiting tacit assumptions have their basis in the cognitive heuristics and biases described in Chapter 4. For instance, because they use simplifying cognitive schemata to organize their ideas and expectations, human decision makers have a blind spot for unexpected events or relationships.

Creativity consists in the ability to break away from existing assumptions, mind-sets and habits.

The creative process

A well-known conceptualization of the creative process distinguishes four steps: preparation, incubation, illumination and verification (Wallas, 1926; see also Bazerman, 1990: 92–4). At the **preparation** stage the decision maker defines the problem in broad terms and takes stock of the available information. At the **incubation** stage this information is pondered over, taking care not to arrive too quickly at an obvious conclusion. The preparation and incubation periods are sometimes very long. Many great inventors have worked at problems for many years, before finding the solution that made them famous. Edison and Marie Curie are examples (Henry, 1991).

At these first two stages the elimination of implicit assumptions restricting the search for solutions is particularly important. The mode of thought leading to creative solutions is believed to be that of 'lateral' or 'divergent' thinking, not following conventional logical chains of reasoning, but by means of association, jumping in unexpected and at first sight irrelevant directions (DeBono, 1971). The **illumination** phase constitutes the heart of the creative process. New ideas appear 'in a flash of insight', or 'all of the pieces fall into place' suddenly (Bazerman, 1990: 94). This is the stage we know least about. The **verification** stage, finally, is were the creative process comes to converge with rational decision processes. The fruits of the creative insight are held against the light of critical reason. Many creative ideas appear to have fatal flaws when confronted with practical limitations.

The relevance of this four-stage model of the creative process lies not in its descriptive accuracy, for there is no knowing whether that is the case. But the model makes clear that while the core of the process – illumination – remains elusive, this core is preceded and followed by stages that can to a certain extent be manipulated. We can try to remove barriers at the preparation and the incubation stages, in order to avoid a premature closure of the mind. This is what the recommendations given below aim at. We can only hope that if these two stages are given sufficient attention illumination will follow. For the verification stage, we can rely on the rules of rational evaluation of options.

Enhancing creativity in managerial decision making

Given the nature of creativity as an assumption-breaking process, the most important advice for enhancing creativity is obvious: remove assumptions that block creativity. The examination of one's assumptions about a problem and its potential solutions should be made a standard part of the decision making process (Bazerman 1990: 95). However, this is easier said than done. The tacitness of the assumptions in question makes it difficult to become aware of them. They may be the very basis of our worldview. Making the questioning of assumptions a standard part of the decision-making process may also have the effect of rendering this inquiry perfunctory and shallow. But the least one can do is be aware of the cognitive heuristics described in Chapter 4, and the biases to which these heuristics frequently lead.

An approach explicitly aimed at removing creativity-blocking assumptions is Gareth Morgan's **imaginization**. The goal of imaginization (Morgan, 1993; see also Handy 1991) is to improve one's ability to understand familiar situations in new ways. It proceeds by replacing the conventional images that we, often quite unconsciously, use to organize our thoughts by new, provoking images. For instance, instead of the outworn imagery of the military commander to understand strategy-making, Morgan proposes the image of termites building their nests. In a termite colony columns of earth are built more or less at random. If columns are sufficiently close together, the termites at a certain point join them at the top with a rounded arch. In this way complex, functional architectures grow without a predetermined plan, in a logical incrementalist way.

The use of a new image or metaphor helps us to discover new aspects of problems. The new image does not necessarily have to be more 'true' or 'accurate' than the old one. In Morgan's view social reality can be seen in many different ways, and is actually created and recreated through interpretation. A new image not only helps us to see familiar phenomena in a new light, it may also be a necessary condition for changing reality. Individuals that become trapped by an image of themselves and their role lock themselves into patterns of behaviour that may become inappropriate. Changing the image is necessary for changing the behaviour.

Another way to unleash creativity would be to rely on intuitive thought processes instead of more conventional logical reasoning. Some of the factors that impede the use of intuition, and thus also tend to block creativity, are known, and one can try to remedy them. A too strong attachment to an existing or desired situation may cause decision makers to deceive themselves, and make them transform reality so that it fits with what they would like to be true. A lack of confidence may also stand in the way of intuitive judgement, for it is much easier to defend an ostensibly rational decision, even when it turns out to be wrong, than a decision based on intuition. Another mistake is to confuse intuition with impulsive action. If intuitive judgement is not complemented with at least a modicum of rational assessment wishful thinking may control the decision making (Agor, 1991).

Some other advice concerns more specifically what managers should do in order to enhance the creativity within their organization (Stein, 1982). Managers should acquaint themselves with the nature of the creative process, and with the psychological characteristics of creative individuals, in order to be able to promote creativity. It would also help if human resources were considered valuable assets rather than a source of labour costs. In the selection of new personnel tests for measuring creativity could play a more important role.

But at least as important as selecting the right subordinates is to have managers who do not stifle creative behaviour of their subordinates (see Box 8.1) (Coffey et al., 1994: 499). These managers are willing to absorb risks for their subordinates, in order to give them the freedom to experiment. They

---

Box 8.1 An early innovator at Johnson & Johnson

Early in his career James Burke left Johnson & Johnson, the company of which he would later become CEO, because he was much too imaginative. 'The company was centralized and stifling, and I was bored.' However, after only three weeks Burke was called back in order to manage the new-product division he himself had insisted Johnson & Johnson needed. Burke set to work, but one of his first new products, a children's chest rub, failed abysmally, and before long he was summoned to the office of the company's fearsome chairman, General Robert Wood Johnson. Burke was afraid that this time he would be dismissed, rather than leave Johnson & Johnson of his own accord. The general asked: 'Are you the one who just cost us all that money?'. Burke could only admit it, but then to his surprise was told: 'Well, I just want to congratulate you. If you are making mistakes, that means you are making decisions and taking risks. And we won't grow unless you take risks'. This sounds extremely open-minded, but someone who had known the old general well observed that a second mistake would surely have terminated Burke's career at Johnson & Johnson.

(Source: Heller, 1989: 79–80)

---

are also able to evaluate half-developed ideas, without always wanting all the details filled in first. Furthermore, these managers are prepared to stretch the rules, when an initiative does not entirely fit within the promulgated policy (cf. Burgelman's, 1983, view on autonomous strategies, discussed in Chapter 6). Finally, it should be emphasized that the stress and pressure on managers that is typical for present-day business organizations does not induce creativity (Agor, 1991; Schwenk and Thomas, 1983). An organization that expects new ideas from its employees should also give them sufficient time to think.

8.3 Improving group decision making

In this section a small selection from the many techniques for improving group decision making discussed in the literature will be presented. These techniques are *brainstorming*, the *nominal group technique*, the *Delphi method*, and *group decision support systems*. But before going into these various approaches, the concept of consensus will be discussed.

Achieving consensus

When group decision processes are not guided by explicit procedures, the group members often interact in a way which is implicitly believed to lead to consensus. In the four techniques for improving group decision making to be discussed below the achievement of consensus plays a crucial role, too. Group members try to convince each other by elaborating arguments and by pointing at supporting evidence. The goal is to find a solution everybody can agree with. Only if this goal cannot be reached are other decision rules used, such as majority vote or fiat.

Consensus and unanimity

There is a subtle difference between deciding on the basis of consensus and on the basis of unanimity. In the case of unanimity all decision makers agree that the selected option is the best. In the case of consensus some of the group members may have a different opinion about what is the optimal alternative, but the option chosen and the argumentation leading to its choice is acceptable to everyone (Hall, 1971). If the group members with a diverging opinion comply in order to avoid an impasse, or to give an impression of unity to the outside world, the difference between consensus and majority vote with post-decision loyalty of dissenting members almost dissolves.

Guidelines for reaching consensus

Several authors have formulated guidelines for decision making by consensus (see Box 8.2). The essence of these guidelines is that striving for a final consensus is important, but this goal should not foreclose a profound discussion. Real consensus is not achieved by covering up latent disagreements, but by bringing them into the open and finding acceptable solutions.

In discussions about organizational strategy, groups may strive after consensus on means as well as on ends Both are an element of the strategic decision-making process, as we have seen in Chapter 2. However, sometimes it is possible to live with differences of opinion concerning ends if those concerned can reach consensus on means. At least for the short and middle term, it is not terribly important if people have different ultimate goals, as long as they for the time being can agree on the policy to follow (Fahey, 1981). Moreover, lack of consensus on means appears to be more detrimental to the effectiveness of the decision-making process than disagreements on ends (Bourgeois, 1980).

Brainstorming

A problem with decision-making groups is that over time group norms develop and group members tend to conform to dominant group opinions. In serious cases, the phenomenon of 'groupthink' may occur (see Chapter 5). As a result

Box 8.2 Rules for achieving consensus

- Present your own position as clearly and logically as possible, but also consider seriously the reaction of the group in any subsequent presentations of the same point.
- See differences of opinion not as an impediment to the decision-making process, but as the basis for a better ultimate solution.
- Avoid seeing differences of opinion in too personal terms. Discard the notion that someone must win and someone must lose in the discussion.
- Do not change your opinion only to avoid conflicts. Only change your mind if you are genuinely convinced.
- Distrust any consensus reached too easily. It may cover up differences of opinion that have not been made explicit.
- In case of an impasse look for the next most acceptable alternative for all parties.
- Avoid conflict-reducing techniques such as majority vote, coin flippings and the like.

(Source: Hall, 1971; Nemiroff et al., 1976)

of these tendencies, the creativity of a decision-making group often declines after having peaked early in the history of the group (Stein, 1982). For this reason, techniques for enhancing group creativity can be particularly useful and the best-known technique for doing this is called brainstorming (see, e.g., Osborn, 1957; Smart and Vertinsky, 1977).

The method

In a brainstorming session group members generate the largest possible number of ideas. Taking a stimulus question as a point of departure, each group member has the opportunity to contribute one idea at a time. The natural tendency to evaluate – and hence criticize – ideas as they are developed is suppressed by explicitly prohibiting idea evaluation in the initial phases of the brainstorming session. This prohibition should also lower the barriers to contribute for members that are particularly shy, have divergent ideas or have low status within the group. During the idea generation, group members are encouraged to build on (but not criticize) ideas produced by others. This cross-fertilization is assumed to produce a synergetic effect.

After the idea generation phase, the group goes on to edit the ideas. In this phase of the process redundancy is removed by eliminating ideas that are not substantially different from others. The remaining unique ideas are subsequently put in broad categories, to allow useful comparisons in the next phase, idea evaluation. In this phase the ideas within each category are ranked on the basis of consensus, and suggestions for the implementation of the most worth-while ideas are developed.

Applicability and limitations

Brainstorming is most suited for problems that can be solved with information that is available within the organization, but which cannot easily be tapped by more conventional methods. This may be the case if the information is dispersed over many individuals at various ranks and in various functions. In this case an *ad hoc* group can be composed for the brainstorming session in order to bring together information from disparate sources. Alternatively, infor-mation may not flow freely within an established group because of group norms emphasizing harmony or because of informal pecking orders. In this situation the brainstorming technique is used in order to break down the established patterns of interaction within the group. Brainstorming appears to be less suitable for extremely complicated issues that call for concentrated decision making and calculation by a small number of people. Brainstorming is also less fit for close scrutiny of an already identified set of choices (Gallupe and Cooper, 1993).

Three problems may occur in brainstorming sessions. In the first place, the process may lead to the production of large numbers of shallow, poor quality ideas if all group members feel compelled to contribute as many ideas as the others (Bazerman, 1990: 100). This problem is a consequence of the elimination of criticism. Secondly, 'production blocking' as discussed in Chapter 5 may occur (Gallupe and Cooper, 1993). Group members that want to contribute ideas have to wait until it is their turn to talk. By that time, they may have forgotten their idea or have lost interest. Thirdly, 'evaluation apprehension' may lead to self-censorship, impairing the creativity which brainstorming is meant to pro-mote (Gallupe and Cooper, 1993).

These last two problems are most virulent if some of the group members dominate the discussion, because of their rank or their character. The problems of production blocking and evaluation apprehension may also be assumed to increase with group size. The optimal group size is probably as small as six people, with a maximum of about 12 people (Gallupe et al., 1992). A possible remedy for these problems, and a possibility to work with larger groups, is the use of electronic brainstorming methods. These will be discussed below, under the heading of 'group decision support systems'.

The nominal group technique

The nominal group technique bears a strong resemblance to brainstorming, but is even more structured. In this method, no verbal communication between group members is allowed at the initial stage, and also in later phases com-munication is restricted. The reason for not allowing verbal communication at the initial – idea generation – stage is that interacting groups may inhibit creativity (as discussed above).

The method

The typical nominal group process consists of four steps: idea generation, recording, discussion and ranking (Delbecq et al., 1975; Moore, 1987). The most important difference with brainstorming is that ideas are initially generated individually and in silence, with each group member writing down his or her responses to a stimulus question. After that, the ideas are presented to the group, mostly in a round-robin fashion, with each group member in turn contributing one of his or her recorded ideas. All ideas are recorded in the form of a phrase or a brief sentence on a flip-chart or blackboard. During the recording stage no discussion takes place, and no idea is dropped. Subsequently the group members clarify their ideas, and comment on those of the others. It is not necessary to achieve a consensus at this stage; all that is needed is that the various positions are clear to everyone. Finally all group members rank in order all proposals individually. The outcome of the nominal group process is mathematically derived by pooling the individual rankings of the members.

Applicability and limitations

The nominal group technique ends with a voting procedure and may therefore give the impression of being a complete decision-making process. This is not normally the case, as the principal outcome of the technique is the generation of ideas. The outcome of the voting process is not meant to have binding force. Moreover, the ideas generated in the nominal group process typically have to be developed further, and not all of the ideas will in the end be selected for implementation (Moore, 1987: 125).

The nominal group technique can be applied to the same kind of problems as the brainstorming method. Experiments suggest that the main advantage of the nominal group technique is the speed of idea generation (and the subsequent decision making). Therefore the technique is particularly well suited to situations in which time is the critical factor (Nemiroff et al., 1976). The lack of rich verbal communication may be felt as a drawback of the technique.

The Delphi method

The next method for group decision making to be discussed, the Delphi method, is again more structured than those discussed previously (see below for origins). In comparison with the nominal group technique, the Delphi procedure has the advantage that the participants (typically experts on the issue in question) do not actually have to meet. They can be dispersed in place and time and still contribute to the process, because the Delphi technique uses written (mail) questionnaires. Another difference with the nominal group technique is that Delphi is an iterative procedure: participants are informed of the opinions of the rest of the panel, after which they can react and adapt their initial response.

The method

Different kinds and uses of Delphis can be distinguished (Goodwin and Wright 1991; Linstone and Turoff, 1975; Moore, 1987). Originally, the method was developed for making future projections and forecasts (the method is named for the Oracles at Delphi in ancient Greece, who were assumed to be able to forecast future events). Our major concern here is with **policy Delphis**, the objectives of which are not to forecast the future but to ensure that all possible options for a policy decision have been considered, to estimate the impact and consequences of policy options and/or to examine the acceptability of a particular policy option (Moore, 1987: 51).

A policy Delphi consists of at least the following four steps (Moore, 1987: 52). In the first step the issue and the questions to be put to the experts are formulated. In the second step these questions are sent to the participants, who respond anonymously. In the third step these responses are fed back to the experts in a composite form, enabling them to compare their own opinion to those of the other experts. In the fourth step the new responses are analysed in order to detect any consensus or remaining divergent opinions. More iterations are also possible, for instance until the composite feedback stays the same, indicating that everyone is sticking with his or her position (Luthans, 1992: 509).

In conducting a Delphi, a small monitoring team is needed in order to prepare the questionnaires and give feedback to the panel of experts. It is important that the monitoring team protects the anonymity of the experts, for this is a major key to the success of the technique. Anonymity eliminates the problem of 'saving face' when an expert adapts his or her opinion in the process (Luthans, 1992: 509). Shifts of opinion are of crucial importance for the technique, as it is assumed that those with less firmly grounded opinion are most inclined to change their mind. As a result the outcome is assumed to become more accurate after each iteration (Goodwin and Wright, 1991: 254).

Application and limitations

The Delphi method is particularly attractive when one is interested in the judgement of a pool of experts, but it is impossible or impractical to organize a face-to-face meeting. In the case of a policy Delphi, it is necessary that the question and/or options are identified before the first questionnaire is made up. The Delphi method has to rely on some other process to do this (e.g. brainstorming by a small group of internal experts) (Moore, 1987: 125). This is particularly important because the credibility of the Delphi process and of the monitoring team partly depends on it.

According to some sources the Delphi method (as well as the nominal group technique) are significantly more effective in the generation of high quality ideas and judgements than unstructured group processes (Van de Ven and Delbecq, 1971). Other sources, however, point at mixed results of experimental tests. The iterative Delphi technique only slightly improves the performance of a given panel compared to the simple average of individual judgements, and is seldom as good as the judgement of the best member of the group. The limited results of the Delphi method are perhaps a consequence of the fact that the extent of information sharing is small (compared with unstructured group interaction) (Goodwin and Wright, 1991: 255).

Group decision support systems

'Group decision support systems' (GDSS) is a generic term used to refer to various kinds of computer-supported group decision-making systems and techniques. Most of the GDSSs can be used to support face-to-face groups as well as groups that communicate through electronic media. For instance, in a **real-time Delphi** a computer conference is substituted for the mail question-naires of the conventional Delphi (Moore, 1987: 51). This allows participants to respond immediately to the comments entered (anonymously) by the other members of the panel. The total time to complete the Delphi is much reduced in this way.

Below we will, by way of example, discuss briefly three GDSSs: decision conferencing, electronic brainstorming, and strategic options development and analysis.

Decision conferencing

Developed in the late 1970s, decision conferencing is one of the older group decision support systems. (The discussion of decision conferencing is based on Goodwin and Wright, 1991: 255–7 and Phillips, 1990.) Decision conferencing is a socially interactive, computer-assisted approach which aims to generate a shared understanding of a problem and to produce commitment to action. The method requires an intensive two-day or three-day session. The decision group (consisting of the major 'problem owners', that is, the people who bear respon-sibility for solving the problem) is assisted by two people from outside the organization. One of these acts as a facilitator, who helps participants structure their discussion, think creatively, identify issues, model the problem and inter-pret results. The other outsider is a decision analyst who attends to the com-puter modelling and helps the facilitator if necessary.

Decision conferencing consists of an iterative process in which the facilitator, on the basis of the discussion by the group members, tries to con-struct a model of their thinking. This model is put into the computer by the decision analyst, who then projects the results on to a screen. The group members, from their holistic judgement, subsequently criticize the model, and propose improvements. On the other hand, the explicated model may also change the judgements of the group members. It is the inevitable discrepancies between the judgements of the participants and the simplifying model which drive the process.

In case of differences of view between group members there is no attempt to obtain agreement about every aspect of the model. Instead, sensitivity analysis is used to identify areas where disagreement or imperfections in the model specification really matter to the results. Gradually, the model becomes more adequate, until finally new iterations no longer result in changes in the model. At this point the model has served its purpose of helping to achieve insight (the model is not a goal in itself). The group can now go on to summarize key issues and conclusions and to create an action plan.

Electronic brainstorming

The process of brainstorming can be supported by computers (see Gallupe and Cooper, 1993 and Jarvenpaa et al., 1988). In an electronic brainstorming session, the participants have at their disposal networked workstations and an electronic blackboard. Instead of contributing their ideas in a round-robin fashion, they simply type in their suggestions. These ideas are disseminated to the other group members without an identifying mark. Thus, anonymity is preserved, and the group members can react more freely than in a conventional brainstorming session. Anonymity also prevents ideas from being adopted solely because they were advocated by powerful group members.

Various techniques are possible. All ideas can be sent to the electronic blackboard, or just a selection. Group members can also be provided with a random selection of all the ideas generated by the other participants, so that no two people are looking at the same screen. Oral communication can be suspended or encouraged.

After the idea generation phase the session enters the editing phase. At this stage the electronic blackboard is very helpful. Redundancy is eliminated, and remaining ideas are categorized. Software is available that helps organizing ideas by key words. Finally, the brainstorming session can be wound up by voting for the various ideas. Here also, software can make life easier, for instance, by helping to convert individual rank orderings into a group decision.

The main advantages of electronic brainstorming (compared with conventional brainstorming) are that production blocking does not occur (many ideas can be entered simultaneously), and evaluation apprehension is avoided because the process is more anonymous. Electronic brainstorming can also be applied to larger groups than conventional brainstorming, groups of up to 50 people present no problem, although the typical electronic brainstorming group is much smaller. Evidence suggests that electronic brainstorming yields more ideas than conventional brainstorming. However, it is not clear if the additional ideas contribute much in the way of decision quality.

SODA (strategic options development and analysis)

SODA is a method geared at structuring unstructured problems (see Eden and Radford, 1990; Rosenhead, 1989). The primary goal of the technique is to provide a management team with a model which clarifies discussion and negotiation of a complex issue. The secondary goal is to build commitment to solving the problem (to develop high levels of 'problem ownership'). The method is suited to small groups of four to 10 participants.

The procedure starts with interviews with individual group members. The goal of these interviews is to construct 'cognitive maps' (see Chapter 4) of individual group members' views of the issue. That is, strategic goals are identified, as well as the factors and actions that directly contribute to or prevent these goals from being reached. Subsequently, in a one to two day workshop a group map or model is constructed through the aggregation and integration of the individual cognitive mappings into a 'strategic map'. The aim is to secure enough agreement about the nature of the problem for the individual team members to be committed to finding possible solutions as a group.

The merging of individual cognitive maps is achieved by identifying and overlaying identical concepts, and by trying to link other concepts. The process is supported by two facilitators, one of whom attends primarily to the content of the model, the other to the discussion process. The content facilitator uses computer software to record and display qualitative arguments and to build the strategic map. The envisaged result of a SODA-session is agreement between key decision makers on the nature of a strategic problem and possibly agreement on the best option to solve the problem.

8.4 Improving organizational strategic decision making

As mentioned earlier, the distinction between the group level and the organizational level is somewhat hazy as far as methods for improving decision making are concerned. In this section we will describe two methods that are different from those discussed above in that more than one group of decision makers is involved. These methods are **devil's advocacy** and **dialectical inquiry**.

Both approaches involve the introduction of conflict into the corporate strategy formulation process (Thomas, 1984b). This is in contrast with the methods discussed earlier, which are more adequately characterized as consensus-enhancing approaches. The rationale for deliberately introducing conflict into the decision process is that consensus may stand in the way of good decision making. If everybody is of the same view, a partial, and possibly distorted picture of reality guides the decision-making process. A diversity of views, if in some way integrated, leads to a better overall perception (Bourgeois, 1985).

Devil's advocacy

Institutionalizing criticism

The devil's advocacy approach consists of institutionalizing criticism of a contemplated course of action. (The discussion of devil's advocacy is based on Schwenk, 1988: 85–107.) It is designed to avoid the danger of premature consensus. The procedure begins after a possible strategy has been developed.

At this point, some individual or group (the 'devil's advocate') is assigned the task of examining the proposal and the underlying analysis for inconsistencies, inaccuracies and irrelevancies. Subsequently, in a confrontation session, the devil's advocate will critique the proposed strategy, which is defended by the organization members who have designed it. On the basis of the debate in the confrontation session, senior decision makers can accept the original proposal, modify it or demand the development of a completely new proposal. The advantage of devil's advocacy is that all sides of a proposal are brought to the light, the negative as well as the positive.

Who can be a devil's advocate?

The role of devil's advocate can be played by one or more organization members or by outsiders. In the case of organization members, it is best to rotate the task, in order to avoid the devil's advocate becoming 'domesticated', that is, becoming known as a carping critic. It is also possible that the role of the devil's advocate becomes a mere ritual, giving decision makers the impression that they have chosen rationally and considered various perspectives. Task rotation diminishes this risk. Possible devil's advocates are 'junior executives with upper management potential' (Herbert and Estes, 1977).

The alternative to assigning the task of devil's advocate to an organization member is to call in an outsider, management consultants being obvious candidates. At any rate, the method can only be expected to work if it is valued by top management and if the devil's advocate is knowledgeable enough to be taken seriously. If the original proposal has been designed by staff analysts or lower or middle managers, and if top management has a relatively high level of understanding of the data, they may choose to play the role of devil's advocates themselves. In this case it is important not to criticize proposals too ruthlessly, for that would undermine confidence and stifle creativity (see Box 8.3).

Application and limitations

Devil's advocacy is a time-consuming procedure and so should only be used when necessary. That is when the organization has to decide on complex and controversial issues. The method appears to assume a situation in which top management can contemplate a detailed strategic proposal relatively non-committally. This is not the case if top management itself has played an important role in the design of the strategy. The method therefore, appears to be most applicable in organizations in which a specialized staff department develops strategic plans, relatively isolated from top management.

The staff specialists, because they have more time, are likely to know more about the strategic plans, and the data and assumptions that underlie them, than line managers (Mintzberg, 1994). They are the 'strategy experts'. Top management may choose to follow their lead for that reason. This can be called the 'expert model' (Cosier, 1987; Mason, 1969). Devil's advocacy can be seen as a reaction to this expert approach implicitly adopted in many large firms with

---

Box 8.3 The CEO as devil's advocate

Some top managers like to play the role of devil's advocate themselves. A famous example is Harold S. Geneen, CEO of ITT until 1979. Geneen organized regular General Management Meetings that, according to Heller (1989: 45), were sometimes 'a cross between Spanish Inquisition and Stalinist show-trials'. A General Management Meeting lasted for three days. During those days, managers from all the countless business units had to present their results and strategies to the highly critical audience, with a public questioning led by Geneen himself. A former vice-president of ITT observes that Geneen 'didn't arrange all that for our benefit; he did it for himself. And I must say that it worked well, he seemed to know everything'. The system did not work well enough, however, to prevent Geneen from adopting diversification as a 'fanatical religion', and from buying scores of corporations that later had to be sold again, often at heavy losses. Presumably a decision-making atmosphere in which unorthodox viewpoints were certain to be cut down relentlessly has contributed to this decline.

(Sources: Heller, 1989: 45–6; Johnson and Scholes, 1993: 66–7)

---

a separate planning department. Its use in smaller or less differentiated organizations seems to be less obvious.

Field and laboratory research strongly suggests that devil's advocacy leads to more effective decisions than the common (although implicit) expert model (the same is true of dialectical inquiry, to be discussed next). The method improves the decision makers' use of ambiguous information, instead of relying solely on sometimes too narrow expert advice. A disadvantage of devil's advocacy is that top management may be unwilling to question a proposal that has already been developed in substantial detail. This will be particularly the case if dominant top managers have been actively involved in the initiative. Under these circumstances in particular an approach that promotes conflicting views would be useful as the risk of groupthink looms large. Another disadvantage of the method is that it may be difficult to find organization members who are willing to play the role of devil's advocate. In Chapter 5 we saw that group members with a different view are found less attractive for that reason alone. It is risky to be the one that always has a different opinion, even if it is your official task. Finally, it is likely that when decisions are made under time pressure (which very often is the case), the impact of the devil's advocacy method will be limited, because the inclination will be to discard the advocate's criticism as irrelevant.

Dialectical inquiry

Some variants of the devil's advocacy approach come very close to the next type of method to be discussed, dialectical inquiry. Cosier developed a model of devil's advocacy in which the advocate not only criticizes the proposed strategy, but also produces an alternative strategy (Cosier, 1981). The opposition of various alternative strategies is an important feature of dialectical inquiry (see Mason and Mitroff, 1981; Schwenk, 1988; Schwenk and Thomas, 1983; Thomas, 1984b).

Challenging assumptions

The essence of the dialectical inquiry approach, however, is not that one strategic plan is compared with another. The comparative evaluation of several alternatives is a standard item of many models of choice. But in the case of dialectical inquiry the intention is to identify the assumptions underlying the original plan, and then, by changing these assumptions, to show how the same set of data can be interpreted to support an alternative plan. Thus the 'antithesis' of a counterplan is placed opposite to the 'thesis' of the first proposal. (The denomination 'dialectical inquiry' refers to the concept of dialectics developed by the philosopher Hegel. In Hegel's philosophy an antithesis is placed in opposition to a thesis, leading to a synthesis in which the opposition is dissolved ('aufgehoben'), because both are united or transcended on a higher plane.) Both plans have their own group of advocates.

Integrating assumptions

The dialectics of the process take place through a structured debate, in which the advocates of both plans present their cases, interpreting the same set of data in different ways. The result of this debate is that attention is focused on the assumptions underlying both strategies, and on the degree to which the expected success of the plans depends on the accuracy of these assumptions. This should lead to a set of better thought-out assumptions, which form the basis for a new strategic plan ('synthesis').

Application and limitations

Dialectical inquiry, just like devil's advocacy, is to be used at a point in the decision process at which ideas with regard to possible policies have already been formed. This means that the method is activated after an organization has gone through the 'awareness' stage of the decision process. It can lead to a reinterpretation of the issues and a reformulation of possible policies. This is captured in Figure 8.4, taken from an article by Schwenk and Thomas. (As is obvious from the figure, Schwenk and Thomas (1983) employ a model of the decision-making process which is slightly different from that presented in Chapter 2. This difference is immaterial as far as the discussion of the use of devil's advocacy and dialectical inquiry is concerned.)

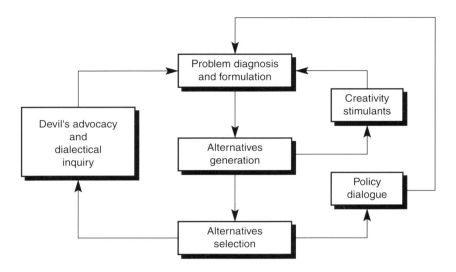

Figure 8.4 Use of aids in the decision formulation process. (Source: Schwenk and Thomas, 1983.)

Devil's advocacy and dialectical inquiry are used during or after the stage of the (initial) selection of alternatives, and may lead to a re-iteration of the steps of the decision process from problem diagnosis through alternatives selection. The creativity stimulants referred to by Schwenk and Thomas are techniques like brainstorming. Strategic options development and analysis (SODA) is an example of a policy dialogue technique.

Dialectical inquiry, just like devil's advocacy, has received empirical support, suggesting that the method does indeed lead to better decision processes (Schwenk, 1988). It also has disadvantages comparable to those of devil's advocacy: top management may resist digging up the assumptions underlying the present or the proposed policy and the procedure is time-consuming (Thomas, 1984b).

In order to give a better impression of the dialectical inquiry approach, one specific variant of the method, 'strategic assumption surfacing and testing' (SAST), will be discussed in some detail (Mason and Mitroff, 1981: chs 3, 4 and 5).

Strategic assumption surfacing and testing

The SAST procedure consists of four phases: pre-meeting activities and introduction, group formation and assumption surfacing, debate of assumptions and integration of assumptions.

Pre-meeting activities and introduction

In the first phase, the participants are selected. The optimal number is between 18 and 24. The participant list should represent all the relevant perspectives on the strategic problem that is going to be dealt with. Furthermore, enough participants with the authority and political power to give weight to the outcome should be included, as well as creative thinkers and people with enough direct, hands-on experience. The participants are supported by one or two facilitators who have experience with the method and knowledge of the underlying ideas.

Group formation and assumption surfacing

In the second phase, a nominal group technique is conducted in order to identify different perspectives. The group members are asked to write down, individually, three to 20 issues that they think are critical to the plan or problem under discussion. They are encouraged to submit unconventional or creative ideas. All ideas are put on a public list, without debate, other than for purposes of clarification. Every individual group member subsequently indicates which five to 10 issues of the aggregated list he or she considers most important. These votes are subsequently used for composing small groups of people with similar perspectives. In this way a maximum of homogeneity within and heterogeneity between groups is achieved.

In the small groups (three to seven members) thus made up, the participants set out to sharpen their particular perspective, and develop a concomitant policy proposal. After that, the groups identify stakeholders, that is, concrete entities that affect and/or are affected by the proposed policy. Examples are individuals or departments within the organization, labour unions, competitors, customers, government agencies, and so on. Next the groups identify the assumptions underlying their policy, by answering, for every stakeholder, the question: 'What must we be assuming about this stakeholder and its future behaviour in order for the plan to be successful?' (Mason and Mitroff, 1981: 101). Contradictory assumptions should not be repressed at this stage.

All the assumptions generated in this way are ranked with regard to their relative importance and their uncertainty (how sure are the group members that the statement is correct?), and plotted on a graph (see Figure 8.5). The pivotal assumptions are those that are relatively important and relatively certain. These are the 'bedrock' assumptions for the policy in question. The assumptions that are relatively important and relatively uncertain can be called 'major question marks'.

Debate of assumptions

In the next phase the groups come together for a plenary debate about the proposed policies and the underlying assumptions. All groups present their cases, and the pivotal assumptions as well the major question marks. Some of the assumptions will be shared by two or more groups. In other cases, opposite

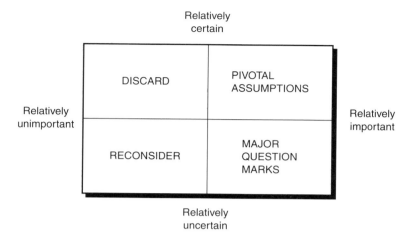

Figure 8.5 Assumption plotting graph. (Source: adapted from Mason and Mitroff, 1981: 48.)

assumptions may be found, or one group may maintain assumptions that are particularly damaging for the viability of the policy proposed by another group. On the basis of these presentations for all policies a list of 'damaging assumptions' is made up. These lists are the point of departure for an unstructured debate between all participants. This debate is hoped to surface more of the background beliefs that lie at the basis of the policies and the assumptions. It continues until all critical issues have been discussed; it is not necessary that all differences of opinion be resolved.

Integration of assumptions

In this last phase of the SAST procedure either new groups are formed, consisting ideally of at least one member of the initial working groups, or the whole process is passed through in a plenary session. The emphasis is now on synthesis, and no longer on the differences between groups. The participants now try to reach consensus on a synthetic set of assumptions, and develop a policy based on these synthetic assumptions. In some cases it will not be possible to obtain a synthesis. The group can then analyse the outcome of the policy proposals under different assumptions, and choose the strategy that does best under various sets of assumptions (see Box 8.4). Another option is to try to reach consensus concerning the data that would be necessary for the group to decide on the contested assumptions, and postpone the decision until these data have been gathered.

A SAST workshop as described above typically has a duration of approximately three and a half days. If there is little time, some of the later phases can be shortened, or even eliminated, but the initial activities are critical.

The outcomes of the procedure include some or all of the following:

Box 8.4 Deciding on the pricing policy for a drug

Mason and Mitroff, in their book *Challenging Strategic Planning Assumptions*, discuss the case of a drug company that had to decide on the pricing policy for an important product. One group of managers was in favour of raising the price, another group of lowering the price, and yet other managers wanted to leave the price at the present level. A SAST session made clear that these differences of opinion had much to do with different assumptions regarding one of the most important stakeholders, namely the drug-prescribing physician. The high-price group assumed that the physician prescribed the best quality drug for the patient. The low-price group on the other hand believed that the physician prescribes the lowest price drug that will serve the patient's needs. The two groups could not come to one shared assumption on this point, but they agreed that the assumption was a major question mark. Careful analysis of assumptions regarding the physician's perception of price eventually led to a consensus. Everybody agreed that if the price of the drug were raised and (if necessary) subsequently lowered physicians would continue to prescibe the drug. However, if the price of the drug was first lowered, and subsequently raised to the old level, physicians were believed not to prescribe the drug as often as before. On the basis of this shared assumption it was decided to raise the price.

(Source: Mason and Mitroff, 1981: 76–8)

- an understanding of the assumptions underlying several policy options;
- a shared identification of pivotal assumptions for any strategy;
- a newly developed strategy synthesizing the insights acquired through the assumption surfacing and testing process;
- a list of information necessary for checking the status of pivotal assumptions.

Disadvantages of devil's advocacy and dialectical inquiry

The strength of devil's advocacy and dialectical inquiry is that these methods allow the organization to break out of a consensus which stifles creativity. However, this advantage comes at a price. Experimental evidence suggests that decision procedures that introduce conflict do indeed produce decisions that are better thought-out, but they also lead to lower levels of satisfaction of the participants (Schweiger et al., 1986). The conflicts that are evoked by devil's advocacy and dialectical inquiry cannot be suppressed at will, once they have served their purpose. These conflicts may weaken the ability of a group to work together effectively in the future. The experiment conducted by Schweiger and associates also made clear that the commitment to actually implement decisions is lower if high conflict decision procedures have been used. This finding is troubling, because one of the strengths of a method like SAST purportedly is the heightened commitment to decisions.

Findings reported in the literature suggest that the introduction of conflict into the decision-making process should occur only after careful consideration (Cosier and Aplin, 1980; Schweiger et al., 1986). If the harmony in a decision-making group is precarious, use of the consensus method is advisable. If there is excessive harmony, and the danger of groupthink looms large, dialectical inquiry is called for. In intermediate cases devil's advocacy is perhaps most appropriate.

8.5 The dialectics of opening and closure

Notwithstanding the inevitability and necessity of programming decision behaviour emphasized in the beginning of this chapter, the discussion of methods for improving decision making in the previous section may confer the impression that it is always good to de-programme decision procedures, and to introduce conflict into previously harmonious decision groups. This is not the case, of course. Maintenance and reinforcement of existing patterns of behaviour is under many circumstances beneficial to the organization. Introducing conflict into decision-making groups – like with the devil's advocacy and the dialectical inquiry procedures – is not without its dangers and disadvantages, as we have seen. In this last section of the chapter we will focus on what can be called 'the dialectics of opening and closure': the interplay between programming and de-programming movements which are both complementary and antipodal. (This section is strongly influenced by Romme, 1992.)

Programming and de-programming

Opposite and complementary movements

Programming and de-programming are opposite movements. Programming decision making provides closure: signals from the environment are interpreted through the use of ready-made schemes, and reactions are chosen from a given response set. Programming allows the decision maker to ward off potentially disturbing variations in the environment, in order to accomplish efficiently day-to-day routine processes. De-programming, on the other hand, consists in the questioning of formerly taken-for-granted cognitive schemes, shared meanings and values, routines and procedures. Existing behavioural programmes are scrutinized and held against the light of reason. De-programming opens up an individual, group or organization to changes in the environment. Thus programming and de-programming are opposite movements, the first towards the pole of fully programmed choice, the other towards fully rational decision making.

But programming and de-programming are also complementary movements. Without programming, there is nothing to de-programme. This is true not only in the most obvious sense, but also because, given cognitive limitations, no individual, group or organization can function without the use of routines, procedures, and so on. On the other hand, without de-programming, programming would lead to ossification and inability to respond to environmental changes. An individual, group or organization which is not able to adapt its response set to changes in the environment has little chance of survival in a competitive world. Then again, de-programming must be followed by re-programming, for without the counterforce of closure, opening would lead to the disintegration of the system (Wing-Tsit Chan, in Romme, 1992: 23).

Opening/closure as a dialectic movement

If programming is seen as the thesis, and de-programming as the antithesis, the movement of opening and closure can be seen as a dialectic, leading to the synthesis of re-programming. This means that the changes that take place, or that we would like to see take place, in the behaviour of a decision maker (whether at the individual, group or organizational level) are not a simple oscillation between the poles of programmed choice and rational deliberation. If the paradigm of dialectics is valid, the opposition between programming and de-programming is transcended in the subsequent movement of re-programming (see the discussion of Hegelian dialectics above). That is, decision making is re-programmed at a higher level of effectiveness, responsiveness, and so on, than existed before the de-programming took place.

However, the dialectical movement does not stop there. With time, the re-programmed decision behaviour tends to ossify, to become ingrained in taken-for-granted routines, to become part of the organizational culture, and to sink below the level of consciousness. This means that after some time a new movement of de-programming is needed, followed by re-programming, and so on *ad infinitum*.

This picture of the development of decision-making behaviour over time is only accurate if the decision maker is able to learn, in the sense that the model underlying his decision behaviour can be adapted when necessary.

Decision making and learning

As pointed out in Chapter 7, two kinds of learning processes can be distinguished: single-loop learning and double-loop learning (Argyris, 1984). Single-loop learning occurs when a mental model of the environment is

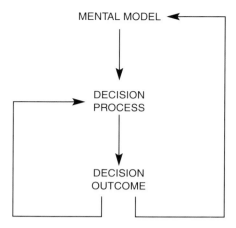

Figure 8.6 Double-loop learning.

acquired, and used for decision making. Through repetitive application, the model is internalized to the point that it becomes subconscious and is used automatically. This is a process that in the terminology of this book would be categorized as decision programming.

The automatic use of internalized mental schemes (we have seen in Chapter 4 that this is identified with the use of intuition) has many advantages, such as rapid response and economizing on scarce cognitive resources. But the big disadvantage is that the decision maker is no longer critical of the model and its limitations. Consequently, the model may be applied out of context, or become inappropriate when circumstances change. This is what Argyris calls 'skilled incompetence' (Argyris, 1990).

To avoid this danger, double-loop learning is necessary. Double-loop learning involves changing the model used to make decisions. With double-loop learning there are two feedback loops from decision outcomes: one to the decision process as it is executed applying the existing model, and one from the decision outcome to the model itself (see Figure 8.6).

The second feedback loop enables the decision maker to reflect critically on the model in use, and to initiate changes when decision outcomes deviate strongly from what was to be expected on the basis of the model. It will be clear that the dialectic progress of decision behaviour fuelled by the succession of programming, de-programming and re-programming can only be expected if the decision-making unit in question is capable of double-loop learning.

The learning organization

Double-loop learning is the key to the prevention of ossification of strategic decision making in organizations. The recipe contains no mysterious ingredients: all that is needed is alertness concerning the decision models and procedures used and their limitations. At the same time, this is the most difficult thing there is. It goes against our nature to question the obvious. An oppressive story by Vladimir Nabokov paints the 'supreme terror' that results if all habitual interpretations of reality give way, and the human mind refuses to accept houses as 'houses', and trees as 'trees' (Nabokov, 1975). Yet this is what those responsible for strategic decision making within organizations should do from time to time: refuse to see the obvious truth that underlies the existing concept of the organization and its relationship with the environment.

Becoming a learning organization

A 'learning organization' is an organization which is capable of constant revitalization of its strategic decision-making processes. This is only possible if continuous learning at the level of individual organization members is encouraged, if processes exist for easy dispersion of knowledge around the organization, and if the organization is able to change quickly its way of acting (Thompson, 1993: 712). While all this is easy enough to understand, it is less clear how an organization can attain these goals. For instance, the recommendation made by some authors that organizations should routinize the learning process appears to be dangerous in the light of the foregoing discussion (Quinn Mills and Friesen, 1992). This could lead to the very ossification the learning organization tries to prevent.

Becoming a learning organization is all the more difficult because of the defence mechanisms that may be activated if the existing organizational structure, culture and procedures, as well as the taken-for-granted worldviews of organization members are attacked. A prime defence routine is to make the key existing patterns of behaviour undiscussable, and to make the fact that they are undiscussable itself undiscussable (Stacey, 1993: 184). This is a strategy often employed consciously or unconsciously by dominating groups in the organization, and the lone dissenter can speak out candidly only at his or her own peril.

Yet the ability to discuss is the linchpin of learning (Nutt, 1989: 342). And at least in environments that change at a fast pace, the ability of individuals and organizations to learn may in the long run be the only sustainable competitive advantage (Stata, 1989). In what way can the organization adapt itself in order to enhance its capacity to learn?

Corporate networking

Apart from following recommendations to stimulate de-programming and re-programming at the level of individuals and groups, contained in the earlier sections of this chapter, the organization as a whole must try to acquire characteristics that make it more capable of learning. Doubtlessly, organizational culture is an important element. For instance, key characteristics of a learning organization have been described as 'real commitment to knowledge' and 'openness to the outside world' (Quinn, Mills and Friesen, 1992). We have discussed the difficult task of changing culture in Chapter 6. A third characteristic regards the organizational structure: a learning organization has a mechanism for internal renewal (Quinn, Mills and Friesen, 1992).

One way for an organization to secure this ability to renew itself is to complement the more traditional organizational structure with more fluid human networks (Mueller, 1991). The requisite informal human networks often already exist within the organization; they only need to be encouraged and empowered. The free-flowing communication within networks is vital to the initiation and acceptance of changes in culture, attitude and mind-set within an organization.

The recommendation to stimulate informal networking is also in line with Mintzberg and Waters' (1983) observations concerning strategy formations in adhocracies, the type of organization associated with the most turbulent environments. In these organizations the formal organizational structure is complemented with – if not substituted by – an informal, project-like structure that is constantly adjusted in line with changes in the environment. Ossification of decision-making processes is avoided in this way. However, this extreme flexibility has its price, and should not be pursued indiscriminately in every context.

Chapter summary

- Decision processes tend to become programmed over time, that is, they are removed from the realm of rational deliberation. A way to revitalize strategic decision making is to de-programme the associated decision processes.

- It is inevitable that de-programmed decision-making processes will be eventually re-programmed.

- Individual decision making can be improved by strengthening rational analysis (decision analysis) and/or by stimulating creativity.

- Creativity is an assumption-breaking process.

- Some techniques for improving group decision making are brainstorming, the nominal group technique, the Delphi method and various group decision support systems.

- Methods for improving organizational decision making are devil's advocacy and dialectical inquiry. These methods entail the introduction of conflict into the decision process. They have the advantage of enabling the organization to break out of a consensus which stifles creativity. The disadvantage is that they disrupt the harmony of decision groups.

- In a learning organization programming (closure), de-programming (opening), and re-programming (closure) follow one another in a dialectic movement, that is, re-programming takes place at a level of effectiveness and/or efficiency that transcends that of the previous phase.

References

Ackoff, R.L. and Emory, F.E. (1972). *On Purposeful Systems*. Chicago, IL: Aldine-Atherton

Agor, W.H. (1991). The logic of intuition: how top executives make important decisions. In *Creative Management* (Henry, J. ed.), pp. 162–76 London: Sage

Allen, G. and Hammond, J. (1976). The use of experience curves in competitive decision making. Boston: Intercollegiate Case Clearing House, Case #9–175–174

Allison, G.T. (1971). *Essence of Decision: Explaining the Cuban Missile Crisis*. Boston: Little, Brown

Allison, S.T. and Messick, D.M. (1987). From individual inputs to group outputs, and back again. In *Group Processes* (Hendrick, C. ed.), pp. 111–43. Newbury Park, CA: Sage

Amburgey, T.L. and Dacin, T. (1994). As the left-foot follows the right? The dynamics of strategic and structural change. *Academy of Management Journal*, **37**, 1427–52

Andrews, K.R. (1971). *The Concept of Corporate Strategy*. Homewood, IL: Irwin

Andrews, K.R. (1980). Director's responsibility for corporate strategy. *Harvard Business Review*, November–December, 30–44

Ansoff, H.I. (1965). *Corporate Strategy*. New York: McGraw-Hill

Ansoff, H.I. and McDonnel, E.J. (1990). *Implanting Strategic Management*, 2nd edn. Hemel Hempstead: Prentice–Hall

Argyris, Ch. (1984). Double loop learning in organizations. In *Organizational Psychology*, 4th edn (Kolb, D.A, Rubin, I.M. and McIntyre J.M., eds.), pp. 45–58. Englewood Cliffs, NJ: Prentice-Hall

Argyris, Ch. (1990). In Stacey R.D., *Strategic Management and Organizational Dynamics*. London: Pitman

Arrow, K.J. (1963). *Social Choice and Individual Values*, 2nd edn. New Haven, CT: Yale University Press

Axelrod, R. (1973). Schema theory: an information processing model of perception and cognition. *American Political Science Review*, **67**, 1248–66

Baligh, H.H. (1994). Components of culture: nature, interconnections, and relevance to the decisions on the organization structure. *Management Science*, **40**, 14–27

Bandura, A. (1986). *Social Foundations of Thought and Action: A Social Cognitive Theory*. Englewood Cliffs, NJ: Prentice-Hall

Barkema, H.G. (1988). Variations in ownership structure, managerial pay packages and managerial effort across firms and industries. *Unpublished PhD Thesis*, University of Groningen

Barnard, C.I. (1938). *The Functions of the Executive*. Cambridge, MA: Harvard University Press

Barnes, J.H., Jr. (1984). Cognitive biases and their impact on strategic planning. *Strategic Management Journal*, **5**, 129–37

Baron, R.S., Kerr N.L. and Miller, N. (1992). *Group Process, Group Decision, Group Action*. Buckingham: Open University Press

Bateman, Th. S. and Zeithaml, C.P. (1989). The psychological context of strategic decisions: a model and convergent experimental findings. *Strategic Management Journal*, **10**, 59–74

Bazerman, M.H. (1990). *Judgment in Managerial Decision Making*, 2nd edn. New York: John Wiley

Beach, L.R. (1993). Four revolutions in behavioral decision theory. In *Leadership Theory and Research; Perspectives and Directions* (Chemers, M.M. and Ayman, R., eds.), pp. 271–92. San Diego, CA: Academic Press

Beer, M., Eisenstat, R.A. and Spector, B. (1990). *The Critical Path to Corporate Renewal*. Boston, MA: Harvard Business School Press

Behling, O. and Eckel, N.L. (1991). Making sense out of intuition. *Academy of Management Executive*, **5**(1), 46–54

Bennis, W. and Nanus, B. (1985). *Leaders: The Strategies for Taking Charge*. New York: Harper & Row

Berger, P. and Luckmann, T. (1966). *The Social Construction of Reality*. New York: Doubleday

Berle, A.A. and Means, G.C. (1932). *The Modern Corporation and Private Property*. New York: Commerce Clearing House

Binmore, K. and Dasgupta, P. (1986). Game theory: a survey. In *Economic Organizations as Games* (Binmore, K. and Dasgupta, P., eds.), pp. 1–45. Oxford: Basil Blackwell

Blake, R.R. and Mouton, J.S. (1964). *The Managerial Grid*. Houston, TX: Gulf Publishing

Bourgeois, J.L. III (1980). Performance and consensus. *Strategic Management Journal*, **1**, 227–48

Bourgeois, J.L. III (1984). Strategic management and determinism. *Academy of Management Review* **9**, 586–96

Bourgeois, J.L. III (1985). Strategic goals, perceived uncertainty, and economic performance in volatile environments. *Academy of Management Journal*, **28**, 548–73

Bourgeois, J.L. III and Brodwin, D.R. (1984). Strategic implementation: five approaches to an elusive phenomenon. *Strategic Management Journal*, **5**, 241–64

Bower, J.L. (1968). *Managing the Resource Allocation Process*. Cambridge, MA: Harvard University Press

Bowman, E.H. (1980). A risk/return paradox for strategic management. *Sloan Management Review*, **21**(3), 17–31.

Braybrooke, D. and Lindblom, Ch.E. (1963). *A Strategy of Decision. Policy Evaluation As a Social Process*. New York: The Free Press

Brown, R. (1988). *Group Processes; Dynamics Within and Between Groups*. Oxford: Basil Blackwell

Brunsson, N. (1982). The irrationality of action and action rationality: decisions, ideologies and organizational actions. *Journal of Management Studies*, **18**, 29–44

Burgelman, R.A. (1983). A model of the interaction of strategic behavior, corporate context, and the concept of strategy. *Academy of Management Review*, **8**, 61–70

Burns, T. and Stalker, G. (1961). *The Management of Innovation*. London: Tavistock

Byrne, J.A. (1994). The craze for consultants. *Business Week*, 25 July, 46–50

Cadland, D.K. (1977). The persistent problems of emotion. In *Emotion* (Cadland, D. K. et al., eds.), pp. 1–84. Monterey, CA: Brooks/Cole

Camerer, C.F. (1991). Does strategy research need game theory? *Strategic Management Journal*, **12**, 137–52

Carroll, G.R. (1988). *Ecological Models of Organizations*. Cambridge, MA: Ballinger

Chaffee, E.E. (1985). Three models of strategy. *Academy of Management Review*, **10**, 89–98

Chandler, A.D. Jr. (1962). *Strategy and Structure; Chapters in the History of the Industrial Enterprise*. Cambridge, MA: MIT Press

Chatman, J.A. and Jehn, K.A. (1994). Assessing the relationship between industry characteristics and organizational culture: how different can you be? *Academy of Management Journal*, **37**, 522–53

Child, J. (1972). Organization structure, environment and performance: the role of strategic choice. *Sociology*, **6**, 2–22

Christensen, C.R., Andrews, K.R., Bower, J.L., Hamermesh, R.G. and Porter, M.E. (1982). *Business Policy: Text and Cases*, 5th edn. Homewood, IL: Irwin

Christensen, C.R., Andrews, K.R., Bower, J.L., Hamermesh, R.G. and Porter, M.E. (1987). *Business Policy: Text and Cases*, 6th edn. Homewood, IL: Irwin

Coffey, R.E., Cook, C.W. and Hunsaker Ph. L. (1994). *Management and Organizational Behaviour*. Burr Ridge, IL: Irwin

Cohen, M.D., March, J.G. and Olsen, J.P. (1988). A garbage can model of organizational choice. In March, J.G. *Decisions and Organizations*. Oxford: Basil Blackwell

Colman, A.M. (1982). *Game Theory and Experimental Games. The Study of Strategic Interaction*. Oxford: Pergamon

Cosier, R.A. (1981). Dialectical inquiry in strategic planning: a case of premature acceptance? *Academy of Management Review*, **6**, 643–8

Cosier, R.A. (1987). The effects of three potential aids for making strategic decision on prediction accuracy. *Organizational Behavior and Human Performance*, **22**, 295–306

Cosier, R.A. and Aplin, J.C. (1980). A critical view of dialectical inquiry as a tool in strategic planning. *Strategic Management Journal*, **1**, 343–56

Cray, D., Mallory, G.R., Butler, R.J., Hickson, D.J. and Wilson, D.C. (1988). Sporadic, fluid and constricted processes: three types of strategic decision making in organizations. *Journal of Management Studies*, **25**, 13–39

Cray, D., Mallory, G.R., Butler, R.J. Hickson, D.J. and Wilson, D.C. (1991). Explaining decision processes. *Journal of Management Studies*, **28**, 227–51

Crozier, M. and Friedberg, E. (1977). *L'Acteur et le Système*. Paris: Editions du Seuil

Cyert, R.M. and March, J.G. (1963). *A Behavioral Theory of the Firm*. Englewood Cliffs, NJ: Prentice-Hall

David, F.R. (1991). *Strategic Management*, 3rd edn. New York: Macmillan

Davis, J. (1973). Group decision and social interaction: a theory of social decision schemes. *Psychological Review*, **80**, 97–125

Davis, S.M. and Lawrence, P.R. (1977). *Matrix*. Reading, MA: Addison-Wesley

Deal, T. and Kennedy, A. (1982). *Corporate Cultures: The Rites and Rituals of Corporate Life*. Reading, MA: Addison-Wesley

Dean, J.W. Jr. and Sharfman, M.P. (1993). Procedural rationality in the strategic decision-making process. *Journal of Management Studies*, **30**, 587–610

Dearborn, D.C. and Simon, H.A. (1958). Selective perceptions: a note on the departmental identification of executives. *Sociometry*, **21**, 140–4

DeBono, E. (1971). *Lateral Thinking*. New York: Harper

Delbecq, A.L., van de Ven A.H. and Gustafson, D.H. (1975). *Group Techniques for Program Planning*. Glenview, IL: Scott, Foresman

De Smit, J. (1982). *Planning Rituals; The Development of a Planning Process for the Dutch University System*. Delft: Delft University Press

Dess, G.G. and Miller, A. (1993). *Strategic Management*. New York: McGraw-Hill

Dessler, G. (1986). *Organization Theory: Integrating Structure and Behavior*, 2nd edn. Englewood Cliffs, NJ: Prentice-Hall

Dewey, J. (1933). *How We Think*. Boston: Heath

DiMaggio, P.J. and Powell, W.W. (1991). Introduction. In *The New Institutionalism in Organizational Analysis* (Powell, W.W. and DiMaggio, P.J., eds.), pp. 1–38 Chicago, IL: University of Chicago Press

DIO International Research Team (1983). A contingency model of participative decision making: an analysis of 56 decisions in three Dutch organizations. *Journal of Occupational Psychology*, **56**, 1–18

Donaldson, G. and Lorsch, J.W. (1983). *Decision-Making at the Top: The Shaping of Strategic Direction*. New York: Basic Books

Driver, M.J. and Mock, T.J. (1975). Human information processing, decision style theory, and accounting systems. *The Accounting Review*, July, 490–508

Dutton, J.E. (1993). Interpretations on automatic: a different view of strategic issue diagnosis. *Journal of Management Studies*, **30**, 339–57

Dutton, J.E., Fahey, L. and Narayanan, V.K. (1983). Toward understanding strategic issue diagnosis. *Strategic Management Journal*, **4**, 307–23

Dutton, J.E., and Jackson, S.E. (1987). Categorizing strategic issues: links to organizational action. *Academy of Management Review*, **12**, 76–90

Eden, C. (1989). Using cognitive mapping for strategic options development and analysis (SODA). In *Rational Analysis in a Problematic World* (Rosenhead, J., ed.), pp. 21–42. London: Wiley

Eden, C. (1992). Strategy development as a social process. *Journal of Management Studies*, **29**, 799–811

Eden, C. and Radford, J., eds., (1990). *Tackling Strategic Problems: The Role of Group Decision Support*. London: Sage

Eden, C. and Simpson, P. (1989). SODA and cognitive mapping in practice. In *Rational Analysis in a Problematic World* (Rosenhead, J., ed.), pp. 43–70. London: Wiley

Eigerman, M.R. (1988). Who should be responsible for business strategy? *Journal of Business Strategy*, November/December, 40–4

Eisenhardt, K.M. and Bourgeois III, L.J. (1988). Politics of strategic decision making in high-velocity environments: toward a midrange theory. *Academy of Management Journal*, **31**, 737–70

Emory, C.W. and Niland, P. (1968). *Making Management Decisions*. Boston, MA: Houghton Mifflin

Etzioni, A. (1986). The case for a multiple-utility conception. *Economics and Philosophy*, **2**, 159–83

Etzioni, A. (1988). *The Moral Dimension: Toward a New Economics*. New York: The Free Press

Evans, J.St.B.T., Over, D.E. and Maktelow K.I. (1993). Reasoning, decision making and rationality. *Cognition*, **49**, 165–87

Fahey, L. (1981). On strategic management decision processes. *Strategic Management Journal*, **2**, 43–60

Fama, E.F. and Jensen, M.C. (1983). Separation of ownership and control. *Journal of Law and Economics*, **26**, 301–25

Ferrell, W. (1985). Combining individual judgements. In *Behavioral Decision Making* (Wright, G., ed.), pp. 111–45 New York: Plenum Press

Festinger, L. (1957). *A Theory of Cognitive Dissonance*. Stanford, CA: Stanford University Press

Fiegenbaum, A. and Thomas, H. (1988). Attitudes toward risk and the risk-return paradox: Prospect theory explanation. *Academy of Management Journal*, **31**, 85–106

Fischhoff, B. and Beyth, R. (1975). 'I knew it would happen'; Remembered probabilities of once-future things. *Organizational Behavior and Human Performance*, **13**, 1–16

Fischhof, B., Slovic P. and Lichtenstein S. (1980). Knowing what you want: Measuring labile values. In *Cognitive Processes in Choice and Decision Behavior* (Wallsten, T.S., ed.), pp. 117–41. Hillsdale, NJ: Lawrence Erlbaum

Forsyth, D.R. (1990). *Group Dynamics*, 2nd edn. Pacific Grove, CA: Brooks/Cole

Frank, R.H. (1988). *Passions Within Reason: The Strategic Role of the Emotions*. New York: W.W. Norton & Company

Fredrickson, J.W. (1986). The strategic decision process and organizational structure. *Academy of Management Review*, **11**, 280–97

Fredrickson, J.W. and Iaquinto A.L. (1989). Inertia and creeping rationality in strategic decision processes. *Academy of Management Journal*, **32**, 516–42

French, J.R.P. Jr. and Raven, B. (1959). The bases of social power. In *Studies in Social Power* (Cartwright, D., ed.), pp. 150–67. Ann Arbor, MI: Institute for Social Research

Galbraith, J.R. (1977). *Organization Design*. Reading, MA: Addison-Wesley

Gallupe, R.B. and Cooper, W.H. (1993). Brainstorming electronically. *Sloan Management Review*, Fall, 27–36

Gallupe, R.B., Dennis, A.R., Cooper, W.H., Valacich, J.S., Bastionutti, L.M. and Nanamaker, J.F. Jr. (1992). Electronic brainstorming and group size. *Academy of Management Journal*, **35**, 350–69

Ghemawat, P. (1991). *Commitment: The Dynamic of Strategy*. New York: Free Press

Gensch, D.H. and Javalgi, R.G. (1987). The influence of involvement on disaggregate attribute choice models. *Journal of Consumer Research*, **14**, 71–82

Godet, M. (1987). *Scenarios and Strategic Management*. London: Butterworths

Goodwin, P. and Wright, G. (1991). *Decision Analysis for Management Judgment*. Chichester: John Wiley

Gordon, G.G. (1991). Industry determinants of organizational culture. *Academy of Management Review*, **16**, 396–415

Gouldner, A.W. (1960). The norm of reciprocity: A preliminary statement. *American Sociological Review*, **25**, 161–78

Graeff, C.L. (1983). The situational leadership theory: a critical review. *Academy of Management Review*, **8**, 285–91

Grandori, A. (1987). *Perspectives on Organization Theory*. Cambridge, MA: Ballinger

Grayson, L.E. (1987). *Who and How in Planning for Large Companies; Generalizations from the Experiences of Oil Companies*. Basingstoke: Macmillan

Greer, D.F. (1984). *Industrial Organization and Public Policy*. New York: Macmillan

Gupta, A.K. and Govindarajan, V. (1984). Business unit strategy, managerial characteristics, and business unit effectiveness at strategy implementation. *Academy of Management Journal*, **27**, 25–41.

Guth, W., Schmittberger, K. and Schwarze, B. (1982). An experimental analysis of ultimatum bargaining. *Journal of Economic Behavior and Organization*, **3**, 367–88

Hall, D.J. and Saias, M.A. (1980). Strategy follows structure! *Strategic Management Journal*, **1**, 149–63

Hall, J. (1971). Decisions, decisions, decisions. *Psychology Today*, November, 51–4, 86, 88

Hambrick, D.C. and d'Aveni, R.A. (1992). Top team deterioration as part of the downward spiral of large corporate bankruptcies. *Management Science*, **38**, 1445–66

Hambrick, D.C. and Mason, Ph.A. (1984). Upper echelons: the organization as a reflection of its top managers. *Academy of Management Review*, **9**, 193–206

Handy, Ch. (1991). The age of unreason. In *Creative Management* (Henry, J., ed.), pp. 269–82. London: Sage

Hannan, M.T. and Freeman, J.H. (1989). *Organizational Ecology*. Cambridge, MA: Harvard University Press

Harrison, E.F. (1987). *The Managerial Decision-Making Process*, 3rd edn. Boston: Houghton Mifflin

Haselhoff, F. (1976). A new paradigm for the study of organizational goals. In *From Strategic Planning to Strategic Management* (Ansoff, H.I., de Clerck, R.P. and Hayes, R.L., eds.), pp. 15–27. Chichester: John Wiley

Hassard, J. and Sharifi, S. (1989). Corporate culture and strategic change. *Journal of General Management*, **15**(2), 4–19

Hatch, M.J. (1993). The dynamics of organizational culture. *Academy of Management Review*, **18**, 657–93

Hauschildt, J. (1986). Goals and problem solving in innovative decisions. In *Empirical Research on Organizational Decision-Making* (Witte, E. and Zimmermann, H.-J., eds.), pp. 3–19. Amsterdam: North Holland

Hax, A.C. and Majluf, N.S. (1984). *Strategic Management: An Integrative Perspective*. Englewood Cliffs, NJ: Prentice-Hall

Heiner, R.A. (1983). The origin of predictable behaviour. *American Economic Review*, **73**, 560–90

Hedley, B.D. (1976). A fundamental approach to strategy development. *Long Range Planning*, **9**(6), 2–11

Hedley, B.D. (1977). Strategy and the 'business portfolio'. *Long Range Planning*, **10**(1), 9–15

Heller, R. (1989). *The Decision Makers*. Falmouth: Hodder & Stoughton

Hendrikse, G.W.J. (1991). Organizational choice and product differentiation. *Managerial and Decision Economics*, **12**, 361–6

Henry, J. (1991). Making sense of creativity. In *Creative Management* (Henry, J., ed.), pp. 3–11. London: Sage

Herbert, T.T. and Estes, R.W. (1977). Improving executive planning by formalizing dissent: the corporate devil's advocate. *Academy of Management Review*, **2**, 662–7

Hickson, D.J., Butler, R.J., Cray, D., Mallory, G.R. and Wilson, D.C. (1986). *Top Decisions: Strategic Decision-Making in Organizations*. Oxford: Basil Blackwell

Hickson, D.J., Hinings, C.R., Lee, C.A., Schneck, R.E., and Pennings, J.M. (1971). A strategic contingencies' theory of intraorganizational power. *Administrative Science Quarterly*, **16**, 216–29

Hill, Ch.W.L. and Jones, G.R. (1989). *Strategic Management: An Integrated Approach*. Boston: Houghton Mifflin

Hitt, M.A. and Tyler, B.B. (1991). Strategic decision models: integrating different perspectives. *Strategic Management Journal*, **12**, 327–51

Hofer, C.W. (1975). Towards a contingency theory of business strategy. *Academy of Management Journal*, **18**, 784–810

Hofer, C.W. and Schendel, D. (1978). *Strategy Formulation: Analytical Concepts*. St Paul, MN: West

Hofstede, G. (1980). *Culture's Consequences: International Differences in Work-Related Values*. Beverly Hills, CA: Sage

Hofstede, G. (1984). Cultural dimensions in management and planning. *Asia Pacific Journal of Management*, January, 81–99.

Hofstede, G. (1991). *Cultures and Organizations: Software of the Mind*. London: McGraw-Hill

Hofstede, G., Neuijen, B., Ohayv, D.D. and Sanders, G. (1990). Measuring organizational cultures: A qualitative and quantitative study across twenty cases. *Administrative Science Quarterly*, **35**, 286–316

Hogarth, R.M. (1980). *Judgement and Choice: the Psychology of Decision*. Chichester: John Wiley

Horvath, D. and MacMillan, C.J. (1979). Strategic choice and the structure of decision processes. *International Studies of Management and Organization*, **9**, 87–112

Horovitz, J.H. (1980). *Top Management Control in Europe*. New York: St Martin

Horwitz, R. (1979). Corporate planning – a conceptual critique. *Long Range Planning*, **12**, February, 62–6.

Huey, J. (1993). Managing in the midst of chaos. *Fortune*, 5 April, 30–6

Huff, A.S. and Reger, R.K. (1987). A review of strategic process research. *Journal of Management*, **13**, 211–36.

Jackson, J.M. (1959). A space for conceptualizing person–group relationships. *Human Relations*, **10**, 3–15

Jackson, S.E. and Dutton, J.E. (1988). Discerning threats and opportunities. *Administrative Science Quarterly*, **33**, 370–87

Janis, I.L. (1982). *Victims of Groupthink*, 2nd edn. Boston: Houghton Mifflin

Janis, I.L. (1989). *Crucial Decisions: Leadership in Policymaking and Crisis Management*. New York: The Free Press

Jarvenpaa, S.L., Rao, V.S. and Huber, G.P. (1988). Computer support for meetings of groups working on unstructured problems: a field experiment. *MIS Quarterly*, **12**, 645–66.

Jay, A. (1967). *Management and Machiavelli*. New York: Holt, Rinehart & Winston

Jegers, M. (1991). Prospect theory and the risk-return relation: some Belgian evidence. *Academy of Management Journal*, **34**, 215–25

Jelinek, M. (1979). *Institutionalizing Innovation*. New York: Praeger

Jepperson, R.L. (1991). Institutions, institutional effects, and institutionalism. In *The New Institutionalism in Organizational Analysis* (Powel, W.W. and DiMaggio, P.J., eds.), pp. 143–63. Chicago, IL: University of Chicago Press

Johnson, D.W. and Johnson F.R. (1987). *Joining Together: Group Theory and Group Skills*, 3rd edn. Englewood Cliffs, NJ: Prentice-Hall

Johnson, E. and Russo, J.E. (1984). Product familiarity and learning new information. *Journal of Consumer Research*, **11**, 542–50.

Johnson, G. (1987). *Strategic Change and the Management Process*. Oxford: Basil Blackwell

Johnson, G. (1988). Rethinking incrementalism. *Strategic Management Journal*, **9**, 75–91.

Johnson, G. (1992). Managing strategic change – strategy, culture and action. *Long Range Planning*, **25**(1), 28–36

Johnson, G. and Scholes, K. (1993). *Exploring Corporate Strategy: Text and Cases*, 3rd edn. New York: Prentice-Hall

Johnson-Laird, Ph.N. and Shafir, E. (1993). The interaction between reasoning and decision making: an introduction. *Cognition*, **49**, 1–9

Kaplan, M.F. (1987). The influencing process in group decision making. In *Group Processes* (Hendrick, C., ed.), pp. 189–212. Newbury Park: Sage

Kapteyn, A., Wansbeek, T. and Buyze, J. (1979). Maximizing or satisficing? *Review of Economics and Statistics*, **61**, 549–63

Katz, D. and Kahn, R.L. (1978). *The Social Psychology of Organizations*, 2nd edn. New York: John Wiley

Kets de Vries, M.F.R. and Miller, D. (1984). *The Neurotic Organization*. San Francisco, CA: Jossey-Bass

Kerr, N.L. (1992). Issue importance and group decision making. In *Group Process and Productivity* (Worchel, S., Wood, W. and Simpson, J.A., eds.), pp. 68–88. Newbury Park, CA: Sage

Kerr, N.L., Davis, J.H., Meek, D. and Rissman, A.K. (1975). Group position as a function of member attitudes: choice shift effects from the perspective of social decision scheme theory. *Journal of Personality and Social Psychology*, **31**, 574–93

Kerr, N.L. and MacCoun, R.J. (1985). The effect of jury size and polling method on the process and product of jury deliberation. *Journal of Personality and Social Psychology*, **48**, 349–63

Kiechel, W., III (1982). Corporate strategists under fire. *Fortune*, 12 December, 34–9.

Kiesler, S. and Sproull, L.S. (1982). Managerial response to changing environments: perspectives on problem sensing from social cognition. *Administrative Science Quarterly*, **27**, 548–70

Kirkpatrick, D. (1993). Could AT & T rule the world? *Future*, 17 May, 19–27

Klayman, J. and Schoemaker, P.J.H. (1993). Thinking about the future: a cognitive perspective. *Journal of Forecasting*, **12**, 161–8

Knight, F.H. (1965 [1921]). *Risk, Uncertainty and Profit*. New York: Harper & Row

Koopman, P.L. and Pool, J. (1990). Decision making in organizations. *International Review of Industrial and Organizational Psychology*, **5**, 101–48.

Kreps, D.M. and Spence, A.M. (1984). Modelling the role of history in industrial organization and competition. In *Contemporary Issues in Modern Microeconomics* (Feiwel, G., ed.), pp. 340–78. London: Macmillan

Lane, Ch. (1989). *Management and Labour in Europe*. Aldershot: Edward Elgar

Langley, A. (1988). The roles of formal strategic planning. *Long Range Planning* **21**(3), 40–50

Langley, A. (1989). In search of rationality: the purposes behind the use of formal analysis in organizations. *Administrative Science Quarterly*, **34**, 598–631

Laughlin, P.R. and Adamopoulous, J. (1982). Social decision schemes on intellective tasks. In *Group Decision Making* (Brandstatter, H., Davis, J. and Stocker-Kreichgauer, G., eds.), pp. 81–94. London: Academic Press

Laughlin, P.R. and Ellis, A.L. (1986). Demonstrability and social combination processes on mathematical intellective tasks. *Journal of Experimental Social Psychology*, **22**, 177–89

Lawrence, P. and Lorsch, J. (1967). *Organization and Environment*. Boston, MA: Harvard Business School, Division of Research

Lea, S.E.G., Tarpy R.M. and Webley, P. (1987). *The Individual in the Economy: A Textbook of Economic Psychology*. Cambridge: Cambridge University Press

Leary, M.R. and Forsyth, D.R. (1987). Attributions of responsibility for collective endeavors. In *Group Processes* (Hendrick, C., ed.), pp. 167–88. Newbury Park, CA: Sage

Learned, E.P., Christensen, C.R., Andrews, K.R. and Guth, W.D. (1965). *Business Policy: Text and Cases*. Homewood, IL: Irwin

Legrenzi, P., Girotto, V. and Johnson-Laird, P.N. (1993). Focussing in reasoning and decision making. *Cognition*, **49**, 37–66

Lévi-Strauss, C. (1969). *The Elementary Structures of Kinship* (Bell, J.H, von Sturmer, J.R. and Needham, R., trans.). London: Eyre & Spottiswoode

Lewin, K. (1947). Group decision and social change. In *Readings in Social Psychology*, (Newcomb, T.M. and Hartley, E.L., eds.), pp. 330–44. New York: Holt, Rinehart & Winston

Liddell Hart, B.H. (1967). *Strategy*, 2nd edn. London: Faber & Faber

Lindblom, Ch.E. (1959). The science of muddling through. *Public Administration Review*, **19**, 79–88

Linstone, H. and Turoff, M. eds. (1975). *The Delphi Method: Techniques and Applications*. Reading, MA: Addison-Wesley

Lorange, P. (1980). *Corporate Planning: An Executive Viewpoint*. Englewood Cliffs, NJ: Prentice-Hall

Loomis, C.J. (1993). Dinosaurs? *Fortune*, 3 May, 32–8

Lundberg, C.C. (1985). On the feasibility of cultural intervention in organizations. In P.J. Frost et al., *Organizational Culture*. Beverly Hills, CA: Sage, pp. 169–85

Luthans, F. (1992). *Organizational Behavior*, 6th edn. New York: McGraw-Hill

Lyles, M.A. (1981). Formulating strategic problems: empirical analysis and model development. *Strategic Management Journal* **2**, 61–75

Mahoney, J.T. (1993). Strategic management and determinism: Sustaining the conversation. *Journal of Management Studies*, **30**, 173–91

Maljers, F.A. (1990). Strategic planning and intuition in Unilever. *Long Range Planning*, **23**(2), 63–8

Malmlow, E.G. (1972). Corporate strategic planning in practice. *Long Range Planning*, **5**(3), 2–9

March, J.G. (1978). Bounded rationality, ambiguity, and the engineering of choice. *Bell Journal of Economics*, **9**, 587–608

March, J.G. (1981). Decision making perspective: decisions in organizations and theories of choice. In *Perspectives on Organization Design and Behavior* (van de Ven, A.H. and Joyce, W.F., eds.), pp. 205–44. New York: John Wiley

March, J.G. and Olsen, J.P., eds. (1976). *Ambiguity and Choice in Organizations*. Bergen: Universitetsforlaget

March, J.G. and Sevón, G. (1988). Behavioral perspectives on theories of the firm. In *Handbook of Economic Psychology* (van Raaij, W.F., van Veldhoven, G.M. and Wärneryd, K.E., eds.), pp. 368–402. Dordrecht: Kluwer Academic Publishers

March, J.G. and Shapira, Z. (1988). Managerial perspectives on risk and risk-taking. In *Decisions and Organizations* (March, J.G., ed.), pp. 76–97. Oxford: Basil Blackwell

March, J.G. and Simon, H.A. (1993 [1958]). *Organizations*, 2nd edn. Cambridge, MA: Blackwell

Martin, J., Sitkin, S.B. and Boehm, M. (1985). Founders and the elusiveness of a cultural legacy. In *Organizational Culture* (Frost, P.J., et al., eds.), pp. 99–124. Beverly Hills, CA: Sage

Maslow, A.H. (1970). *Motivation and Personality*, 2nd edn. New York: Harper & Row

Mason, R.O. (1969). A dialectical approach to strategic planning. *Management Science*, **15**, B403–B414

Mason, R.O. and Mitroff, I.I. (1981). *Challenging Strategic Planning Assumptions*. New York: John Wiley

Maule, A.J. (1985). Cognitive approaches to decision making. In *Behavioral Decision Making* (Wright, G., ed.), pp. 61–84. New York: Plenum Press

Mazzolini, R. (1981). How strategic decisions are made. *Long Range Planning*, **14**(3), 85–96

Meyer, J.W. and Rowan, B. (1977). Institutionalized organizations: formal structure as myth and ceremony. *American Journal of Sociology*, **83**, 340–63

Miles, R.E. and Snow, C.C. (1978). *Organizational Strategy, Structure, and Process*. New York: McGraw-Hill

Milgrom, P. and Roberts, J. (1992). *Economics, Organization, and Management*. Englewood Cliffs, NJ: Prentice-Hall

Miller, D. (1986). Configurations of strategy and structure: towards a synthesis. *Strategic Management Journal*, **7**, 233–49

Miller, D. (1987). Strategy making and structure: analysis and implications for performance. *Academy of Management Journal*, **30**, 7–32

Miller, D. (1993). The architecture of simplicity. *Academy of Management Review*, **18**, 116–38

Miller, K.L. (1994) I came, I saw, I conquered. *Business Week*, 11 July, 191–2

Miller, D. and Friesen, P.H. (1984). *Organizations: A Quantum View*. Englewood Cliffs, NJ: Prentice-Hall

Miller, D., Kets de Vries, M. and Toulouse, J.-M. (1982). Top executive locus of control and its relationship to strategy-making, structure, and environment. *Academy of Management Journal*, **25**, 237–53

Miner, J.B. (1992). *Industrial-Organizational Psychology*. New York: McGraw-Hill

Mintzberg, H. (1973). *The Nature of Managerial Work*. New York: Harper & Row

Mintzberg, H. (1978). Patterns in strategy formation. *Management Science*, **9**, 934–48

Mintzberg, H. (1979). *The Structuring of Organizations*. Englewood Cliffs, NJ: Prentice-Hall

Mintzberg, H. (1981). What is planning anyway? *Strategic Management Journal*, **2**: 319–24

Mintzberg, H. (1983a). *Power in and around Organizations*. Englewood Cliffs, NJ: Prentice-Hall

Mintzberg, H. (1983b). *Structure in Fives: Designing Effective Organizations*. Englewood Cliffs, NJ: Prentice-Hall

Mintzberg, H. (1985). The organization as political arena. *Journal of Management Studies*, **23**, 133–54

Mintzberg, H. (1988). Planning on the left side and managing on the right. *Harvard Business Review*, 54 (July–August), 49–58

Mintzberg, H. (1989). *Mintzberg on Management: Inside Our Strange World of Organizations*. New York: The Free Press

Mintzberg, H. (1990a). The Design School: reconsidering the basic premises of strategic management. *Strategic Management Journal*, **11**, 171–95

Mintzberg, H. (1990b). Strategy formation: schools of thought. In *Perspectives on Strategic Management* (Fredrickson, J.W., ed.) pp. 105–235. New York: Harper & Row

Mintzberg, H. (1994). *The Rise and Fall of Strategic Planning*. New York: Prentice-Hall

Mintzberg, H. and McHugh, A. (1985). Strategy formation in an adhocracy. *Administrative Science Quarterly*, **30**, 160–97

Mintzberg, H., Raisinghani, D. and Théorêt, A. (1976). The structure of unstructured decision processes. *Administrative Science Quarterly*, **21**, 246–75

Mintzberg, H. and Waters, J.A. (1982). Tracking strategy in an entrepreneurial firm. *Academy of Management Journal*, **25**, 465–99

Mintzberg, H. and Waters, J.A. (1983). The mind of the strategist(s). In *The Executive Mind* (Srivastva, S., et al., ed.), pp. 58–83. San Francisco, CA: Jossey-Bass

Mintzberg, H. and Waters, J.A. (1985). Of strategies, deliberate and emergent. *Strategic Management Journal*, **6**, 257–72

Mintzberg, H. and Waters, J.A. (1990). Does decision get in the way? *Organization Studies*, **11**, 1–6.

Mirvis, P. and Berg, D. (1977). *Failures in Organization Development and Change*. New York: John Wiley

Moore, C.M. (1987). *Group Techniques for Idea Building*. Newbury Park, CA: Sage

Moreland, R.L. (1987). The formation of small groups. In *Group Processes* (Hendrick, C., ed.). Newbury Park, CA: Sage

Moreland, R.L. and Levine, J.M. (1992). Problem identification by groups. In *Group Process and Productivity* (Worchel, S., Wood, W. and Simpson, J.A., eds.), pp. 17–47. Newbury Park: Sage

Morgan, G. (1993). *Imaginization: The Art of Creative Management*. Newbury Park, CA: Sage

Mueller, R.K. (1991). Corporate networking: How to tap unconventional wisdom. In *Creative Management* (Henry, J., ed.), pp. 153–62. London: Sage

Myers, D.G. and Lamm, H. (1976). The group polarization phenomenon. *Psychological Bulletin*, **83**, 602–27

Nabakov, V. (1975). *Tyrants Destroyed and Other Stories*. London: Weidenfeld and Nicolson

Narayanan, V.K. and Fahey, L. (1982). The micro-politics of strategy formulation. *Academy of Management Review*, **7**, 25–34

Nelson, R.R. (1991). Why do firms differ, and how does it matter? *Strategic Management Journal*, **12**, 61–74

Nelson, R.R. and Winter, S.G. (1982). *An Evolutionary Theory of Economic Change*. Cambridge: Belknap Press of Harvard University Press

Nemiroff, P.M., Pasmore, W.A. and Ford, D.L. (1976). The effects of two normative structural interventions on established and *ad hoc* groups: implications for decision making effectiveness. *Decision Sciences*, **7**, 841–55

Noorderhaven, N.G. (1990). Private competence and public responsibility. *Unpublished PhD Dissertation*, University of Groningen

Nutt, P.C. (1984). Types of organizational decision processes. *Administrative Science Quarterly*, **29**, 414–50

Nutt, P.C. (1989). *Making Tough Decisions. Tactics for Improving Managerial Decision Making*. San Francisco, CA: Jossey-Bass

Nutt, P.C. (1993). The formulation processes and tactics used in organizational decision making. *Organization Science*, **4**, 226–51

Ölander, F. (1975). Search behavior in non-simultaneous choice situations: Satisficing or maximizing? In *Utility, Probability, and Human Decision Making* (Wendt, D. and Vlek, C., eds.), pp. 297–320. Dordrecht: Reidel

O'Reilly, C. (1989). Corporations, culture, and commitment: Motivation and social control in organizations. *California Management Review*, **31**, 9–25

Osborn, A. (1957). *Applied Imagination*. New York: Scribner

Paré, T.P. (1994). Jack Welch's nightmare on Wall Street. *Fortune*, 5 September, 50–5

Pascale, R. (1985). The paradox of 'corporate culture': Reconciling ourselves to socialization. *California Management Review*, Winter, 29–38

Payne, J.W. (1985). Psychology of risky decisions. In *Behavioral Decision Making* (Wright, G., ed.), pp. 3–23. New York: Plenum Press

Payne, J.W., Bettman, J.R. and Johnson, E.J. (1992). Behavioral decision research: A constructive processing perspective. *Annual Review of Psychology*, **43**, 87–131

Perrow, C. (1961). The analysis of goals in complex organizations. *American Sociological Review*, **26**, 854–66

Peters, Th.J. and Waterman, R.H. (1982). *In Search of Excellence; Lessons from America's Best-Run Companies*. New York: Harper & Row

Pettigrew, A.M. (1973). *The Politics of Organizational Decision Making*. London: Tavistock

Pettigrew, A.M. (1977). Strategy formulation as a political process. *International Studies of Management and Organization*, **7**, 78–87

Pfeffer, J. (1981). *Power in Organizations*. Marshfield, MA: Pitman

Pfeffer, J. and Salancik, G.R. (1978). *The External Control of Organizations: A Resource Dependence Perspective*. New York: Harper & Row

Phillips, L.D. (1990). Decision analysis for group decision support. In *Tackling Strategic Problems: The Role of Group Decision Support* (Eden, C. and Radford, J., eds), pp. 142–53. London: Sage

Piaget, J. (1970). *Psychologie et Epistémologie*. Paris: Denoël

Pieters, R.G.M. (1988). Attitude-behavior relationships. In *Handbook of Economic Psychology* (van Raaij, W.F., van Veldhoven, G.M. and Wärneryd, K.E., eds.), pp. 147–204. Dordrecht: Kluwer Academic Publishers

Pieters, R.G.M. and W.F. van Raaij (1988). The role of affect in economic behavior. In *Handbook of Economic Psychology* (van Raaij, W.F., van Veldhoven, G.M. and Wärneryd, K.E., eds), pp. 108–42 Dordrecht: Kluwer Academic Publishers

Plutchik, R. (1985). On emotion: the chicken-and-egg problem revisited. *Motivation and Emotion*, **9**, 197–200

Porter, M.E. (1980). *Competitive Strategy: Techniques for Analyzing Industries and Competitors*. New York: The Free Press

Postrel, S. (1991). Burning your britches behind you: can policy scholars bank on game theory? *Strategic Management Journal*, **12**, 153–5

Prelec and Herrnstein (1991). Preferences or principles. In *Strategy and Choice* (Zeckhauser, R.J., ed.), pp. 319–39. Cambridge, MA: MIT Press

Quinn, J.B. (1978–1979). Strategic change: 'Logical Incrementalism'. *Sloan Management Review*, **20**, 7–21

Quinn, J.B. (1980). *Strategies for Change: Logical Incrementalism*. Homewood, IL: Irwin

Quinn, J.B., Mills, D. and Friesen, B. (1992). The learning organization. *European Management Journal*, **10**(2), 146–56

Quinn, J.B., Mintzberg, H. and James, R.M. (1988). *The Strategy Process: Concepts, Contexts, and Cases*. Englewood Cliffs, NJ: Prentice-Hall

Raiffa, H. (1991). Coping with common errors in rational decision making. In *Strategy and Choice* (Zeckhauser, R.J., ed.), pp. 341–57. Cambridge, MA: MIT Press

Rice, F. (1994). How to make diversity pay. *Fortune*, 8 August, 44–9.

Robert, H.M., III (1971). *Robert's Rules of Order Revised*. New York: William Morrow

Robey, D. and Taggart, W. (1981). Measuring managers' minds: the assessment of style in human information processing. *Academy of Management Review*, **6**, 375–83

Robbins, S.P. (1990). *Organization Theory*, 3rd edn. Englewood Cliffs, NJ: Prentice-Hall

Rohlen, Th.P. (1973). 'Spiritual education' in a Japanese bank. *American Anthropologist*, **75**, 1542–62

Romme, A.G.L. (1992). A self-organization perspective on strategy formation. *PhD Thesis*, University of Limburg

Rosenhead, J., ed. (1989). *Rational Analysis in a Problematic World*. London: John Wiley

Rotter, J.B. (1966). Generalized expectancies for internal versus external control of reinforcement. *Psychological Monographs* No. 609. Washington: American Psychological Association

Rowe, A.J., Mason, R.O., Dickel, K.E., Mann, R.B. and Mockler, R.J. (1994). *Strategic Management: A Methodological Approach*, 4th edn. Reading, MA: Addison-Wesley

Rumelt, R.P., Schendel, D. and Teece, D.J. (1991). Strategic management and economics. *Strategic Management Journal*, **12**, 5–29

Saloner, G. (1991). Modeling, game theory, and strategic management. *Strategic Management Journal*, **12**, 119–36

Schein, E.H. (1985). *Organizational Culture and Leadership*. San Francisco, CA: Jossey Bass

Schelling, Th.C. (1978). *Micromotives and Macrobehavior*. New York: Norton

Schneider, S.C. (1989). Strategy formulation: the impact of national culture. *Organization Studies*, **10**, 149–68

Schoeffler, S., Buzzell, R.D. and Heany, D.F. (1974). Impact of strategic planning on profit performance. *Harvard Business Review*, **52**(2), 137–45

Schoemaker, P.J.H. (1982). The expected utility model: Its variants, purposes, evidence and limitations. *Journal of Economic Literature*, **20**, 529–63

Schoemaker, P.J.H. (1993). Strategic decisions in organizations: rational *and* behavioural views. *Journal of Management Studies*, **30**, 107–29

Schweiger, D.M., Sandberg, W.R. and Ragan, J.W. (1986). Group approaches for improving strategic decision making: a comparative analysis of dialectical inquiry, devil's advocacy, and consensus. *Academy of Management Journal*, **29**, 51–71

Schwendiman, J.S. (1973). *Strategic and Long-Range Planning for the Multi-National Corporation*. New York: Preager

Schwenk, C.R. (1984). Cognitive simplification processes in strategic decision-making. *Strategic Management Journal*, **5**, 111–28

Schwenk, Ch.R. (1988). *The Essence of Strategic Decision Making*. Lexington, MA: Lexington Books

Schwenk, Ch.R. and Thomas, H. (1983). Formulating the mess: The role of decision aids in problem formulation. *Omega*, **11**, 239–52

Selznick, Ph. (1957). *Leadership in Administration*. Evanston, IL: Row Peterson

Shafir, E., Simonson, I. and Tversky, A. (1993) Reason-based choice. *Cognition*, **49**, 11–36

Sheldon, A. (1980). Organizational paradigms: a theory of organizational change. *Organizational Dynamics*, **8**(3), 61–71

Sherman, S. (1994). Leaders learn to heed the voice within. *Fortune*, 22 August, 64–70

Shrivastava, P. and Grant, J.H. (1985). Empirically derived models of strategic decision making processes. *Strategic Management Journal*, **6**, 97–113

Shrivastava, P., Mitroff, I.I. and Alvesson, M. (1987). Nonrationality in organizational actions. *International Journal of Management and Organization*, **17**, 90–109

Shugan, S.M. (1980). The cost of thinking. *Journal of Consumer Research*, **7**, 99–111

Simon, H.A. (1955). A behavioral model of rational choice. *Quarterly Journal of Economics*, **69**, 99–118

Simon, H.A. (1957). *Models of Man*. New York: John Wiley

Simon, H.A. (1960). *The New Science of Management Decision*. New York: Harper & Row

Simon, H.A. (1964). On the concept of organizational goal. *Administrative Science Quarterly*, **9**, 1–22

Simon, H.A. (1965). *The Shape of Automation*. New York: Harper & Row

Simon, H.A. (1972). Theories of bounded rationality. In *Decision and Organization* (McGuire, C. and Radner, R., eds.), pp. 161–76. Amsterdam: North Holland

Simon, H.A. (1976). *Administrative Behavior*. New York: The Free Press

Simon, H.A. (1987). Making management decisions: the role of intuition and emotion. *Academy of Management Executive*, **1**(1), 57–64

Slovic, P., Fischhoff, B. and Lichtenstein, S. (1977). Behavioral decision theory. *Annual Review of Psychology*, **28**, 1–39

Smart, C. and Vertinsky, I. (1977). Designs for crisis decision units. *Administrative Science Quarterly*, **22**, 640–57

Smith, G.F. (1989). Defining managerial problems: a framework for prescriptive theorizing. *Management Science*, **35**, 963–81

Smircich, L. (1983). Concepts of culture and organizational analysis. *Administrative Science Quarterly*, **28**, 339–58

Smircich, L. and Stubbart, T. (1985). Strategic management in an enacted world. *Academy of Management Review*, **10**, 724–36

Smith, G.D., Arnold, D.R. and Bizzell, B.G. (1991). *Business Strategy and Policy*, 3rd edn. Boston: Houghton Mifflin

Snow, C.C. and Hambrick, D.C. (1980). Measuring organizational strategies: Some theoretical and methodological problems. *Academy of Management Review*, **5**, 527–38

Spender, J.-C. (1989). *Industry Recipes: The Nature and Sources of Management Judgement*. Oxford: Basil Blackwell

Spender, J.-C. (1993). Some frontier activities around strategy theorizing. *Journal of Management Studies*, **30**, 11–30

Stacey, R.D. (1990). *Dynamic Strategic Management for the 1990s; Balancing Opportunism and Business Planning*. London: Kogan Page

Stacey, R.D., ed. (1993). *Strategic Management and Organizational Dynamics*. London: Pitman

Starbuck, W.H. (1983). Organizations as action generators. *American Sociological Review*, **2**, 91–102

Starbuck, W.H., Greve, A. and Hedberg, B.L.T. (1978). Responding to crises. *Journal of Business Administration*, **9**, 111–37

Starmer, Ch. (1993). The psychology of uncertainty in economic theory: a critical appraisal and a fresh approach. *Review of Political Economy*, **5**, 181–96.

Stasser, G. (1992). Pooling of unshared information during group discussions. In *Group Process and Productivity* (Worchel, S., Wood, W. and Simpson, J.A., eds.), pp. 48–67. Newbury Park, CA: Sage

Stasser, G., Taylor, L.A. and Hauna, C. (1989). Information sampling in structure and unstructured discussions of three- and six-person groups. *Journal of Personality and Social Psychology*, **57**, 67–78

Stata, R. (1989). Organizational learning – the key to management innovation. *Sloan Management Review*, Spring, 63–74

Staw, B.M. (1980). Rationality and justification in organizational life. In *Research in Organizational Behavior* (Staw, B. and Cummings, L., eds.), Greenwich, CT: JAI Press

Staw, B.M. and Ross, J. (1980). Commitment in an experimenting society: an experiment on the attribution of leadership from administrative scenarios. *Journal of Applied Psychology*, **65**, 249–60

Staw, B.M. and Ross, J. (1987). Behaviour in escalation situations: antecedents, prototypes, and solutions. *Research in Organizational Behaviour*, **9**, 39–78

Steidlmeier, P. (1993). Institutional approaches in strategic management. *Journal of Economic Issues*, **27**, 189–211

Stein, M.I. (1982). Creativity, groups, and management. In *Improving Group Decision Making in Organizations* (Guzzo, R.A., ed.), pp. 127–55. New York: Academic Press

Steinbrunner, J.D. (1974). *The Cybernetic Theory of Decision*. Princeton, NJ: Princeton University Press

Steiner, G.A. (1969). *Top Management Planning*. New York: Macmillan

Steiner, I.D. (1972). *Group Process and Productivity*. New York: Academic Press

Stigler, G.J. and Friedland, C. (1983). The literature of economics: the case of Berle and Means. *Journal of Law and Economics*, **26**, 237–68

Suttle, B.B. (1987). The passion of self-interest: the development of the idea and its changing status. *American Journal of Economics and Sociology*, **46**, 459–72

Taggart, W. and Robey, D. (1981). Minds and managers: on the dual nature of human information processing and management. *Academy of Management Review*, **6**, 187–95

Taggart, W., Robey, D. and Kroeck, K.G. (1985). Managerial decision styles and cerebral dominance: an empirical study. *Journal of Management Studies*, **22**, 175–92

Taylor, R.N. (1975a). Age and experience as determinants of managerial information processing and decision making performance. *Academy of Management Journal*, **18**, 74–81

Taylor, R.N. (1975b). Psychological determinants of bounded rationality: Implications for decision-making strategies. *Decision Sciences*, **6**, 409–29

Terpstra, V. and David, K. (1991). *The Cultural Environment of International Business*, 3rd edn. Cincinnati, OH: South-West Publishing Co.

Thomas, H. (1984a). Mapping strategic management research. *Journal of General Management*, **9**(4), 55–72

Thomas, H. (1984b). Strategic decision analysis: applied decision analysis and its role in the strategic management process. *Strategic Management Journal*, **5**, 139–56

Thomas, H. and Pruett, M. (1993). Introduction to the special issue: perspectives on theory building in strategic management. *Journal of Management Studies*, **30**, 3–10

Thomas, J.B. and McDaniel, R.R. Jr. (1990). Interpreting strategic issues: Effects of strategy and the information-processing structure of top management teams. *Academy of Management Journal*, **33**, 286–306

Thompson, J.L. (1993). *Strategic Management: Awareness and Change*, 2nd edn. London: Chapman & Hall

Tirole, J. (1988). *The Theory of Industrial Organization*. Cambridge, MA: MIT Press

Tuckman, B.W. and Jensen, M.A.C. (1977). Stages of small group development revisited. *Group and Organizational Studies*, **2**, 419–27

Tversky, A. (1972). Elimination by aspects: a theory of choice. *Psychological Review*, **79**(4), 281–99

Tversky, A. and Kahneman, D. (1974). Judgement under uncertainty: heuristics and biases. *Science*, **185**, 1124–31

Tversky, A. and Kahneman, D. (1985). The framing of decisions and the psychology of choice. In *Behavioral Decision Making* (Wright, G., ed.) pp. 25–41. New York: Plenum Press

Tversky, A. and Kahneman, D. (1992). Advances in prospect theory: Cumulative representation of utility. *Journal of Risk and Uncertainty*, **5**, 297–323

Van Cauwenbergh, A. and Cool, K. (1982). Strategic management in a new framework. *Strategic Management Journal*, **3**, 245–265

Van Maanen, J. and Barley, S.R. (1985). Cultural organization: fragments of a theory. In *Organizational Culture* (Frost, P.J., et al., eds.), pp. 31–53. Beverly Hills: Sage

Van Raaij, W.F. (1988). Information processing and decision making. Cognitive aspects of economic behaviour. In *Handbook of Economic Psychology* (van Raaij, W.F., van Veldhoven, G.M. and Wärneryd, K.E., eds.), pp. 74–106. Dordrecht: Kluwer Academic Publishers

Van Veldhoven, G.M. (1988). Dynamic aspects of economic behavior: Some determinants. In *Handbook of Economic Psychology* (van Raaij, W.F., van Veldhoven, G.M. and Wärneryd, K.E., eds.), pp. 52–73. Dordrecht: Kluwer Academic Publishers

Von Winterfeldt, D. and Edwards, W. (1986). *Decision Analysis and Behavioral Research*. Cambridge: Cambridge University Press

Wallas, G. (1926). *The Art of Thought*. New York: Harcourt Brace Jovanovich

Walliser, B. (1989). Instrumental rationality and cognitive rationality. *Theory and Decision*, **27**, 7–36

Walter, S.M., ed. (1980). *Proceedings of the White House Conference on Strategic Planning*. Washington, DC: Council of State Planning Agencies

Wärneryd, K.-E. (1988). Social influences on economic behavior. In *Handbook of Economic Psychology* (van Raaij, W.F., van Veldhoven, G.M. and Wärneryd, K.E. eds.), pp. 206–48. Dordrecht: Kluwer Academic Publishers

Weber, E.U. (1994). From subjective probabilities to decision weights: the effect of asymmetric loss functions on the evaluation of uncertain outcomes and events. *Psychological Bulletin*, **115**, 228–42

Weick, K.E. (1979). *The Social Psychology of Organizing*, 2nd edn. New York: Random House

Weick, K.E. (1983). Managerial thought in the context of action. In *The Executive Mind* (Srivastva, S. et al., eds.), pp. 221–42. San Francisco: Jossey Bass

Weick, K.E. (1985). The significance of corporate culture. In *Organizational Culture* (Frost, P.J., et al., eds.), pp. 381–9. Beverly Hills, CA: Sage

Weigelt, K. and Camerer, C. (1988). Reputation and corporate strategy: Review of recent theory and applications. *Strategic Management Journal*, **9**, 443–54

Wheelan, T.L. and Hunger, J.D. (1990). *Strategic Management*. Reading, MA: Addison-Wesley

Whipp, R., Rosenfeld, R. and Pettigrew, A. (1989). Culture and competitiveness: Evidence from two mature UK industries. *Journal of Management Studies*, **26**, 561–85

White, R.K. (1971). Selective inattention. *Psychology Today*, November, 47–86

Whyte, G. (1986). Escalating commitment to a course of action: a reinterpretation. *Academy of Management Review*, **11**, 311–21

Whyte, G. (1989). Groupthink reconsidered. *Academy of Management Review*, **14**, 40–56

Whyte, G. (1993). Escalating commitment in individual and group decision making: a prospect theory approach. *Organizational Behaviour and Human Decision Processes*, **54**, 430–55

Wilson, D.C. (1980). Organizational strategy. *PhD Thesis*, University of Bradford

Wilson, D.C. (1982). Electricity and resistance: a case study of innovation and politics. *Organization Studies*, **3**, 119–140

Wilson, D.C., Butler, R.J., Cray, D., Hickson, D.J. and Mallory, G.R. (1986). Breaking the bounds of organization in strategic decision making. *Human Relations*, **39**, 309–32

Winter, S.G. (1987). Knowledge and competence as strategic assets. In *The Competitive Challenge: Strategies for Industrial Innovation and Renewal* (Teece, D.J., ed.), pp. 159–84. New York: Harper & Row

Witte, E. (1972). Field research on complex decision-making processes – the Phase Theorem. *International Studies of Management and Organization*, **2**, 156–82

Woodward, J. (1965). *Industrial Organization: Theory and Practice*. London: Oxford University Press

Wrapp, H.E. (1984). Good managers don't make policy decisions. *Harvard Business Review*, **62**(1), 8–21

Wright, G. (1985). Decisional variance. In *Behavioral Decision Making* (Wright, G., ed.), pp. 43–59. New York: Plenum Press

Zuckerman, M., Kuhlman, D.M., Joireman, J., Teta, P. and Kraft, M. (1993). A comparison of three structural models for personality: the Big Three, the Big Five, and the Alternative Five. *Journal of Personality and Social Psychology*, **65**, 757–68

Index